TEN RIVERS

ADVENTURE STORIES FROM THE ARCTIC

ED STRUZIK

Published by CanWest Books Inc.
A subsidiary of CanWest MediaWorks Publications Inc.
1450 Don Mills Road
Toronto, ON
Canada, M3B 2X7

Library and Archives Canada Cataloguing in Publication

Struzik, Ed, 1954-
     Ten rivers run through it : adventure stories from the Arctic / Ed Struzik.

ISBN 0-9736719-4-7

     1. Rivers—Canada, Northern. 2. Struzik, Ed, 1954- —Journeys—
Canada, Northern. 3. Natural history—Canada, Northern. 4. Canada,
Northern—Description and travel. I. Title.

FC3956.S85 2005   917.19   C2005-903875-6

Sponsored in part by:

CANADIAN PARKS AND WILDERNESS SOCIETY

Book Design by Mad Dog Design Connection
Maps by Richard Pape
Photographs courtesy of Ed Struzik
Printed and bound in Canada by Transcontinental

First Edition

10 9 8 7 6 5 4 3 2 1

Some things should last forever. Some things are irreplaceably Canadian. In partnership with industry, government, scientists and local communities, CPAWS chapters across Canada are working to create new parks and conserve our wilderness.

Ten Rivers is part of the Henderson Book Series, made possible due to the kind and generous support of Mrs. Arthur T. Henderson. The Canadian Parks and Wilderness Society gratefully acknowledges Mrs. Henderson's support of the Society's efforts to promote public awareness of the value of Canada's park and wilderness areas.

CPAWS
CANADIAN PARKS AND WILDERNESS SOCIETY

For more information, contact:
Canadian Parks and Wilderness Society
250 City Centre Ave., Suite 506
Ottawa, Ontario, K1N 6K7
613-569-7226   Fax: 613-569-7098
info@cpaws.org
www.cpaws.org

For Julia, my favourite paddling partner.

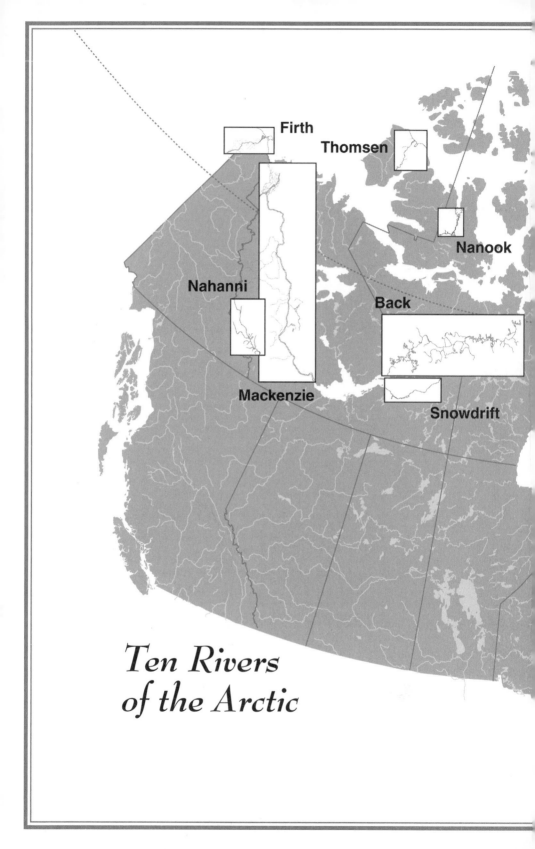

Firth

Thomsen

Nanook

Nahanni

Back

Mackenzie

Snowdrift

Ten Rivers of the Arctic

Contents

Introduction

When I was a boy of seven or eight, my father would occasionally drive me to the country to go fishing. My father was not a happy man. He had lost his country, his family, his home and any chance at an education when he went to war in 1939 at the age of just 18. Working impossibly long hours as a miner, labourer and farmhand in his newly adopted country had taken its toll on him. He was already burning out by the time I was old enough to appreciate that he and my mother had a life other than the one that revolved around me.

But there was something about that trout stream that we went to on hot summer days that seemed to remind my father of the promise of Canada. It was a small stream as I recall, barely a half-metre deep in many spots. But in the clear, deep pools that remained ice cold in the shade of the old growth stands that lined its banks, there were huge trout hiding beneath the cutbanks, waiting to strike at whatever my father tied to my line.

Like most children, I was exhilarated by the hits and tugs that would come each time I waved my rod over the glassy surface. But what really pleased me most was the look on my father's face when he saw a deer passing by or a fish at the end of my line. On those rare occasions that I did catch a fish, he'd place his hands on his hips, puff out his chest in an exaggerated way and shake his head in amazement. Then, after carefully unhooking each one, he'd consider the possibilities for the frying pan before deciding whether to put the fish back into the stream. My father's pleasure would return in the evening when he and my mother would pick away at the bones and savour every last morsel of the supper their little boy had caught for them. This was the type of day of the life in Canada that they had dreamed of.

I had almost forgotten that stream by the time my father passed away more than 25 years later. He had been ill for some time and his struggle with alcoholism and other demons had left us somewhat estranged. I had been living in the Northwest Territories, and following the funeral, I decided to return to that stream of my childhood in the hopes that it might remind me of happier times.

I had driven to that spot so often I thought I would never forget how to get there. But there was now a highway running along the gravel road we had once followed in our old 1954 Pontiac and the wooden bridge that we would use to get across the railroad tracks had been replaced by a concrete overpass. It was some time before I finally found a familiar landmark that put me back on the right course. But the stream that I was searching for was nowhere to be found.

Initially, I suspected that I was on the wrong gravel road. But when I found nothing on the routes to the east and the west of where I thought I was supposed to be, I began wondering whether that waterway had ever existed. It was getting late by the time I returned to where I had started. As a last resort, I knocked on the door of a farmhouse. The young man who answered was polite enough when I asked about the stream that I was certain trickled through his property. But he told me matter-of-factly that if there was water running there, he'd know about it.

I was, truth be told, a little embarrassed having taken this desire to revisit my youth so far. But before I had a chance to turn away, the man shouted towards the kitchen: "Grandpa, do you know anything about a trout stream around here." An old man shuffled out of the kitchen asking: "Who wants to know?"

It was then I discovered that the stream was not simply part of the geography of my imagination. Water did rise from springs, fens and a lake somewhere upstream before trickling in little rills over sand, rock, and through the sedge meadows and forests. "But you won't find it," the old man informed me. "It eventually dried out and the farmer who bought up the land ended up plowing over the muddy ditch that it turned out to be." The old man wasn't sure what happened, but I suspect that like many other small streams in Canada, logging, urban development, countless cattle crossings, and a warming climate had eroded, diverted and reduced the flow of the stream to the point that it finally dried up or had no place to go.

On the drive back, I realized something about myself that should have been obvious long ago. Ever since I had left home, I have been searching for the stream that would replace that perfect one of my youth. For a while I thought I had found it in the Pukaskwa and Missanaibi in northern Ontario. But that changed when I moved to Alberta and canoed the Bow, the Wild Hay, the Little Smoky and the Kakwa. In the Yukon, however, my definition of a perfect stream took on new meaning. There, I was mesmerized by the blue-green waters of the Kathleen River flowing into a lovely lake that some people consider to be even more picturesque than Lake Louise in Banff National Park. I caught my first Arctic greyling in that lovely stream, and nearly drowned trying to paddle its length. Kathleen gave me the first untreated river water that I drank without fear of becoming ill, and I will be forever thankful for that.

The unique allure of the Kathleen, however, eventually gave way to the attractions of the Big Salmon, the Alsek, the Snake and other more remote rivers of the Yukon. And then I moved to the Northwest Territories where the Horton, Burnside, Hood, Thelon, and many other rivers I canoed forced me over and over again to redefine what it was I was searching for. The farther north or east I went into the tundra wilderness, it seemed, the closer I got to what it was I was after.

It wasn't just the sense of adventure, it was the thrill of standing in the middle of 50,000 migrating caribou, or calling out to loons and wolves and getting an answer back. It was also the realization that I was seeing the world the way Aboriginal People and the first European explorers saw it before most of southern Canada was settled and developed. As a child I had read many dry accounts of those early explorations, but it was only after having retraced several of those trips that the stories really came to life.

It was exhilarating following in the path of Matonabbee and Samuel Hearne on the Coppermine and Burnside, Akaitcho and John Franklin on the Yellowknife, and Maufelly and George Back on the great Barren Land river that now bears Back's name. And it was painfully sad standing over the graves of John Hornby, Edgar Christian and Harold Adlard along the banks of the Thelon where the three slowly starved to death in 1927.

Arctic river trips aren't for everybody. For some, the rain, snow, the bugs, the long portages and the damp sleeping bags can be a little overwhelming. On the Anderson River many years ago, I once watched with morbid fascination as an RCMP officer — a tough as nails sort of guy — slowly went nuts trying to cope with the challenges we faced on that three week trip. When the plane finally came in to pick us up, he was frantically waving his hands in the air like someone who had been stranded on a desert island for months and was fearful that the plane might miss him.

Even the most difficult journeys have their highlights if one comes well prepared. There really is nothing like a gourmet meal at the end of a long day in the wilderness, or having a hot drink by a fire on a cold, foggy night hearing but not seeing a small herd of caribou on the other side of the river being chased by a pack of wolves.

I've had the pleasure of paddling and hiking with a lot of remarkable people over the years – grizzly bear, wolf and polar bear biologists, archeologists and paleontologists, artists, writers, lawyers, engineers, and guides. Many of them brought with them a special connection to the river that added another dimension to the trip. Watching Justin Trudeau running through Hell's Gate on the Nahanni River was a hoot because his father was largely responsible for ensuring that Virginia Falls will never be dammed. Sitting beside Ivvavik national park warden Merv Joe on a hilltop over-looking Joe Creek on the Alaska/Yukon border was also special. The mountain stream was named after his Inuvialuit grandfather who trapped in the area. It was also instructive to do a trip down the Hornaday with my friend I. S. MacLaren, a remarkably insightful Arctic historian who specializes in wilderness travel literature. He maintains quite correctly that there is a great disparity between what explorers jot down in their journals at the end of a day and what they put on paper for the public to read.

I hadn't thought of including myself in that assessment until Tom Carpenter, a friend and gifted magazine editor, wrote an arti-cle a number of years ago entitled, "Every Year They Go to The Wilderness and Bring Back Half the Truth." It was a hilarious rant about a canoe trip he had done on the Barren Lands following in the footsteps of British explorer George Back. Magazine writers lie, Tom insists. They leave out the part about there being no facilities. They don't tell you that because of the way the body reacts to stress during the first five days of a trip, you're not likely to make use of them anyway. Nor do they say anything about the rising bacteria count in the food you've brought along and its effect. "After paus-ing for several days like a sprinter resting before a meet," he writes of his own experience, "your bowels react to the microbial change in your sealed container of spaghetti sauce by accelerating day after day in a terrifying attempt at a personal best."

Tom suggests that adventure writers and magazine editors have no interest in telling the truth because it would be bad for circula-tion. "People read those stories because the adventure sounds like something they want to do." He does, however, concede that the absence of information about portages and other hardships may not be altogether deliberate. Wilderness writers ignore lots of stuff, he says "because no one has the energy at the end of a day of portag-ing. Midway through my first afternoon of walking, when I thought

I was going to be paddling, I already planned an expose. And yet all I could manage was this list: 'Long, confusing, wet, dusty, bears, hills that go up not down, hot, hot, hot, buggy beyond belief, stones underfoot, Ed's (our leader) demented sense of distance, hidden bridge disguised as a natural logjam. . ."

Tom's story never did get published, but before you read the chapter on the Back River in this book, it might be instructive to note that the "demented" Ed he aims at in his article is none other than me.

Over the years, my search for the perfect stream has taken me down more than 40 northern rivers of appreciable length. The stream that comes closest to the perfect one of my youth is the Wind. It flows out of the Wernecke Mountains in the north central Yukon before spilling into the Peel and Mackenzie. The Wind doesn't look anything like the one I fished and played along so many years ago. But paddling it with my wife, and favourite canoeing partner, Julia, my 12-year-old son Jacob and my eight-year-old daughter Sigrid in the summer of 2005 brought back some wonderful memories of what it was like to be a child experiencing the natural world in all of its glory and promise. It was up to them to make their own fun, and they didn't waste a minute of it. They paddled, fished (catch and release with barbless hooks), hiked, swam, lit campfires, roasted marshmallows and put their arms up in the air trying to fool a bunch of caribou into thinking they had antlers. The one time they succeeded in drawing in three big bucks was one of the highlights of the trips. Seeing my son in the bow responding effortlessly to the approach of a rock, a sweeper or a rapid was another fine moment. So was the question my daughter asked me at the end of the long journey. She wanted to know which northern river we were going to do next year.

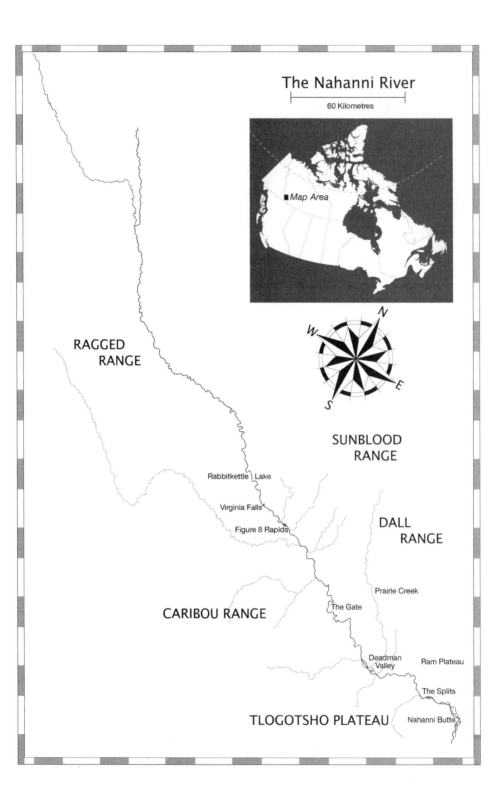

The Nahanni River

60 Kilometres

Map Area

N
W E
S

RAGGED
RANGE

SUNBLOOD
RANGE

Rabbitkettle Lake

Virginia Falls

Figure 8 Rapids

DALL
RANGE

Prairie Creek

CARIBOU RANGE

The Gate

Deadman
Valley

Ram Plateau

The Splits

TLOGOTSHO PLATEAU

Nahanni Butte

Nahanni River

Nahaa Dehé Náilicho — Big Water Falling

In the summer of 1999, a boyish looking, 19-year-old drove into the dusty town of Fort Simpson in the Northwest Territories, high on the rush of adrenaline one gets at the outset of a great adventure. Stepping out of the beat-up Volkswagen Rabbit that he had driven across the country from his parents' home in Ancaster, Ontario, William Sommer walked into the Nahanni National Park office to file a trip report for a kayak trip down the South Nahanni River. Sharon Weaver was the Parks Canada warden on duty. She remembers Sommer as tall, slim with brown hair and brown eyes. Two other things that struck her were that he wore a dark blue Hiker's Haven jacket — not a brand typically worn by serious outdoor enthusiasts — and that he planned to run the river on his own.

The Nahanni is not the most difficult river in the world, but neither is it for the faint of heart. Located along the east side of the mountainous Yukon border, it plunges through a series of four spectacular canyons, churning up rapids, boils and whirlpools with sinister names such as Hell's Gate, or misleading ones like Tricky Current and Lafferty's Riffle, which can be equally challenging. The river is inaccessible by road, and the only practical way to get there from Fort Simpson is by bush plane.

Only a few hundred people canoe, kayak or raft the river each year, and nearly half of those who do, do so accompanied by experienced guides. The others are, almost without exception, highly skilled paddlers with formidable credentials when it comes to whitewater and wilderness. For many of them, the South Nahanni is what Everest is to mountaineers – remote, breathtaking and mysterious. The country is also rich with legends of lost gold, murder, headless men, and of tropical gardens and Indian spirits that dwell in the vents of the river valley's hotsprings. Dozens of people have been swallowed up along this 500-kilometre-long stretch of water over the years. At least 24, possibly more, have died or disappeared without a trace since non-natives started venturing into the country at the turn of the century.

Weaver was surprised but not entirely caught off guard. Every once in a while, a couple of novices, usually young, naive adventurers from Europe, arrive with an inflatable boat, a big bag of rice and fishing gear and only the remotest idea of what it takes to successfully pull off a two-to-three-week river trip like this. In these cases, the wardens do their best to talk them out of the journey. Mostly, they're successful. Occasionally, they're not. Weaver pegged Sommer as another naive young adventurer. "He tried to give me the impression that he was a really skilled paddler with lots of wilderness experience, but the more I asked questions, the more evasive he became," Weaver recalls. "That's when I called in Chuck, our superintendent. I was pretty certain this guy was in over his head, and that he wasn't going to listen to a 20-year-old woman."

Chuck Blyth is a tall, lanky 55-year-old who was, in earlier years, a dead ringer for a post-Beatles John Lennon (a son looks like Neil Young). Having travelled up and down the river at least a couple of dozen times, he has seen his share of mishaps and near disasters, many involving skilled paddlers. Blyth has a disheveled look that suggests that he has perhaps spent a few too many years in this remote part of the world but looks, in his case, are deceiving. Gentle, articulate and fatherly, Blyth talked to Sommer as he would to his own teenage sons. "I tried to make it clear that I would strongly advise against anyone going down the river on his or her own," he said. "And I really thought I had talked some sense into him when he left the office and told me that he would think about it. When I didn't hear from him again, I figured that was the end of it. He had either gone home or driven off to do something more within his range of skills."

Nearly a month later, the Parks Canada office in Fort Simpson received a call from Elisabeth Sommer looking for her son. She had not heard from him in more than a month, and was calling to find out whether anyone knew where he might be. At first, the person who took the call didn't know who she was talking about. Only after she had asked around did Weaver and Blyth recall the young man from Ontario.

Steve Catto, Nahanni's top warden, immediately filed a missing person report with the RCMP. After tracing Sommer's credit card purchases and interviewing gas-station attendants, investigators tracked the young man from Fort Simpson along a narrow gravel road that would have led Sommer on a punishing drive to the northeast corner of British Columbia. Instead of heading south at Fort Nelson, as investigators expected, Sommer turned north along the Alaska Highway to Watson Lake in the Yukon. From there, he drove northeast, farther and farther into no-man's land along the little-used Campbell route, before finally pulling onto a muddy, unmaintained road that leads to an abandoned mine high in the mountains along the Northwest Territories border.

A few kilometres from the mine, just below a washed-out section of road, Catto, a RCMP investigator and the pilot found Sommer's abandoned VW Rabbit. Inside, there was a calling card, vaccination papers for his dog and some brochures on Nahanni.

Elite paddlers occasionally enter the South Nahanni from this old mine site. But to get there, they must first descend the Little Nahanni, an extremely challenging stretch of whitewater that feeds into the bigger, more famous river. Figuring that this is what Sommer had had in mind, Catto had the pilot helicopter downstream that evening. Less than an hour into the flight, they spotted part of a tent wrapped around a log in the water, a kayak floating upside down in the willows along shore, and a life jacket 100 metres away. After retrieving the boat and personal flotation device, they also found an old gas stove, a cast iron frying pan, a big sack of potatoes, a Bible, a Pelican case and camera and a diary that recorded some of the young man's last thoughts.

———

Two years later, William Sommer is in the back of my mind when I embark on my own 62 day trip down the Nahanni, Liard and Mackenzie rivers. Unlike him, however, I have more than two dozen Arctic river trips under my belt, a number of which are far more challenging than the Nahanni. Still, I am nervous. Sommer was not the first to die in this watershed. And with it being late June, still very early in the season, floodwaters are promising to make the river that much more dangerous.

In truth, I have little time for second thoughts. The Nahanni, which spills into the Liard and then the Mackenzie, is the first stage of my three-river, summer-long journey. My plan is to go into Virginia Falls with Weaver and a group of wardens on the first river patrol of the year. This way I can save the cost of flying in alone, and get insights into the Nahanni that I might not get by going solo all the way. At some point – I haven't decided when or where – I plan to go my own way.

These best-laid plans, however, are not meant to be. After having spent several sleepless nights making last-minute preparations, I arrive in Fort Simpson only to discover that none of the food, clothes and equipment I packed for the 2,000-kilometre trip have made it with me. They'd been bumped from the plane in Yellowknife to make room for more important cargo. And there is no sign of the kayak that I had shipped to Fort Simpson. "Our float plane is waiting to go," says Barry Troke, the park warden who greets me at the airport. He's sympathetic but tied to a tight schedule. "If you're going to hitch a ride with us, I'm afraid you're going to have to decide now whether you want to go."

For a brief moment, I consider the possibility of giving up on the Nahanni portion of the trip. But I can't imagine passing on what promises to be the highlight of the summer. And so, with Troke's help, I round up a toothbrush, some rain gear and a lightweight sleeping bag. If it's going to rain or snow, as it can on the Nahanni in June and July, I realize I am going to be one cold puppy.

It's a rough flight to Virginia Falls. After crossing the vast stretch of undisturbed muskeg west of Fort Simpson, the twin-engine plane bounces over the rolling, verdant hills of the Nahanni Range before reaching the first of the river's four deep canyons. Deadmen Valley, Headless Creek, Murder Creek and the Funeral Range – the names of these and other landmarks below are more haunting reminders of why the Nahanni is known as the "Dangerous River," or the "Valley of Vanishing Men."

Once more, I agonize over what it is I am getting into. While I am now no longer going to be alone in a kayak, I'm not sure what to make of my partners who are using a combination of raft, canoe and rubber boat to take us downstream. In paddling, I have always had the advantage of choosing my partner and sharing or dictating the decision-making. Now I am little more than a hitchhiker, beholden to these wardens, but wary of becoming partners with those whose talents are unknown to me.

But there isn't much opportunity to consider the alternatives. As the white spray of Virginia Falls comes into view, the turbulence of the flight has Adele Laramee, the seasonal park interpreter, putting her head between her knees with an air-sickness bag in hand. Park biologist Doug Tate is also looking a little green around the gills. It is all I can do to snap a few photographs before succumbing to the same paralyzing nausea.

Few experiences are as exhilarating as flying in a bush-plane that is about to land on the Nahanni a few hundred metres above Virginia Falls when the wind is blowing downstream. In this case, it is routine for the pilot to first skim over the intended landing area, while gauging the direction of the wind and scanning the river for logs and debris. Then, he heads back down toward the Funeral

Range where the river has carved a 90-metre deep, eight-kilometre long canyon out of the limestone mountains. About a kilometre from the falls, he banks hard to the left to avoid a cliff. He steers the plane back toward the cascading water along an unnerving line of descent over Sluicebox, a boiling mass of whitewater that marks the beginning of the falls. While it's a tricky manoeuver, for the pilot, it's an exhilarating experience for the passenger. Virginia Falls is an impressive sight from any angle at any time. From the beginning of the river's descent, the 35-metre plunge is twice the height of Niagara Falls, and is split in two by a towering spire. But when you're gliding over the falls — and it looks like you're almost flying into the maelstrom — it seems that much more daunting. This, I think to myself, is a hell of a way to start a trip.

That night, we are camped above the falls, sorting out the food and gear, and making sure that all the paddles, the raft and rubber boat parts have come along from the plane ride. With nothing but a camera and the clothes that I am wearing, it doesn't take me long to get organized. So while the others are busy checking off their long to-do and equipment lists, I venture downstream along the riverbank. The river looks enormous, swollen as it is by the rain and snow melting off the mountainsides upstream. A couple of huge trees floating in the middle of the river are being sucked underwater at Sluicebox Rapids. I watch and wait to see if they get spat back before they go over the falls. They don't. I then try to imagine what would happen to a five-metre canoe going through here. It makes me shudder to think about it. Some of the best canoeing in the North comes during the spring-run off when most of the big boulders are submerged. Often, the greatest challenge is getting through the rollers and haystacks without getting swamped. But on a big mountain river like the Nahanni, all that extra water flooding through a narrow valley has no place to go but down or around in circles. What you get then are lots of whirlpools and boils that can suck a canoe under or spin it out of control.

Near the end of the trail, I grab hold of the thin trunk of a small lodgepole pine growing out of the rock a foot away from the edge of the cliff, and look 60-metres down at the spire that splits the falls in two. Paddlers affectionately call this Mason's Rock, after artist/filmmaker and paddler extraordinaire Bill Mason, who once described the Nahanni "as the greatest canoe trip in the world." To the Dene of the Mackenzie River Valley, the spire represents one of the spirits of the Naha, a tribe of mountain warriors who wore sheepskin clothing and armoured vests made of tightly woven sticks. Legend has it that this fierce people would descend from the mountains from time to time to raid the Dene camps below. By the time the victims pulled themselves together to track down the marauders, they would only find a burning campfire.

This isn't the only spirit the Naha believed in. Upstream at the hotsprings near Rabbitkettle Lake, Ndambadezha, "protector of the people" is said to inhabit one of the vents that rises out of the enormous beehive-shaped tufa mounds. It is this spirit, so the legend goes, that went down to Nahanni Butte and drove away two giant beavers that would drown boaters with a slap of their enormous tails. One beaver ended up at Trout Lake near Fort Simpson, the other went all the way to Tulita at the confluence of the Mackenzie and Great Bear rivers.

The Naha eventually disappeared. No one knows why or where they went to. But similarities between the local Dene dialect and the Navajo language in the United States has led some to believe that the Navajo are descendants of the Naha. Others hold the notion that the Naha remained in small pockets and were responsible for the disappearance of dozens of white men who ventured up the Nahanni searching for gold during the early part of the 20th century. In 1908, the bodies of two of these men, Métis brothers Willie and Frank McLeod, were found near a creek flowing into the Nahanni with their heads missing. A message carved into a sled runner left nearby stated cryptically, "We have found a prospect."

Mesmerized by the sight and sound of this thundering water, I can appreciate why the Naha felt that there was a powerful force living here.

And looking into the brink of Virginia Falls, it is also evident how someone could suddenly and inexplicably disappear, as one 20-year-old guide apparently did in 1978 after he ventured off alone to scout the river. In spite of an exhaustive ground, air and river search, his body was never found. Speculation at the time was that he might have faked his own death. Most people, however, believed otherwise until California police called 20 years later to say they had picked up a man with the same name and date of birth. Parks Canada records suggest only that this may have been a coincidence.

———

Fenley Hunter was already well aware of the hazards of the Nahanni when he and two others travelled upstream along the river in the summer of 1928. Unlike those who came before him searching for gold or fur, Hunter's primary goal was to see this roaring cataract. He wasn't disappointed. "It is just as good as Niagara, only smaller in scale," he wrote in his journal early on the morning of August 22. "I have not yet measured them yet, but estimate them to be well over 200 feet. The entire river falls into a box canyon with calm waters just below the falls and much mist. I wish Virginia could see them as I have named them after her."

———

Virginia was Hunter's daughter, a girl still early in her teenage years. She was with her mother in Flushing, New York, when her father, a wealthy American businessman-turned-adventurer, headed north that summer with George Ball and Albert Dease, two small-time outfitters from northern British Columbia. It was quite the expedition. The plan was to go up the Nahanni with little more than a collapsible canoe, an outboard motor, hunting rifles and a supply of dry food. Once they got to the falls and beyond to the headwaters of the great river, Hunter envisioned hiking overland to the Gravel, (now known as the Keele River) and building a birchbark or skin canoe. From there, he intended to float downstream to the

Mackenzie River to Fort Norman (now known as Tulita). Somehow, Hunter believed he would still have time to push on for another 400 kilometres before ascending the Peel and Rat rivers over a mountain pass to the Yukon, and then down the Bell and Porcupine rivers to Fort Yukon in Alaska.

For all Hunter knew at the outset of his great adventure, the falls were nothing more than the stuff of legend. Long before he headed north, the Dene had spoken with awe and reverence about these cataracts whenever they came into Fort Liard in their huge moose-skin boats to trade their furs. They claimed that the falls could be heard six kilometres away. But none of the white traders in Liard knew if they were describing myth or reality. The two were often indistinguishable in many Dene tales. Charles Camsell, the Canadian deputy minister of mines during the 1920s, thought there was something to them. The son of a Hudson's Bay Company factor, Camsell had grown up in the region spellbound by these stories. So when he ran into Hunter at the Rideau Club in Ottawa, he challenged the American explorer to verify the stories. Intrigued by the possibility, Hunter wrote to his friend Charles French, the fur trade commissioner for the Hudson's Bay Company in Winnipeg, to see what he could tell him. French wrote back informing Hunter that "he could tell him less about the Nahanni than any river in Canada."

In 1923, Hunter, Dease and a Swede by the name of Charlie Olsen had made a 1,126-kilometre canoe trip through northern British Columbia and the Yukon across wilderness that had not yet been mapped. But that apparently hadn't prepared Hunter for the challenges he would face on the Nahanni. "This place is a heartbreaker," he wrote at one point. "The Nahanni is unknown and will remain so until another age brings a change in the con-formation of these mountains. It is an impossible stream, and a stiff rapid is met on average every mile, and they seem countless." Nor was he was he pleased with his partners Ball and Dease. George "is a good soul, but my God, he is dumb," Hunter wrote. "His boots leak, his hat is (always) lost and his gun is rusty as an old iron." Hunter lamented

that there was no one with whom he could share the natural wonders of the trip. "The world I am now living in is a man's physical
world and mentally a child's. The boys are good fellows, and all one
could expect, but there is no happiness, almost no humour, and very
little talk. . . There is so much of Nature and the beauty of the
country that might be discussed, yet all this I have to figure out and
enjoy by myself as best I can. A one-man outfit has its advantages,
but the thorns go along with the roses."

To his surprise, Hunter found the Nahanni to be a relatively
busy place that summer. He and his colleagues crossed paths with
prospectors Sherwood and Poole Field who were heading toward the
Flat River in search of gold, and Gordon Matthews and Raymond
Patterson who were setting themselves up to spend the winter
prospecting and trapping along the Flat River. Planes constantly
buzzed overhead, dealing with a flu epidemic that was wiping out
the area's Aboriginal Peoples.

Hunter's expedition was down to its last bag of flour, some
sugar, tea and coffee and a smidgen of jam by the time they arrived
at the falls. With snow already falling on the mountaintops, Hunter
realized that there was no sense in pushing farther upstream. So he
decided to retreat to Fort Simpson. But that didn't end the journey.
Back at Fort Simpson, Hunter hopped aboard a Hudson's Bay
Company boat going down the Mackenzie to the trading post at
Arctic Red River. At Arctic Red, he bought a boat in which he poled
up the Peel and Rat to Summit Lake in the Yukon and down the
Bell and Porcupine rivers to Alaska. By the time he arrived at his
final destination in mid-October, ice was holding fast on parts of
the river.

Hunter, Ball and Dease were not the first outsiders to reach
Virginia Falls. Raymond Patterson and Albert Faille had earned that
distinction a year earlier. The name "Virginia," however, stuck, which is
poignant considering what transpired shortly after Hunter returned to
New York. Both Virginia and her mother were shocked to hear that he
was abandoning them in favour of a life with his secretary. Virginia saw
her father only once before she died in Pennsylvania in 1995. She

never visited the falls, nor did she tell anyone but her closest family members that one of the most celebrated landmarks in the world was named for her. So devastated was she by her father's abandonment, she hid a copy of a *Canadian Geographic* magazine article that gave her her one and only glimpse of her namesake.

———

Mornings on northern rivers are my favourite time of day. A perfect morning begins with a mist on the water, a bite in the air that is one degree too cold for mosquitoes, and the smell of coffee percolating over a snapping campfire as it puffs up curls of smoke. Mornings are also "sweeter in the knowledge of what the afternoon is to bring," as the American writer Edward Abbey once put it. Lying in my tent that first morning, I am dreading the three-kilometre portage that this afternoon demands.

Not that I'm ungrateful for the kindness of the wardens in letting me tag along. I just want to relax in solitude. Nor am I concerned about the slog that all paddlers have to do in order to get around the falls. I've trudged across a great many portages and I can honestly say those around La Roncière and Wilberforce falls in the central Arctic and Hanbury canyon in the Thelon River country make the downhill hike around Virginia seem like a cakewalk. But today I despair at the idea of being weighed down like a mule. All I want is to go back down the path that I had walked the night before to look at and feel the river thundering into the gorge.

The portage, however, offers its own rewards. It is a geological wonder, a voyage back in time where one bears witness to the death of a river. The route follows an ancient arm of the South Nahanni that eventually dried out after being blocked by glacial debris. The descent, at least initially, is gradual and we have no trouble walking the boardwalk that Parks Canada has built to protect the permafrost from eroding. Things become a little more challenging beyond the site of the ancient waterfall on the river. Not only does the boardwalk end here, the trail steepens across a series of slippery switchbacks that end at a cobblestone beach.

It is cool and raining down by the river, and the brilliant rainbow that had lit them up hours earlier, has vanished. Chilled by the mist, the steady rain and the sweat, everyone dips into their dry bags for an extra layer of clothing. Taking pity on me, Doug Tate, the biologist, offers me a fleece jacket that I thankfully accept. Before us lies Fourth Canyon, the last gorge that Hunter would have encountered while working his way upstream. Also known as Five Mile or Painted Canyon, it radiates with the same yellow and orange limestone that lights up the Grand Canyon in the United States. No doubt, Hunter's retreat through here 75 years ago was a lot easier than navigating a small, unstable boat upstream through whitewater. Still, it must have been intimidating. As picturesque as it was from above the night before, the river below looks like a nasty stretch of water. In these flood conditions, huge trees have been swept downstream toward a long series of high standing waves and protruding boulders.

The Nahanni is not an easy study. Most mountain rivers flow straight because it doesn't take long for pounding water to erode whatever stands in its way. The South Nahanni is rare, a meandering big mountain river, or as one former park warden once described it, "a gentle river gone mad." There is an explanation to account for this antecedence. The South Nahanni was formed on an open sub-Arctic prairie many millions of years before the mountains rose up. Because the uplift of land developed more slowly than the erosive forces of the stream, the river has maintained its winding course.

The trick in paddling through Painted Canyon is to ferry upstream towards the falls as far as you can before crossing over. That way, you avoid the danger of the powerful current slamming your canoe into the rock wall along the first bend. Most paddlers have no trouble doing this, but every once in a while some swamp in the high waves in the middle of the river or overturn after hitting a boulder. Several years ago, park wardens watched in amazement when an inflatable boat literally exploded, scattering all of its occupants, after slamming into one of these rocks. The passengers bobbed downstream for some distance before they could be fished out.

Ultimately, Doug Tate and I have no trouble picking our way through this stretch of river in the canoe while the others follow in the raft. Doug is big and strong, and a much better paddler than he had earlier led to me to believe. Watching the mountains slip by, I realize for the first time how glorious it is to finally be in the stern of a canoe, heading downstream on an adventure that I expect will last two months or more. The lost kayak and missing gear are no longer a concern. I decide not to worry about them until we return to Fort Simpson.

———

Apart from the men who died on the Nahanni, there were those who lived on the river that became legends in their own right. Trappers Gus and Mary Kraus, former Klondike Mountie Poole Field, outfitter Dick Turner, and perhaps the most famous of them all, Albert Faille. Faille prospected in Nahanni country for nearly 50 years before he was found dead in his outhouse in Fort Simpson. Most non-natives adored him for his reclusive nature and for his distinctive handmade red pants that he often wore. Some Deh Cho natives, on the other hand, regarded him as a grouchy old coot. I will always remember him as the character he was in a National Film Board documentary – old, wrinkled and stooped because of the broken back that he suffered while on a trapline – but stubborn in his determination to portage up hill around the falls. Faille never did find the motherlode of gold that he was looking for. Nor did he share much of what he knew about the people and the country, although he was not convinced that the McLeod brothers were murdered. He thought it more likely that they left it too late to return and starved to death. But word was that he was convinced that some form of skullduggery took place near the confluence of the Nahanni and Clearwater Creek just below Painted Canyon. To him, it was Murder Creek.

In the summer of 1912, Martin Jorgensen and Osias Meilleur hiked up the Clearwater still hot on the trail of the prospect that the McLeods had reportedly found before their headless bodies had been discovered. While Jorgensen stayed on to build a cabin for the winter, Meilleur headed out in the fall with the understanding that the two would meet the following summer. But Jorgenson was no where to be found when Meilleur returned. Meilleur, however, wasn't worried. He met with some Dene hunters who claimed they had seen Jorgensen a few weeks earlier making his way up the Flat River several kilometres downstream.

Meilleur returned to the Clearwater camp once again in 1914. This time, he found the remains of a burned-down cabin, a revolver and loaded rifle, and Jorgenson's clothes scattered about. There was still no sign of Jorgensen, and Meilleur neglected to report it to the Mounties. The story takes a twist in 1913 when Jorgensen had apparently handed a note to a trapper asking that it be delivered to his friend Billy Atkinson (another report suggests it was actually his partner Poole Field) who lived in the Yukon. Atkinson never did get the note, but his former wife, Mary, did. She gave it to Field, her new husband. The note contained a map urging Atkinson to come quickly because Jorgenson had found the gold they had been looking for.

The next year, Field and Atkinson set out to see if they could solve the mystery of Jorgenson's disappearance. Part-way up the Clearwater, they found the burned-down cabin, and the scattered clothes but they also found Jorgenson's body lying face down between the burnt-out hollow and the river. They could find no sign of his rifle or pistol. No one ever figured out what had happened. In 1916, after the Mounties arrived to exhume Jorgenson's body, they closed the case because so much evidence had been tampered with, and because too much time had elapsed. Faille, however, went to his grave in 1973 convinced that Jorgensen was murdered.

Heading downstream of the Clearwater toward Mary River and Hell's Gate, we argue over how Jorgensen might have come to his end. Park warden Carl Lafferty suggests that a pot-bellied stove or an empty fuel drum which Jorgensen used to heat his cabin may have caught fire. "He could've been heading towards the river to get water before being overcome with smoke inhalation," he says. "But

I don't know," he second-guesses himself in short order. "The way I heard it, Poole Field left the site with a spooky feeling that they were being watched. It also bothered him that there was no sign of the gun. It was a Savage rifle, a fancy gun, not something that Jorgensen would have misplaced."

Lafferty loves speculating about these stories. Like many people from Nahanni Butte, Fort Liard and Fort Simpson, he can trace his roots back to the days when these legends were in the making. In 1922, his great-great-granduncles, Jonas and Jim Lafferty, made their mark on the Nahanni while staking out a coal claim along a small tributary that today bears their surname. While they were boating back to Fort Simpson, the two nearly drowned going through a rapid at the confluence of the Nahanni. The rapid has been called Lafferty's Riffle ever since.

Carl's favourite story is one about May Lafferty, likely a distant relative, who was somehow related to Poole and Mary Field. Poole and Mary had partnered up in the Yukon after Field had lost his first wife in 1915. Four years later, they took his one surviving daughter and a Japanese American prospector by the name of Jujiro Wada and moved to Nahanni Butte.

According to Carl, the Poole family was camped out at May Creek, a tributary of Mary River in 1921 when May bolted off. "May was an odd duck, probably for good reason," explains Carl. "She was treated very poorly; some say like a slave. Tired of the abuse, she apparently got up one night and ran away."

Determined to bring her back, Field persuaded a Dene hunting party camped nearby to help find her. Yohee, Boston Jack, Tesou, Big Charlie and Diamond C were widely regarded as the best trackers in the region, but they couldn't catch up with May. They knew they were on her trail because she had discarded clothing along the way. In fact, she had shed so much of what she was wearing the trackers were convinced she must have been naked. Field had pretty much given up hope that she would be found alive when they spotted her tracks at the bottom of a 1,525-metre mountain that was virtually unclimbable. With nothing to suggest that she might have turned back, they began their ascent expecting to find a body. The climb was so dangerous that some of the men went back down. Those who finally got to the top were shocked to discover her moccasin prints

"Field called off the search after nine days," says Carl. "Some say she froze to death. Others insist she met up with a trapper and ended up in the Yukon. I've even heard it said that she somehow ended back up in Fort Simpson when she was an old lady. Given all of the time that has passed since, we'll never know."

American writer Norman Maclean wrote that fishing is a world created apart from the others, and within it are special worlds of their own. Canoeing, I've come to appreciate, is very similar. There's the dreamy world when you're leaning back in the canoe, with eyes closed and one arm dangling in the water, soaking up the sun and listening to the silt sliding along the side of the boat. Then there's the adrenaline-infused world in which one struggles to find a line in the water that will deliver you safely through a nasty set of rapids. Finding that line at Hell's Gate on the Nahanni can exasperate even the most experienced paddlers when the river is in flood.

We are camped on a small sand and gravel-covered island just above these rapids. Wendy Grater, a veteran wilderness guide and expert paddler, has been brought along to do some rescue training with the wardens. No matter how long we look at them, I can't help but marvel at the hydraulics that makes this stretch of whitewater so famous. Here, a few kilometres upstream of the Flat, the river takes a sharp turn to the right before slamming into a rock wall and splitting into two distinctive whirlpools. In the summer of 1928, Albert Dease, an expert boatman, spent nearly two hours looking at the rapids before letting Fenley Hunter know he could make them. Hunter, however, wasn't so sure. Examining the "double whirlpool" from the top of the cliff which the water slams into, he reckoned that "if you don't cross the line of five-foot combers in the middle of the river before you reach the bluff – goodbye."

The year before, Raymond Patterson also sat contemplating these Rapids-that-Run-Both-Ways, as Faille called them, for quite some time. He could only come up with: "Well, that's the queerest piece of water that I ever did see." Patterson tried three times to get upstream. Twice, the big waves flung him back into the canyon. And just as it looked like he would succeed on the third attempt, a gust of wind blew down river, swinging the bow of his boat into the whirlpool. "It was like the heave of one's cabin bunk at night in some Atlantic storm," he wrote in *Dangerous River*, the book that made the Nahanni famous when it was first published in the 1953. "Persistency is one thing and plain obstinacy is another," he added before noting that it was then that he beached his canoe, unpacked his axe and cleared the path through the trees that is used by portagers to this day.

Hell's Gate has claimed its share of victims. It's believed that three Germans drowned here in the summer of 1963 when their party of six barrelled through the whitewater and overturned. No one really knows for sure what happened. Joe Duntra, a trapper from Nahanni Butte found one of their bodies, far downstream beside a smashed-up canoe that still had food and other supplies lashed to it. The other two were presumed to have drowned until Duntra and an RCMP officer headed up the Flat River and found, perched beside a handmade stretcher, a wooden cross with a big sign over it that read "Dead Man Here." The body had apparently been there for some time. "The head was gone and parts of the arms were gone, the bones were gone," Duntra is quoted as stating in a report. "We looked all over and we found a shoulder blade. It was quite a ways away. He left a diary. . . some other kind of nationality. So somebody read it, and it said that he had gone for 48 days with nothing to eat. He had been shooting at ptarmigan and squirrels and so on, but. . ."

———

Ten minutes past Hell's Gate, which we get through without incident, Direction Mountain comes into view. This height of land towers above the confluence of the Nahanni and Flat rivers, and signals the "fearful boil" at Wrigley Whirlpool. Also known as Tricky Current, this is where the Dene from the Wrigley area on the Mackenzie River traditionally got together after portaging from the North Nahanni River. It's raining hard by the time we arrive, and the floodwaters are higher than ever. But warden Barry Troke is still intent on jumping in so that his fellow wardens can practice their river rescue skills with Wendy Grater.

The rescue, however, isn't nearly as routine as we expect it to be. Caught in the rapid's powerful whirlpool, Troke is spun round and round while we watch helplessly as the forceful current sweeps our raft and canoe downstream. No amount of muscle can power us back toward him. For a brief moment, I have this sickening feeling that he is going to sink and disappear. He doesn't seem to be able to swim free. Troke, however, pulls himself out of it by giving up on the struggle, and allowing the whirlpool to spin him back into the main current, and then downstream where he is hauled back into the raft.

Robert and Neil Cameron, a father and son team from Calgary, weren't quite as fortunate when they were paddling toward this section of the river in the summer of 1999. Neither one of them knew it at the time, but the Nahanni was in one of its worst June floods in a hundred years. The river was moving so fast that it took them just one day instead of the three that it normally takes to get from Rabbitkettle Lake to Virginia Falls. They couldn't figure out what was splashing through the water at night until they woke up the next day to find giant trees literally flying past them. It wasn't until they turned the first bend in Painted Canyon, however, that they realized that this wasn't normal. There, a monstrous four-and-a-half-metre pyramid of brown water awaited them. With no time to get to steer way from it, they literally climbed up the wall of water. Mercifully, they got spat out on the other side without getting flipped.

Having barely escaped with their lives, they had no intent of going through Hell's Gate the next day. What they didn't realize until it was too late was that somehow they had gone through the famous rapids. The floodwaters had made them unrecognizable. So the rapids that they were studying the next day were actually Wrigley Whirlpool. All Neil Cameron remembers after that is being submerged in water that was so full of air he could barely get back to the surface to catch a breath. Somehow, the two managed to get to shore where they were greeted by a giant swarm of ants that had been flooded out of their nests underground. The canoe and everything else they had was no where to be seen.

"All they had with them after they dumped was a Bic lighter, two jack-knives, three breakfast bars and a bear banger, " says Troke. The day after the men swamped, a helicopter and two planes flew over, but neither one caught sight of their distress signal. Then, the weather turned. The clouds dropped to the ground and it started to rain - a cold rain. Father and son knew they were in for the long haul since no one would fly in such weather, so they started eating bugs and the swarming ants. A handful of ants, the Camerons discovered, taste a bit like caesar salad. The key to eating them, they also learned the hard way, is to bite them first before they get a chance to bite back.

Neil lost 25 pounds in five days and Robert nearly succumbed to hypothermia in his damp neoprene suit. What saved the pair, says Troke, was the Bic lighter and the schedule they had filed with Parks Canada. When the Camerons failed to arrive in Fort Simpson as planned, Troke had a hunch they might be in trouble, so with the first break in the weather, he brought in a helicopter.

Troke says he'll never forget what he saw when he hopped out of the helicopter and started walking toward them. "Their faces were black, which, I guess, was natural after a week of standing over a smoky campfire trying to keep warm," he says. "But I couldn't help wonder why their teeth were black as well. Apparently they stayed alive by eating bugs. It was really strange. During the short time we were talking to them along the riverside to see if they were okay, Neil was swatting bugs and handing them to his dad. His father just popped them into his mouth like it was a reflex action."

Paddlers will always argue about which of Nahanni's natural wonders is the most breathtaking. Without question, Virginia Falls is an easy one, it would be on many lists. So would the towering cliffs of First Canyon. The Cirque of the Unclimbables would also get a high rating if enough people got a chance to see this cathedral of granite mountains that rise like giant fingers pointing to the heavens. But they are so remote, so difficult to get to, and so often covered in clouds that very few people ever get a chance to experience them.

For me, it's the geological gem that is found in Third Canyon where the river takes a sharp turn before cutting a narrow, steep sided slit through rock streaked red with iron. This is known as The Gate, a landmark that should not be confused with Hell's Gate. Passing though this peaceful stretch of water in 1927, Patterson was almost overcome with emotion, "the whole thing was like a great gateway through which I glided silently, midget like," he wrote. "I have seen many beautiful places in my lifetime, but never anything of this kind."

We arrive at The Gate late in the evening when the sun, low on the horizon, has shone an alpenglow of light on Pulpit Rock, a spire that rises up from a shoulder of granite. It is still, mercifully, too hot for the bugs to torment us with serious enthusiasm, so a cold bath in an icy stream flowing out of the hills is in order. While setting up my tent afterward, I wonder aloud why so many trees have been stripped of their lower branches and why debris is piled high on the hillside.

"A flash flood back in 1997," says Lafferty, setting up his tent next to me. Lafferty seems to know everything that has happened in the park. "No one saw it coming. It had been hot and clear for more than a week when the river started rising in the middle of the night. It was amazing no one was killed."

Those who were on the river say they will never forget what happened in the dark of night. One group upstream of The Gate had barely enough time to pack up and jump into their rafts before the island on which they were camped disappeared. They floated helplessly downstream unable to find a safe place to pull out. In the confusion, one person fell out and was briefly trapped beneath the raft until the others were able to fish him out. Another group landed on shore in their canoes hanging on to tree trunks and wondering if the world was coming to an end.

The cause of flood remained a mystery until Lafferty and a colleague headed upstream in a helicopter searching for other people who might have been on the river at the time. Along Clearwater Creek, they discovered that the entire top of a mountain had toppled over into the path of the stream, blocking the flow of water for weeks. A big lake formed, bursting through the earthen dam, and unleashing a wall of water. "We figure that initially, it was maybe six foot high," says Lafferty. "Had there been anyone camped at the confluence of the Clearwater and the Nahanni that night, I have no doubt they would have drowned in their tents."

Flash floods on the Nahanni are rare, but not unheard of. The most dangerous are those that occur on some of the big river's tributaries. Some of these creeks are bone-dry by midsummer. But when the heavy rain comes, as it often does at the end of a hot, muggy day, they re-emerge like serpents, raging down valleys and swallowing up everything that stands in their way. This is what happened in Dry Canyon in July 1995 when a small group of hikers were walking along looking for caves and for Dall's Sheep, a thin-horned white sheep found in Alaska, Yukon and North West Territories. Alerted by lightning in the distance, and the sound of something rumbling toward them, the party's guide ordered everyone to climb up the hill as fast as they could. Everyone did as they were told. Only part way up, one young man, Harry Spook, turned back to retrieve his day-pack.

———

Big Bend is a hairpin turn on the river that marks the spot where the Funeral Range ends and the Headless Range begins. We are below Second Canyon at the head of Deadmen Valley, aiming to get to the warden cabin there when Doug Tate and I decide to pull out partway downstream at the spot where the McLeod brothers were found. A more forlorn looking place on the river would be hard to find. Headless Creek flows out of a valley closed in by a thick tangle of willow and a few stands of stunted pine and spruce. Hellaciously buggy as it is when we disembark, I figure this was as good a place as any for the men to have died. A film director couldn't find a location more melancholy.

No Nahanni story is as strange as the tale of Willie and Frank McLeod. Some say their headless bodies were tied to a tree when their brother Charlie found them. Others have suggested that the Naha killed them. So many versions have been told that it is almost impossible to figure out which is true.

Dick Turner and Raymond Patterson probably did the best job of pulling together the pieces of this mystery while they were exploring the country in the 1920s. Brother Charlie McLeod was still alive, as were others who knew the victims. According to Patterson's, Willie, Frank, and Charlie, sons of a Hudson's Bay Company factor in Fort Liard, had grown up in the area and were caught up by an Indian tale of treasure high in the Flat River region. Determined to find out if there was gold in those hills, they spent years conspiring to find a way of getting into that unmapped part of the world.

The opportunity evidently presented itself in Edmonton during the winter of 1903. They hopped a train to Vancouver and headed up the coast to Wrangell Island on the Alaska Panhandle. There, in the dead of winter, they assembled a dog team to take them up the Stikine River to Telegraph Creek along the British Columbia and Yukon border and eventually over the Continental Divide. Come spring, the brothers found themselves on a tributary of the Flat (Gold Creek) where they met some Indians coming out with "big stuff, two- and three-dollar gold nuggets."

The McLeods weren't well rewarded for their toil and trouble that summer. All they found was a tiny toothache-remedy bottle full of small nuggets that they subsequently lost when the boat they built out of wooden sluice boxes swamped as they tried floating through the treacherous Cascade of the Thirteen Steps. So, back they went to Gold (now Bennett) Creek and got themselves a moose, some more gold dust, and another boat they made out of the last of the sluice boxes. This time, against all odds, they managed to get themselves back to Liard in their "crazy bateaux."

Charlie had learned his lesson. But that brush with death and disaster was not enough to deter Willie and Frank. Convinced there was a fortune to be had, they worked all winter for the Hudson's Bay Company before hooking up with a Scottish engineer named Weir the following spring. Instead of taking the circuitous route along the coast, they went straight up the Nahanni and Flat rivers.

Almost two years later, Charlie began the search that ended at Headless Creek. There, he found his brother's bodies as well as the note carved in a sled runner that read "We have found a prospect." That was not unusual since Willie was known to carve messages in trees. What was unusual was the location and condition of the bodies. "Charlie buried them without their heads," his nephew stated in a newspaper interview some time later. "One brother was found lying down in their night bed face up, and the other was lying face down, three steps away, with his arm outstretched in a vain attempt to reach his gun, which was at the foot of a tree, only another step from where he fell."

Since Charlie had found no gold nor any sign of the rumoured third man, many speculated that Weir had murdered them. One version put Weir back in Telegraph Creek with $8,000 in nuggets. Another suggested that the RCMP traced Weir to Vancouver with $5,000 in gold before losing the trail. All that a Parks Canada report offers is that a third skeleton later found in Deadmen Valley could have belonged to the Scottish engineer.

Maybe there never was a third man. Perhaps the McLeod brothers had starved to death as the RCMP concluded after an investigation many years later. Wolves or bears could have accounted for the missing skulls. But with all the unexplained deaths that occurred in the years that followed, many people were left more convinced than ever that something evil lurked in the Valley of Vanishing Men. First Jorgensen died under suspicious circumstances in 1912. Then trapper Phil Powers was found dead in his burned-down cabin at Irvine

Creek, a tributary of the Flat, in 1931. RCMP investigators scratched their heads over that one for a long time. Their report concluded that the fire had been ignited some time early in the winter of 1931. But a note nailed to an untouched cache nearby stated "Phil Powers – Finis – 1932." And then, Bill Epler and Joe Mulholland failed to show up in Fort Simpson in the spring of 1936 after they went into the Rabbitkettle Lake country to do some trapping. Maybe it goes with the dangers that come with travelling through this country, but every few years, it seems, something happens in Nahanni country that keeps the legends going.

The search for gold, silver and other treasures on the Nahanni never stopped as most people thought it might when the area became a national park in 1971. Prospectors simply shifted their attention to the park boundaries where Canada's Department of Indian and Northern Affairs continues to encourage mineral development even when it makes no economic sense. During the late 1970s a group of investors led by Texan brothers Nelson Bunker Hunt and William Hunt came up with a crazy plan to corner the world's silver market by building a huge mine a few kilometres outside of the park on Prairie Creek. Prairie Creek is a cool, clear running stream that flows through Deadmen Valley before spilling into the Nahanni. Scientist and economists warned that the project would run into financial and environmental trouble. They were soon proven right. A few weeks before their Cadillac Mine was to go into production, the price of silver crashed. The Hunt brothers filed for bankruptcy, and left Indians Affairs responsible for the hundreds of drums of cyanide and other chemicals that had been brought in to separate silver from the ore. Indian Affairs, however, did nothing about the toxic mess for more than two decades until it was pointed out that many of the drums were badly rusted and in danger of leaking.

The lesson was never learned. In 2003, the Dene of the Dehcho offered a huge part of their land to expand Nahanni's boundaries so that the headwaters of all the rivers flowing through the park would be protected. In spite of that offer, Indian Affairs has been unwilling to dissuade another company from reviving the Prairie Creek project.

———

The sun is blazing down like a hot iron as Doug Tate and I make our way up Prairie Creek, the day after we arrive at the warden's cabin in Deadmen Valley. We are searching for the elusive upland sandpiper, a pigeon-sized bird that nests on the ground and often perches in trees. This is one of the few places north of the 60th parallel that the bird can be found but all we see are mountain bluebirds. Enervated, I feel the beginnings of a bad headache. Damn this stupid pigeon! I should have stayed at the warden's cabin with the rest of the gang. And then it happens. A bear pops out from behind some trees, forcing us to play a game of hide and seek for several minutes.

Having spent considerable time hunting in this wildlife rich valley, Raymond Patterson wrote that there are "more bears (here) to the acre than any place I have ever seen." Mindful of that observation, I stay as close to Tate as possible — he has the bear spray; mine is at the airport in Fort Simpson with all the rest of my gear. Patterson also noted that "blowing sand, lightning, thunder, rain and gales" are "typical Deadmen Valley stuff." When it storms, he wrote, the place looks "just like hell." Alerted to the sound of something rumbling in the distance, I am no longer wondering where the bear has disappeared to. Looking up at the blue sky, I ask Tate whether it's rock that's being moved along the creek bed that is making the noise. "No," he says, pointing to an enormous, anvil-headed column of cumulous cloud rising up over the mountains behind us. Not wanting to be caught on the wrong side of the river when this one hits, we hightail it back to our canoe, following the fresh tracks of a couple of wolves. By the time we reach the boat and push off, the first gust of cold air gives us a good slap. Then a deafening clap of thunder forces us to duck. Looking back, I see a wall of sand moving across Prairie Creek toward us. For a fleeting moment, I weigh the merits of a quick electrocution over a long, cold drowning. Waiting for us up on shore at the warden's cabin, thankfully, are a line of outstretched hands. Two of them pull Doug and me up onto the riverbank. The others lift the canoe out of the water. Blasphemous as it may sound to wilderness purists, I don't regret for a minute taking refuge in the wardens' cabin and eating supper by a warm stove.

———

Most northern rivers, I've come to learn, offer an epiphany somewhere along the way. On the Coppermine, it's the shiver one gets looking down at Bloody Falls where, more than 200 years ago, a band of Dene from the south slaughtered two dozen Inuit men, woman and children who had camped there. On the Thelon, it's the gloomy stand of trees on the edge of the Barren Lands where John Hornby, Edgar Christian and Harold Adlard are buried. The three starved to death in 1927 as a result of bad luck, poor planning and unfortunate timing. And at Belanger Rapids on the Burnside River, it's the spot where John Franklin and two other men nearly drowned while crossing the river in 1820 on canoe trip in which only nine of 20 men survived.

For me, on the Nahanni, it's the 34-kilometre stretch of river that takes you through First Canyon from Deadmen Valley to Kraus's Hotsprings. The highest cliffs in Canada, higher than those found in Yellowstone's Grand Canyon, are found here. So is one of the finest wilderness campsites in the world. Neil Hartling, a Yukon guide who has led dozens of trips down this river, insists that it's sacrilegious to do anything but float through this section of river.

Poole Field gave First Canyon its name, and likely encouraged others to be practical in naming the others Second, Third and Fourth. You can pay a price before you enter this one. Just downstream of Dry Canyon, there is an island where the river picks up speed before turning sharply to the left. A huge slab of dolomite sticks out of the right bank of this bend and it nearly did in trapper

George Sibbeston when he boated through earlier in the century. Paddlers can easily avoid the worst of what George's Riffle offers by staying left of river centre or going right of the island if there is enough water in that channel. The first option can be a hoot, and on hot days, there's a bonus waiting for paddlers in the cool waters at Whitespray Spring. Here water gushes out of a series of caves and underground channels from the karstlands above. It is as clear and clean as any water you'll find anywhere in the world.

Time passes slowly as we float silently through First Canyon. Up above, the clouds are nearly touching the spires and turrets along the clifftop. From time to time, stones slide or bounce down the naked rock, echoing off the canyon walls before splashing into the water. Only moss, lichen and the odd pine or spruce tree grow along these cliffs. The steep walls won't allow in enough sun for much else to grow. Carl Lafferty points to the entrance of a huge cave high above us. Grotte Valerie, one of the best known of the 120 caves in First Canyon, is 1,900-metres long and its subterranean passages vary in size from crawling tunnels to enormous chambers filled with 350,000 year-old stalactites and stalagmites. Back in the 1970s, a French scientist discovered a frozen waterfall that ended in a large chamber now known as Gallery of the Dead Sheep. Sometime between 2,000 and 10,000 years ago, more than 100 Dall's sheep wandered in and slid down this icefall.

Snow covers the mountains 30-metres above our camp at Lafferty Creek. I had been looking forward to this day for some time — paddling through Lafferty Riffle with Lafferty himself. Now, I am not quite so eager. Carl is wedded to doing it in 'Bob', the rubber canoe that he is so attached to. Why, I don't know. As its name suggests, the thing bobs up and down relentlessly, stubbornly resisting the stroke of a paddle. Worse still, is that from the get-go, you kneel in a pool of water that slowly works its way beneath your rain gear and up your pants. It's damn cold this morning, and the pants and shirt I have been wearing for more than a week are permanently damp and dirty like dish rags. Running on the spot, I try to warm up before hopping into Bob. Carl, all toasty in a dry suit, is grinning from ear to ear. Almost immediately, the water creeps up my legs. Kraus's hotsprings can not come too soon.

The rapids at Lafferty's Riffle are most formidable when the river levels are low, created as they are by the outwash from the creek in Lafferty Canyon. So, they don't present much of a challenge to us as the water continues to rise. Any hope I have of warming up at the hotpools, however, are dashed when we discover them submerged two feet below the waterline. Off and on for more than 30 years, Gus and Mary Kraus made their home here until they moved to Little Doctor Lake in 1970. Twenty paddlers went down the river that year and Gus felt that was too many. Mary Denya was born at Fort Liard in 1912. She spent six years in a convent before marrying her first husband Pascal Ekenale, who was Dene like herself. He died in 1942. A native of Chicago, Kraus settled in the Nahanni region when both Canada and the United States were in the depths of a deep Depression in the 1930s, and when gold was one of the few things that still had tremendous value. He and Mary met shortly after her husband died. They couldn't have picked a better spot to grow their vegetables when they weren't hunting or trapping on the Nahanni. Without a doubt, the hotsprings were the inspiration for the legend of the tropical gardens of Nahanni. Flowing out of the ground at temperatures reaching as high as 38.8 C, they account for the exotic looking plants and maybe the humming bird that Patterson claims to have seen.

Gus Kraus saw a great many strange things happen on the Nahanni before he died in 1992 (Mary lives in a nursing home in Fort Simpson). One of the strangest occurred in the fall of 1959 when he and game warden Frank Bailey flew into McMillan Lake just south of the Flat River to check on five men who had come in to prospect. Since none had a hunting licence, Bailey offered to take them out if they so desired. The men declined, saying they had enough flour, beans and tea and coffee to keep them healthy until a supply plane arrived on snow skis in January. The supply plane, however, didn't show up and by the time Yellowknife-based bush pilot Chuck McAvoy dropped in on them by chance the next spring, there were only two remaining. Both were in bad shape. The survivors told a grim story. One man was so desperate when the plane failed to show, he tied a stick of dynamite to his chest and lit the fuse. The two others went overland to Nahanni Butte to get help, but were never seen again. Kraus was sent out to find them but he never found a trace.

———

It takes a very long day or two short ones to get from Kraus's Hotsprings to the tiny hamlet of Nahanni Butte where the Nahanni flows into the Liard. At The Splits, the big river becomes braided, shallow and slow. Here we come across the bow of a canoe sticking straight up out of a pile of logs that have jammed along the river bank. Speculation is that it belongs to Neil and Robert Cameron. We try long and hard, but we can not extricate it from this woody grave. Like the logs, it has become part of the river.

———

This is how it occasionally ends for some adventures on the Nahanni. Some go home lucky to be alive. Others don't go home at all. Standing there on the riverbank, watching the wardens empty what they can out of the canoe, I can't help think about William Sommer and what had driven him to continue on with his journey when a friend he had planned to do it with backed out at the last minute because his parents felt it was too dangerous. What was it, I wonder, that motivated him to go alone even when it was pointed out to him in Fort Simpson that it was a very dangerous thing to do?

Sommer, according to his brother Eric, was a deeply spiritual person who apparently had trouble coming to grips with his worthiness and his relationship with God. But his diary suggests that God is what he found on the river after he lost his maps in three-to-four foot high waves before they inexplicably floated back toward him. He took that to be a sign that God was going to protect him. "Even if something does happen to me, I am sure that in life and death, God will be the Father, and I will be his son, and without the will of my heavenly Father, not a hair will fall from my head," he wrote in his diary.

Steve Catto is pretty certain that Sommer drowned the second or third day of the trip well before the serious whitewater begins. After capsizing, he may have hit his head on a rock, passed out and drowned. There is also a more remote possibility that Sommer and his dog were off hiking somewhere when his kayak came loose from the willows on shore. Realizing that his only way out was overland he may have set out, got lost, run into a bear or drowned trying to cross the river. His family ultimately decided not to prolong the search after it was clear the boy would not be found alive. Eric says it was their way of letting him become part of the legend that he wanted to experience.

During our last hour on the Nahanni, I am thinking about William Sommer getting into his VW Rabbit at his parents' home that May day in 1999, waving goodbye, and nervously, but excitedly, heading off on a trip. I can see him in my mind's eye walking into the Nahanni National Park office in Fort Simpson as I had done, pumped with adrenaline. And I can see him standing on the side of that washed-out road near the old mine site wondering what to do next when a four-wheel drive comes by and offers to take him to his point of departure. Maybe he thought himself invincible. Many young men do. I am not religious, but I can't help but admire how his father Murray comforts himself with a proverb: "I love them that love me, and those that seek me early shall find me."

Beaufort Sea

Inuvik
Tsiigehtchic

Colville Lake
Fort Good Hope

Norman Wells
Tulita

Great Bear Lake

Willow Lake R.

Fort Simpson

Great Slave Lake

The Mackenzie River

300 Kilometres

Map Area

N
W   E
S

Mackenzie River

Deh Cho — The Big River

Midnight light in the Arctic has a way of playing tricks on a city boy, especially one who had been paddling along the Mackenzie River for 14 hours a day for nearly two weeks straight. Initially, I thought nothing of the distant sky billowing with violet-blues and magentas. It looked more like the northern fogs that roll in late at night after things cool down. But it was still too hot and muggy for things to mist up; so, I pored over the map, more concerned with finding a breezy island to protect me from the mosquitoes and blackflies. And then it happened. A brilliant light flashed in the north, followed by a cool gust of wind that sent a wave rippling upstream past my kayak. The giant beaver had slapped its tail.

Thunder followed lightning. Before the crack had a chance to reach me, I cursed myself for pushing so late into the night and not noticing this storm looming. I stuffed the maps between my legs and started for shore. It was too late. Looking up, I watched helplessly as an even more powerful gust of wind brought in a wall of white spray that caught me broadside and nearly flipped me over. A huge rolling wave followed and partially filled my boat since I hadn't the time to button down the spray skirt.

This weather is classic for July in the Mackenzie Valley. One minute it could be the hottest place in Canada; the next, leaden clouds might sail overhead, spitting pellets of ice at embattled birds and unfortunate souls like me. Nearly a kilometre from shore, I could only survive by straightening out, riding the curling waves as they rolled upstream and angling into shore at every opportunity. I didn't even think about trying to retrieve the map, the spare paddle or my hat, which were now swirling in sinister boils and whirlpools.

These can be terrifying times for a solo paddler, knowing that another big wave could sink you in seconds. Even the best panic in these situations. Not sure if they have seen the worst of what's to come, some make a break for shore and risk being flipped sideways. Knowing tent, sleeping bag and food were securely stuffed deep inside the kayak, I was not tempted to risk a long, midnight swim and maybe a three-or-four day walk to safety. I took a deep breath, braced for the rollercoaster ride that lay ahead, and said a prayer to Yamoria, the beneficent spirit of the Mackenzie Valley, a spirit powerful enough to chase away giant beavers.

The Mackenzie is a huge river, exceeded only by the Amazon and the Mississippi/Missouri rivers in the area it drains. From its headwaters on the Peace and Finlay rivers in northern British Columbia, it flows for more than 4,200 kilometres before spilling into the Beaufort Sea. Four kilometres wide in places, the river can be easily be mistaken for a big lake. Just when think you have found the perfect landing, the powerful currents that snake silently through the muddy water can sweep you past your target. With lightning striking all around, it was hit and miss for maybe an hour before I finally got close enough to jump, waist-deep, into an eddy and drag my water logged tub onto the slippery, boulder-strewn shore. The rain was lashing down sideways. Tired, sopping wet and cold, I didn't give a damn that setting up my tent in this gale was going to be a nightmare. I was thankful not to be struggling with the rollers, swimming in the surge that was sweeping six-metre-long trees past me.

My trip down the Mackenzie had begun two weeks earlier in the town of Fort Simpson, where the Mackenzie and the Liard rivers combine on a northwest course down the big valley to the delta and, finally, the Beaufort Sea. The Mackenzie Valley is home to a number of First Nations: the Dene of the Dehcho in the south, the Inuvialuit and the Gwich'in in the north, and the Dogrib Dene and the Dene of the Sahtu who are sandwiched between. There are no more than 9,000, mostly aboriginal people, living in an area the size of California.

Some elders believe the river is haunted by giant monsters and spirits, and a real-life prehistoric-looking creature that was, until recently, dismissed as a figment of overactive imaginations. Fish grow big here. In the summer of 2001, a gigantic, 33.6 kilogram lake trout was hauled out of Great Bear Lake. The Winnipegger who caught it, a woman who had never fished before, spent two hours landing the monster while die-hard fishermen shook their heads in envy. Grizzlies, on the other hand, grow no more than two-thirds the size of their southern cousins. Stressed by the long winters, and a shorter foraging period before hibernation, females don't begin reproducing until they are nine years old, nearly twice the age of most other grizzlies.

Peter Pond never understood the full measure of the Mackenzie while drafting the first map of the valley in the 1770s. Most of what Pond, a North West Company fur trader, penned was based on conversations he had had with the Copper Dene while he was stationed in the Athabasca region in what is now northern Alberta. But he was convinced that the stream the Dene saw flowing out of the west end of Great Slave Lake was the same water Captain James Cook had charted when he had sailed up the Pacific coast a few years earlier. Were this true, it would have provided Pond's North West Company with the long sought-after route across Canada to the Orient. More important, it held out the possibility of new trade. As it was, the Hudson's Bay Company's monopoly was confined to the lands that drained into Canada's middle north. Pond never did test his theory, wrong though it turned out to be, but his protégé, Alexander Mackenzie, did.

On the morning of June 3, 1789, Mackenzie, four voyageurs and a party of aboriginals under the leadership of a Dene named Nestabeck, (whom Mackenzie called English Chief), set off from Fort Chipewyan in northern Alberta. So convinced were they that the river would take them to the Orient, they took along rubles to trade with the Russians.

The early going was rough. After spending the better part of a long day on Lake Athabasca, near the present-day Northwest Territories border, they headed down the mighty Slave where they were forced to portage around four deadly rapids – the Casette, the Pelican, the Mountain and the Rapids of the Drowned. Over the length of 26 kilometres, the river dropped 33 metres. The river was a veritable minefield of giant "haystacks," six-metre-long diagonal waves collapsing on each other and deep holes into which big spruce and aspen trees disappeared.

There was little sign of summer when Mackenzie and his crew arrived at Great Slave, the 10th largest lake in the world. Ice still held fast to the shoreline and they struggled for nearly three weeks. They dragged their flimsy canoes 150 kilometres before finding, with considerable difficulty, the narrows through which the lake drained into the river they sought. The Dogrib Dene warned Mackenzie not to pass through there, believing a monster would swallow anything that went beyond this gate to the North. Contemptuous of most everything aboriginal, Mackenzie ignored their advice.

The Mackenzie meanders for more than 1,400 kilometres from Great Slave, past Fort Simpson, Wrigley, Tulita, Norman Wells, Fort Good Hope, Tsiigehtchic, Inuvik and Aklavik before braiding in dozens of directions and spilling into the brackish Beaufort Sea. Ultimately, Mackenzie made it to the Arctic coast and back to Fort Chipewyan in 102 days. Upon learning, halfway through, that the river, which now bears his name spilt into the Northern Sea and not the Pacific, Mackenzie dubbed it the "River of Disappointment." In a letter to Lord Dorchester, the Governor of

British North America, he lamented that his trip "did not answer the intended purpose," but merely proved that Pond's "assertion was nothing but conjecture, and that a Northwest Passage is impractical."

Historians have been kind to Mackenzie. In his book *Caesars of the Wilderness*, Peter C. Newman insists Mackenzie is a "legitimate Canadian hero." Others have praised him for his empathy with his men and for the way he treated the Aboriginal Peoples. At night in the tent, I read his narrative for inspiration, but I confess that by the time I finished, I had found no such empathy. Unlike John Franklin, who confessed to being brought to tears by the kindness of his guide Akaitcho, or Samuel Hearne who saw in his Dene guide Matonabbee, the "nobleness and elegance" of manners that "might have been admired by the first personages of the world," Mackenzie believed the Dene's stamina, intelligence, and appetite were inferior to his own. Nestabeck apparently sensed this early, but got nowhere when he confronted Mackenzie about his show of disrespect. Perversely, Mackenzie was pleased that he had got under his skin: "This was the very opportunity which I wanted, to make him acquainted with my dissatisfaction for some time past."

Only once did Mackenzie show a hint of compassion. When Nestabeck wanted to shoot Red Knif (sic), the Dogrib whom they had engaged on the shores of Great Slave Lake, for not knowing where the entrance to the great river was located, Mackenzie reluctantly intervened. "Indeed, none of us are well pleased with hime (sic)," he noted in his diary, perhaps after duly considering a summary execution. "But we don't think with English Chief that he merits such severe punishment."

The rest of the time, it seems, Mackenzie either coerced or kidnapped whatever Dene he met. He forced them into servitude, and then hunted them down when they ran away. Why he bothered is a mystery. He considered their advice and stories "so very fabulous" that he refused to include them in his narrative, which is a pity considering the anthropological richness of what they had might have conveyed. "Suffice it to say," he wrote, " that they would wish to make us believe that we would be several winters getting to the sea, and that we should be old men by the time we would return, that we would encounter many monsters (which can only exist in their own while (sic) imaginations. Besides that, there are two impracticable falls or rapids in the river, the first thirty days' march from us."

After one more journey — a more successful trip across the Rockies searching for an overland route to the Pacific – Mackenzie finally returned to Scotland. He married a 14-year-old girl from a wealthy family, obtained a share in the North West Company and resisted any opportunity to return to the northwest of Canada — even though he had sired at least one illegitimate son there.

In Fort Simpson, I discovered that many Métis and Dene are thankful Mackenzie never returned. They see Mackenzie's journey as the catalyst for the colonial government that followed and cast them as second-class citizens in their own land. More than a few think Mackenzie should have been shot rather than treated with politeness by their ancestors, while a more moderate majority would rather see his name erased from the map and the river renamed Deh Cho, the Dene word for Great River.

The residents of Fort Norman and Fort Franklin, small communities in the Mackenzie Valley, have already changed their village names to Tulita and Deline. And who would begrudge them that? For many Dene and Métis, Franklin was merely an overstuffed tenderfoot who, in the summer and fall of 1821, nearly starved himself and his men to death when he ignored the advice of his guide and headed overland to the Arctic Coast as winter set in.

While at Fort Simpson, I tried to get a sense of what lay ahead. I tried to imagine the origin of many of the European names on the map. To the west of the Mackenzie lay the Black Stone Range, the Red Stone Range and the Flint Stone Range. To the east were the Great Bear and Little Bear rivers. Also on the map were the names Stinky Creek and Dodo Mountain.

I had already travelled down the Nahanni and Liard and into Fort Simpson where I stayed before journeying down the Mackenzie. It was cold and raining. The food and gear that had been bumped from a plane were waiting for me at the Parks Canada office on the Nahanni, but my kayak was still no where to be had. Not that I cared too much. I had spent 12 days on the Nahanni without a change of clothes, no air mattress and a summer sleeping bag. At Fort Simpson, I only wanted to find a hot shower, a warm bed and a meal that hadn't been cooked over a campfire.

But both the Nahanni Inn and the only other small hotel were full. Then someone told me that Nick Sibbeston, a Canadian senator who had once been premier of the Northwest Territories, had a bed and breakfast in a big house he had recently built on the outskirts of the village. A phone call later and I was eating bannock and moose stew with Sibbeston, and hearing the first of many different takes on the history of the Mackenzie Valley.

In private, Nick Sibbeston, then 60 years of age, had a gentle, graceful nature that seemed far removed from his tough, combative political style. He was first elected to the Northwest Territories legislature in 1970 when he was just 27 years old, but quit in disgust when he realized to what extent the territory was run by a federally appointed commissioner. A law degree and a marriage followed before he re-entered politics in 1979 with the aim of sweeping Ottawa-appointed bureaucrats out of government and returning power into the hands of the people. His many critics laughed when he said he would some day become leader of the government. And they laughed again when he became the government leader and insisted on being called premier. People stopped laughing when the title stuck.

He was hell-bent on changing the political culture. During his rookie term in the Northwest Territories legislature, for example, he was singled out by the Speaker who suggested that he wear a tie. "Only if you take off that silly British robe," Sibbeston retorted. Then, he was ejected from the legislature for cuffing Tagak Curley on the side of the head after Curley, the Inuit member from Rankin Inlet, taunted him during *Question Period*. But Sibbeston really turned heads the day he performed a striptease. "I do not wish to have anyone here – the Commissioner, or anybody – tell me that I have to wear a suit and tie," he pronounced. "So today, I wish to take

my suit and tie off and wear something that reflects the Dene cus-
tom and culture and way of dressing." He put on a pair of moccasins
and a moose-hide vest and announced that he was "throwing off the
chains of colonialism."

Sibbeston turned out to be a trendsetter. The many who followed him into the Office of Premier all took pride in wearing traditional clothing. Today, the Speaker, wears a black robe adorned
with tufts of moose hair.

It didn't take long to figure out why Sibbeston and others living along the Mackenzie Valley are determined to change the
political culture and to reinterpret the history of the North.
Sibbeston's sense of place and identity had been moulded almost
from the day he was born out of wedlock to a father he would never
know and to a Dene mother who was an alcoholic. Like many Dene
and Métis children, he was sent to a residential school, prohibited
from speaking in his native tongue and forced to wear white man's
clothing. Even now, a boat ride along the Mackenzie is an emotional experience for Sibbeston. All he remembers about the trip
to the residential school at Fort Providence is that he couldn't stop
crying. He also remembers that only one of the many nuns ever did
anything to make him feel at home. "These people were supposed
to love God and be charitable," he said. "All but one that I met were
mean. They were never happy. They never smiled. It was, at times,
brutal."

Sibbeston believed his residential school experience and the
fact that he had never known his father accounted for the many
dark periods in his life. In search of more information about his
family, and possibly a cure for his depression, he set off to pursue a
rumour that his father had been George Dalziel, a legendary bush
pilot, whose flights up and down the Mackenzie and Nahanni in the
1930s and 1940s were well documented by several newspapers,
including the *New York Times*. Dalziel had arrived from British
Columbia in 1932, buying his first plane two years later. He had
survived a couple of crashes and some brutal winters in the bush.
Dalziel ignored the rules. He hunted and trapped where he wanted

and smuggled illegal animal trophies. The RCMP clearly didn't like him but the trappers did. To them, Dalziel was a modern-day Robin Hood who had flown in frozen turkeys when the trappers were half-starving on the Nahanni one brutally cold Christmas. He also flew them out for medical treatment when a flu epidemic hit.

"There seemed to be a lot of similarities," Sibbeston told me. "He was a renegade like me, always one step ahead of the law. He was reputedly kind. And he loved to fly, which most of my children do."

Sibbeston eventually tracked down some of Dalziel's offspring living in British Columbia and was delighted to learn that they were willing to provide DNA samples. "The tests turned out to be 99.9 per cent certain that we were directly related," he told me. "I just got the results the other day. George Dalziel was, indeed, my father."

Sibbeston dealt with his depression by travelling down the Mackenzie into the wilderness to take counsel from George Boots, a wise, old man of the river who lived, year-round, at the confluence of the Mackenzie and Willowlake rivers. Dene leaders often sought advice from Boots, then 91. They called him Joa and would come to pray in his makeshift chapel. While some regarded him as a powerful prophet like André André (or Naedzo) in Deline who had powers that transcended those of ordinary mortals, others saw Boots as simply a deeply religious holy man.

Since the 1850s when the first missionaries boated down the Mackenzie River, aboriginal spiritual beliefs were, and have continued to be, incorporated into Christian teachings. The most successful missionaries – those who tallied the most converts – realized that they were most effective if they diminished the traditional Christ-on-the-Cross image and sold the Saviour as the perfect Dene, a free man in the wilderness who resisted the temptation of evil spirits. Everything else followed easily since the Holy Trinity – the Father, Son and Holy Ghost – was in keeping with the benevolent spirit-worship practised by the Dene.

Boots was five years old when an Oblate missionary came down the Mackenzie in a leaky birchbark canoe with little more than a sack of rotting potatoes, some flour and tea. Mesmerized by the priest's devotion, his Bible stories and his hymns, Boots embraced Christianity and didn't undermine his Dene spirituality. He held onto that faith throughout the many years he lived in the wilderness.

When I had finally caught up with Boots at Willowlake River, I was a little taken aback. Barely five-feet tall, Boots looked more like Yoda from *Star Wars* — except with round-rimmed glasses and a baseball cap — than a prophet. But I took counsel. I was impressed that his statuesque, 34-year-old Dene wife had offered to live with him because she had been so taken by his goodness and spirituality. I was also impressed by the fact that he still went moose-hunting up the Willowlake River every fall.

Boots was bewitching in an unnerving way. While a friend translated, he never once took his eyes off of me to consider a response. There was not a touch of meanness in his demeanour. He was a man at peace with his world. Boots assured me that I would be a much better human being after my trip. The Deh Cho, he said would cleanse me of my sins as long as I offered a gift – a string of tobacco or a prayer – each time I set off in my kayak. He also warned me of the spirit monsters that I might meet along the way.

The monsters he described were almost identical to the beast that had once terrorized the people on the Nahanni. In the Mackenzie Valley, however, there were three giant beavers that slapped their tails to drown boaters. According to Boots, the beavers had eventually been chased from Great Bear Lake, down Great Bear River to Tulita by the spirit-warrior Yamoria. Using a bow and arrow, Yamoria finally killed the beavers at the confluence of the Great Bear and Mackenzie rivers.

"Look carefully when you get there," Boots told me, "and you will see, on the south side of the mountain, three dark mounds. Down below in the river, there will be big tree trunks sticking out of the water. The mounds are the sites where Yamoria stretched out the hides of the beasts. The poles you'll see in the river are the ends of the arrows he used to kill them.

"Before you get to this spot," he added, "Look closely for a fire burning on the side of the river. That's where Yamoria cooked and ate the meat of these monsters. If you see this fire at night, you will live a long life."

My initial inclination was to dismiss the advice just as Mackenzie had dismissed the Dene who advised him. But Sibbeston had convinced me. So had Camille Piché, a Catholic missionary I knew and respected. Piché claimed to have seen too many extraordinary and inexplicable things during his quarter century in the North to dismiss the possibility that there were other forces at play in the Dene world.

I didn't give the story much thought until I was long past Willowlake River. The river was wide and slow, as it had been since I left Fort Simpson. I was struggling to make progress through the rain and the powerful headwinds. Cold, wet and hungry, I hugged the shoreline, which was steep, muddy and tangled, to avoid the bigger waves in the main current. There was no place to pull in. It was depressing. Then, the wind calmed, the rain stopped and a wall of thick fog crept in, blanketing the river from shore to shore. Above the fog, thunder cracked. And then, dramatically, the fog lifted, revealing a shoreline smouldering in smoke. It was too weird for words. But there it was the fire that Boots had told me to look out for. I later learned that the smouldering river banks were coal seams that had been burning for hundreds of years but was content to think I would live a long life.

When I finally landed on the sandy shore of Tulita, where the Mackenzie and Great Bear rivers meet, Dene leaders from across the Mackenzie Valley were convening for their annual gathering. For the first time on the trip, it was sunny, so I spread my soggy tent and wet clothes across a bleached tree trunk. Looking up at Bear Rock, the massive hill that hovers over the confluence of the rivers, I saw the three dark mounds that George Boots had described as the tree trunks poking out of the river.

The Dene national assembly is always an important political event but more than usual was at stake at this meeting. Stephen

Kakfwi, the premier of the Northwest Territories was there, as was Joe Handley, the finance minister and future premier. Both wanted to talk to the Dene chiefs about a proposed multibillion-dollar natural gas pipeline through the Mackenzie Valley and about a plan to build six massive hydroelectric dams. "Fur will never come back," Handley told them. "And there is limited potential for commercial fishing and forestry in the Northwest Territories. Hydro will drive industry down the road and provide us with revenues through electricity exports to southern Canada and the United States."

Handley envisioned two dams in the Mackenzie Valley, a $1.2 billion, 600-megawatt project along the Great Bear River just upstream of Tulita, and a massive $23-billion, 10,500-megawatt project at the Sans Sault Rapids on the Mackenzie between Norman Wells and Fort Good Hope. Most of those in attendance didn't know what to make of his speech. But George Blondin, a respected elder, was fearful of what development would bring.

"The days of Dene medicine men are quickly coming to an end because so few people are living on the land and by the laws of the Creator." Blondin said. "The Dene ways are disappearing."

———

All of this, of course, transpired in the weeks before that stormy night on the Mackenzie.

When I woke up from the nightmare, my feet were still propped up against the tent poles where I had planted them hours earlier to prevent the whole thing from collapsing. The storm that had nearly drowned me was over but its remains were being soaked up by my down sleeping bag. It was so calm and silent, I felt I was suspended in time. A hum, which I mistook for a big bumblebee, made me realize that this was the first time in nearly three weeks that there was no wind. But the buzz grew louder before becoming a thump, thump. A helicopter was flying overhead. Popping my head out of the tent, I looked up and saw a round orange ball burning through the grey fog. The helicopter circled like a UFO trying to figure out what form of intelligence would be paddling a kayak through this muddy wilderness. Then it left and I considered what flavour of porridge I would have with my morning coffee. I wished I had brought along a fishing rod.

Before the porridge had a chance to boil, the chopper returned and landed on an outcrop of flat rock no more than 100 metres from my tent. Two men hopped out. One carried sandwiches and a bag of homemade donuts. The other had a large Thermos of coffee. They were two forest-firefighters on their way from Norman Wells to see if the thunderstorm had doused a huge fire. After the violent rainstorm, which they said had been one of the worst on record, they took pity and paid me a visit. It was the first time on the trip that anyone had stopped to find out what I was doing.

———

It was warm and cloudy when I finally arrived at Norman Wells, an anomaly in the Mackenzie Valley. It is the only community that doesn't trace its origins to a fur-trading post, but rather to two half-century-old pipelines. One sends oil south to Alberta and the United States; the other once pumped fuel across the Mackenzie Mountains to the Yukon during the Second World War.

The Dene call this area "Le Gohlini," meaning "where the oil is." They had once used the yellow goo that oozed from the river-banks to patch their canoes. The Dene led geologists to the site in the early 1900s and Imperial Oil sent the first drilling team here in 1920. Company engineers had never seen anything quite like it. Unlike most crude, which becomes thick and sticky when it gets very cold, this oil poured like water in temperatures that dipped to -50 C, making it much easier to pump. During those early years, demand was limited to the needs of the communities upstream.

During the Second World War, after the Japanese had attacked westcoast refineries and bombed Pearl Harbor, the U.S. government decided to draw from these deposits, believing Whitehorse to be part of Alaska. The American officials called upon James H. Graham, the Dean of Engineering at the University of Kentucky, to determine how it could be done.

Initially, no one bothered to consult the Canadian government but once informed Canadian officials had serious doubts. They reluctantly gave their approval, knowing perhaps that the Americans would probably build it anyway, just as they had the Alaska Highway two years earlier. In return, the Americans agreed to hire a few Canadians, but for lower pay.

The 960-kilometre-long pipeline was built by 2,500 military personnel and 22,500 civilians at a cost of more than $134 million. But oil didn't flow for more than a year. When the war ended, the Americans abandoned the pipeline and didn't bother cleaning up the broken-down trucks, bulldozers, camps and bridges. That debris is now part of a heritage hiking trail and a national historic site. Each year, a few brave souls make the long journey to relive this chapter in northern history.

Fewer still paddle the full length of the Mackenzie. The river has never had much appeal to canoeists or kayakers, save for a few Germans who have been inspired by the journals of Johann Steinbruck – a Hessian mercenary who travelled with Mackenzie in 1789 after fighting with the British in the War of American Independence, and then deserting. The river is too big and muddy for most. And given the opportunity to paddle the more picturesque and challenging Mountain or the Natla and the Keele rivers, which flow into the Mackenzie, most people would forego the big river.

Still, there are places that make the trip worthwhile: Camsell Bend, just downstream of Fort Simpson, where the mountains come into view; Willowlake River, where the water flows clear and cool out of the Horn Plateau, and the spot where the Great Bear and Mackenzie rivers meet in panoramic splendour. What puzzled me about my journey so far was that, apart from a moose, a few caribou and six black bears that had harassed me, I had not seen much wildlife.

At the Canadian Legion in Norman Wells during Friday Happy Hour I asked Alisdair Veitch, a government biologist, why so few animals were seen in the valley. He smiled. "Why don't you come with me tonight?" he suggested. "We've got to fly up to the Mackenzie Mountains to check out a report from some local hunters about a mountain sheep they killed. They think that maybe there was something wrong with it."

Less than an hour into the plane ride, I realized why Alisdair had smiled. We had spotted a black bear, a grizzly bear, some caribou, two moose, a golden eagle and an animal that has been absent for so long from this part of the world that recent sightings have been dismissed as a symptom of an overactive imagination: a muskox. Other than the caribou, the muskox — with curled horns, a long, shaggy coat and short stocky legs — is the only hoofed animal to survive in the Arctic at the end of the Pleistocene epoch 10,000 years ago. A Dene legend says the woodland muskoxen were driven from the sub-Arctic forests by shamans long ago, as a punishment to those who had questioned their powers.

Alisdair, however, saw it differently. "When the buffalo disappeared from the Prairies," he told me, "the Hudson's Bay Company turned its attention north. They were paying as much as $24 for a muskox hide. When you compare that to the $5 people up here were getting for a beaver pelt, it's not surprising why so many of the animals disappeared so fast."

A hunting ban was imposed in 1917 and the muskox has returned to the Mackenzie Valley. Alisdair and his colleagues estimated that there were as many as 2,000 muskoxen in the Sahtu region, which includes most of the Mackenzie Valley — from Willowlake River to Fort Good Hope, and from Great Bear Lake to the Yukon border. "It's funny but the people up here have been reluctant to hunt the animals," he said. "Only three muskoxen have been shot by residents in the last six years. It's the same story with grizzlies. The people in the Sahtu have a right to shoot them but few do. Maybe it's because many see the grizzly as sacred. Sahtu is the Dene word for grizzly bear," he explained. "In any case, because of that, we may have one of the biggest grizzly bear preserves in the world — even though very little of this land is legally protected."

There was only one other passenger in the single-engine, four-seat plane on the flight from Norman Wells to Colville Lake, the most remote community in the Sahtu. But that young man, a resident of the community I guessed, nodded off seconds after buckling his seat belt. Alone, I was left to chat with the pilot who had no clue about the community where we were going to, nor anything about the so-called "End-of-Earth" people who lived there with Bern Will Brown, the Catholic missionary who had led a few of his followers deep into the wilderness more than 40 years ago.

Situated near the edge of the treeline, Colville Lake and its 98 Dene residents didn't rate a mention in the Canadian Encyclopedia. But here is where the Earth ended for the Dene of the Mackenzie Valley, and where it began for their traditional enemy, the Inuit who lived in the barrens along the Arctic coast. Brown had been to Colville Lake in 1962 to set up a mission where the Dene could maintain the traditional lifestyle that had become increasingly threatened by alcohol and various other social evils that were slowly migrating up the river valley. There were only two families there but dozens made the long overland trip with Brown.

Brown resigned from the priesthood 30 years ago after he fell in love with and married Margaret Steen, an Inuvialuit woman who cooked and cleaned for the tiny parish Brown had founded. Although he continued to lead the community in prayer on Sundays, offer Communion and bury the dead, he was making a living as an artist and flying out fishermen from his tiny lodge on Colville Lake.

Only after the pilot dropped us off on the dusty dirt airstrip on the edge of town did I have second thoughts about what it was I was getting into. I had sent Brown a letter months before informing him of my intention to visit. All I had received in reply was a note telling me that it was not in his power to stop me, and that he might be busy catering to his clients when I arrived. Seconds after we stepped off the plane, the other passenger beetled off on an all-terrain cycle. Alone in the hot sun with no one to greet me save for the mosquitoes and big horseflies, I felt a little like Cary Grant in

North by Northwest, who finds himself alone on the side of the high-way on the dusty Prairie waiting for someone who is not going to show up. I considered hopping back on the plane but before I had a chance the pilot was already blowing dust up on the runway to head back to Norman Wells.

I grabbed my small pack and started walking toward town. None of the three people who passed offered a greeting. From the hilltop, I could see the town below nestled beside a stunningly beau-tiful lake. The town looked deserted except for one man who was walking away from me, so I picked up the pace to catch up with him. When I asked where I might find Brown, he pointed to a cluster of cabins and walked off without saying a word.

One by one, I found each of the cabin doors locked. Peering into empty spaces through a couple of windows, I began to worry about what I would do without food, a tent or a sleeping bag. There was no hotel. This was, without a doubt, the most unfriendly place I had been to so far on this trip. Then, after what must have been one of the longest half-hours of my life, a husky, white-haired man appeared from nowhere. "You must be the writer," he growled. It was Brown – sounding, if not looking, his 80 years.

"I got to go fly out and pick up a couple of American fisher-men out on the lake," he said, turning back toward me. "In the meantime, if you're staying, I guess you can park yourself in that six-man cabin over there."

Once inside of the cabin, I knew everything was going to be fine. There was a coffee maker, tea, clean sheets and pillows, a bucket for drinking water and a big picture window that provid-ed me with a stunning view of Colville Lake. It wasn't until Brown returned a few hours later, however, that I really felt good about the possibilities. Sitting at the table with him and Margaret, I was treated to a wonderful meal of fresh lake trout, whitefish, rice and apple pie. When supper was over, Brown shuf-fled over to a big Lazy Boy chair, lit up a fat cigar and clicked on the big satellite television set that tuned into the *NBC Nightly News*. "This is the Happy Hour in Colville Lake with Tom Brokaw," he said with a chuckle. "We'll see you in the morning and I'll tell you the story of my life then."

———

The legendary test pilot Chuck Yeager once said that if you want to grow old flying planes, you had to know when to push and when to back off. I was encouraged to see that quote posted on the log wall of Brown's kitchen the next morning just before we set off for a remote fishing lodge on Great Bear Lake where Brown was hoping to sell a few paintings to wealthy Americans. Whatever comfort I took in this, however, vanished as Brown pointed to the various spots where pilots had crashed. Each time he came to the end of these tragic stories, he grabbed a rosary and said a prayer. I was also not encouraged when he said that he was the oldest pilot still flying in the Northwest Territories, and suffering from a cancer to boot, which he was refusing to have treated until the fall because it entailed an extended trip to Edmonton. "Couldn't do that to Margaret," he growled. "Too much work to do. If I crash," he added somewhat philosophically, "I'll know that I lived a good life, and that she will be taken care of."

Brown was born in Rochester, New York, in 1920. He grew up in a devout Catholic family who introduced him to such books as *Mid Snow and Ice* that documented the history of the Oblate missionaries in the Canadian North between 1850 and the 1920s. Inspired by their faith and a sense of adventure, he resolved to join the Order even though it was dominated by Flems, Frenchmen, French-Canadians, and not a single American. He arrived in 1948 and served in Tulita, Nahanni Butte, Norman Wells, Camsell Portage and Uranium City before he was given the challenge of establishing the parish at Colville Lake.

Brown was probably more famous 30 years ago than when I paid my visit. Back then, he routinely received visits from dignitaries such as Canadian Prime Minister Pierre Trudeau and members of the Royal Family. Known as the "Padre of the Logs," Brown took each of these visits in stride. When the Commissioner of the

Northwest Territories once radioed to inform him that the Queen might visit, Brown replied only that he would dig a new privy for the occasion.

The Queen never showed up to use the outhouse, but her husband, Prince Philip, did. Brown told me that he will always remember how the Prince was greeted by a party of young, radical Dene leaders. Among them was Frank T'Seleie, of Fort Good Hope, who presented the Prince with the so-called Dene Declaration, a manifesto that enunciated the Dene's right to self-determination and nationhood. "I got to hand it to the Prince," Brown said. "He stayed cool, accepted the piece of paper and handed it to one of his aides. I'll bet you, he never looked at it."

Brown continues to receive letters from the Museum of Civilization, the Smithsonian Institution in Washington and other large museums seeking artifacts he holds in a museum in yet another log cabin at Colville Lake. His vast collection includes a 39,000-year-old mammoth tooth, various Stone Age tools, an assortment of fossils and primitive works of art. "It's the only museum in the country that was built without a dime of government money," he said.

Brown was not only Colville Lake's priest, but also the postmaster, newspaper editor, dentist, nurse and lodge owner. It saddened him that the community was no longer the idyllic place it had been. Alcohol, once a stranger, had become a regular guest – and one of the reasons a young man had broken into Brown's home a few years ago, stolen a safe and hammered it open. "He and his friends mistakenly thought there was money in it," Brown said. "But there was no need for them to destroy all of the papers and correspondence I had saved for so many years. That stuff was irreplaceable."

Brown had begun to lock everything in a fail-proof safe, but the vandalism continued. The RCMP, who fly in only when called upon, hadn't been able to stop it. Virtually every window in Brown's cabins had been broken, and recently, someone made off with his beloved American flag that had flown in front of his cabin. "Alcohol is one thing. But the real problems started about 10 years ago after we first got electricity. Before that, people went out on the land or lake to do some fishing, hunting or trapping. Now they can't get away from the TV."

The sales were slim at the fishing lodge, just enough to cover for the cost of the fuel used to get there and back. Heading home, Brown lamented the fact that the Americans had had no *Boojalay*, as he pronounced Beaujolais, or any other wine that he could surprise Margaret with. "Just remembered that we've been married 30 years today," he said thoughtfully. "Wonderful woman, Margaret." Another prayer followed, this one in thanks. Then, he asked if I had ever flown a plane before. "No," I answered emphatically. "Well, here's your chance," he said, giving me a quick lesson. He told me to take it down gradually once I saw the first signs of Colville Lake, and wake him when we reached 500 feet. Then he nodded off to sleep.

———

I had lost a great deal of weight during the six weeks I had travelled down the Nahanni, Liard and the Mackenzie, but managed to gain some of it back when I returned to Norman Wells from Colville Lake. Everyone in the Wells, it seemed, wanted to fatten me up before sending me onto Fort Good Hope, 180 kilometres downstream. One night, I was fed barbecued moose steaks and caribou ribs, the next night pizza at a local restaurant.

I was most worried about the leg of my journey that followed. I had been unable to find much reliable information about the Sans Sault and Rampart rapids, and had not been happy to learn that each one was powerful enough to produce 10,000 megawatts of power. Nor was I pleased when someone in the Wells told me to look for the grave of Daniel Donald Lockhart who had drowned while running the Sans Sault 40 years earlier. I hadn't dreamed these rapids could be widow makers.

The weather was on my side when I finally left Norman Wells. The sky was a deep blue and there was a fine breeze coming in from the northwest. After about a half-day's paddle, the country became more mountainous. At Judith Island, I wistfully imagined that one of the peaks in the distance was Dodo, a landmark that caught my eye when I had studied the map in Fort Simpson.

That first night, I enjoyed my finest campsite yet — set on nothing but a sandbar that had risen in the middle of the river when the waterline receded during a recent hot spell. There was not a patch of vegetation, but the site was completely bug-free.

The next morning, I woke to another warm, cloudless day. I sat by the river with a pot of coffee and buried my bare feet in the cool sand as I waited for the bannock to finish frying on my tiny, single-burner stove. This, I thought, was as good as the trip had been so far. It didn't occur to me how hot the day would become. By noon, the thermometer read 28 C. By 4 p.m., it had hit 34 C. Without trees or clouds for shade, I repeatedly filled my baseball cap with water and poured it over my head as I paddled downstream. Desperate for relief, I finally hopped onto another sandbar in the middle of the river and lay flat in the shallow water. I poked my head up from time to time and wondered what a Dene fisherman or hunter might think should one happen by. No one, however, came. This stretch of wilderness between Norman Wells and Fort Good Hope was deserted.

I've always enjoyed the adrenaline rush one gets upon hearing the approach of a big rapid or waterfall. But when I was greeted by the San Sault Rapids, where the Mountain River flows out of the high country in the west and into the Mackenzie, I felt nothing but a headache coming on. Kayaking solo is stressful; when you have no idea of what lies ahead, it is more so. You know that if you swamp or flip over, there is no one to throw you a lifeline or fish you out.

I looked toward the shore for Donald Daniel Lockhart's grave, thinking that I might stop and pay my respects. But my heart was not into bushwhacking through the buggy, tangled shoreline, so I offered a prayer from my boat instead. I stood up to survey what lay downstream. I could see that the river bifurcated. While the west channel looked and sounded as if it were the safest, I wondered what would greet me after it turned. I puzzled over this for half-an-hour until the stifling heat and the big biting horse-flies forced me to move on.

I can't recall such an anticlimactic event in all my years of paddling, nor feeling so good about such a surprise. The Sans Sault may be powerful enough to light the cities of California but not from the west channel. There were a few bounces, but you would almost have to be standing up, going sideways, to be in danger of tipping. Perhaps the rapid is more challenging in higher water, but at the time I went through, there was nothing on that section of river to worry about.

I could have said the same of the Ramparts, which I reached a couple of days later. There, the four-kilometre-wide river squeezes through vertical limestone cliffs that stand no more than 400 to 800 metres apart. This was easily the narrowest part of the Mackenzie. By rights, the river should have been running wild through the gorge. But with depths of more than 300 metres, the water had had plenty of room to escape. And so, like Mackenzie who "did not find the current stronger than elsewhere," I breezed through.

It was 1 a.m. when the river gently spit me out on the other side of the Ramparts. In the distance, I could barely make out the giant cross that marked Fort Good Hope where 600 Dene made their homes. Two hours later, the sky was a deep, dark blue. I set myself on top of a hill across from a Catholic church as lightning flashed above a vast plain of swamp and forest. I heard the faint rumbling of thunder and could smell rain in the air. I felt a need to breathe in deeply, but after nearly 20 hours on the river, I had little strength to savour the freshness. Nor could I watch the light show that was heading my way; instead, I collapsed on top of my sleeping bag.

Sleep, however, was painfully short. By 7 a.m., the sun was blazing like a furnace and my head was pounding from dehydration. Too hot to continue lying inside my nylon oven, I headed down the steep hill for water. But my water purifier refused to produce a drop. It had had to deal with so much silt through these many weeks that it had given up. My head pounded harder as I climbed the hill to the town's only store. "It's closed," said a man who passed in a shiny new pick-up truck. "You'll be lucky if it opens before noon."

Fort Good Hope was a ghost town. There was no hint of the drama that had occurred there 30 years ago, when Thomas Berger, a judge from British Columbia, flew in to hear how people felt about the natural gas pipeline that had been proposed by Calgary-based Foothills Pipeline. It was the first time anyone from the South had bothered to ask native northerners how they felt about anything and Frank T'Seleie, then chief, wasn't about to pass on the chance to speak. T'Seleie rocked the hearings when he declared that, "it is for the unborn child, Mr. Berger, that my nation will stop this pipeline. It is so the unborn child can know the freedom of this land that I am willing to lay down my life."

T'Seleie then turned to Bob Blair, the head of Foothills Pipelines Ltd., and accused him of being a "20th-century General Custer. You have come to destroy the Dene Nation. You are coming with your troops to slaughter us and steal land that is rightfully ours. You have come to destroy a people who have a history of 30,000 years. Why? For 20 years worth of gas?"

I bumped into T'Seleie by the river later that day and he remembered the discussion. "That line about General Custer," he said. "I knew by the look on his (Blair's) face and others in the room that I had finished them off. You could sense it in the air." T'Seleie had just returned from university in Ontario to resume his role of chief. He still bristled recalling those days, when he and other young Dene were dismissed as radical malcontents. But he had mellowed and was one of many Mackenzie Valley leaders who had chosen to support the latest pipeline proposal. In the new endeavour, an Aboriginal-owned company owned a one-third interest.

"You know, the world has changed over the last 25 years," T'Seleie told me. "We're masters of our house in many ways. Many of us have settled our land claims, and we have the power to make sure that this pipeline is done the right way. This gas is going to go south, maybe not today or tomorrow, but it's going to go. I don't think we can afford to be left out."

When the store finally opened at noon, I bought the last six
bottles of water and a box of Kraft Dinner, a surprising craving
since I would never eat it at home. I decided it would be cooler on
the river than hanging around the hot, dusty town. But before I left,
I made arrangements to see inside Our Lady of Good Hope.

From the outside, nothing suggested why the Historic Sites and
Monuments Board of Canada had declared the church a national
historic site in 1977. You might see such a single-storey, wood-
framed, Red River-style church in any small Prairie town. A white
picket fence surrounded it and a graveyard stood to one side. The
steeple above the entrance appeared to be the only distinguishing
feature. But when Jonas Kakfwi, the caretaker, unlocked the doors, it
was all I could do not to fall on my knees and pray. It was exquisite.
Golden stars had been scattered across the royal blue, straight-gabled
ceiling and several colourful frescoes depicting biblical scenes had
been painted in Gothic style. Five exquisitely carved angels seemed
to support the altar below a painted panel depicting Jesus Christ.

Inspired by the Chartres Cathedral in France, the Oblate missionaries who had built this church during the 1860s had hoped to
astound their converts with their artistry and, in turn, inspire awe in
their faith. They were apparently successful. According to church
records, some families would travel for more than 10 days in the
bitter cold simply to attend Midnight Mass at Christmas.

North American scholars took more than a century to recognize the genius of Emile Petitot, one of the missionaries who had
built the church. Petitot's story is strange and tragic. After arriving
from France in 1862, he had served in northern Alberta and the
southern Mackenzie Valley before being sent to Good Hope in
1864. The transfer was punishment for what the bishop described
as a "fatal attachment to a child."

Petitot's time in Fort Good Hope was well spent. In addition
to his contributions in the building of the church, Petitot made a
number of remarkable journeys that took him down the Mackenzie
to the Beaufort Sea and Fort Yukon in Alaska and overland
to Colville Lake and beyond. He was favourably received almost

everywhere by the Dene and Inuit. The Hareskin Dene near Good Hope called him as "Yat-I-Nezun," or "Father Good." The Gwich'in farther north called him "Nne-la-Gottine," the intelligent priest.

These trips took a toll on Petitot's health — twice he nearly died of cold and starvation, and another time he was almost killed by the Inuit who had blamed him for a mysterious illness that had stricken many of them. But Petitot still took the time to draw, map and write down the stories told to him by the Dene and Inuit. He also produced dictionaries of the Inuit and Dene languages that scholars still use. Many of his documents, in fact, have been used in land-claim negotiations to prove historical occupancy.

But Petitot's colleagues — Father Jean Séguin and Brother Joseph Patrick Kearney — distrusted his eccentricities, erratic behaviour and attachment to young Dene men. In several letters to the bishop, they complained of Petitot's fits of violence, hysterical claims that the world was ending and his accusations that Séguin had murdered Jesus Christ and the Virgin Mary. Twice, they said Petitot had tried to murder Séguin, once with an axe, another time he tried to strangle him. Once, they had to tie him to his bed after finding him running naked outdoors in -40 C temperatures. When Petitot insisted that he had to be circumcised to be accepted by the Gwich'in, Séguin had had enough and demanded that the bishop remove Petitot from the parish.

What doomed Petitot were his relations with a 14-year-old boy — a man by Dene standards, in those days — who frequently travelled with him. The implication was that their relationship was sexual — although this was never proven. Between 1879 and 1881, Petitot was transferred to Alberta and then posted to missions at Fort Pitt and Cold Lake. Although Vital Grandin, the bishop responsible for the Mackenzie District, believed Petitot showed no signs of insanity when he visited in 1880, Grandin was convinced that Petitot had a mental disorder that manifested in private. So, when Petitot visited Grandin in February 1881, at the church's headquarters in St. Albert, Alberta, Grandin had already made up his mind to send Petitot back to France.

Petitot refused and returned to Fort Pitt where he married a Métis woman from the Frog Lake reserve. Convinced that Petitot had lost his mind, Grandin sent two Oblates to bring him back. Using physical force, they separated Petitot from his wife, but he managed to escape. When Petitot showed up at the parish of his old mentor, Bishop Henri Faraurd, in the central Alberta town of Lac La Biche, Faraurd refused to receive him and allowed another party of Oblates to hunt Petitot down and take him away in irons. Petitot was put on a train to Montreal where he was committed to a mental asylum. He remained there for a couple of years until his sister, who had repeatedly begged for his freedom, paid his passage to France.

In Mareuil-les Meaux, Petitot worked as a proofreader, author and printer while he tried, without success, to become a Protestant missionary overseas, believing it the only way he would be reunited with his wife. During that time, the Societé de Geographique de Paris recognized Petitot for his explorations and map-making endeavours and Royal Geographical Society awarded him the prestigious Back Prize. In 1886, Petitot was forgiven by the church, officially released from his vows and allowed to become pastor of the parish at Mareuil-les-Meaux. He died there in 1917, much beloved.

There was no relief from the heat when I finally left Fort Good Hope. Half sick, suffering from exhaustion, but still not whipped, I paddled robotically, aware of nothing except the fact that I was constantly thirsty and no longer sweating. By evening a stiff wind blowing out of the north finally cooled things down. Realizing that waves were likely to follow, I headed toward the first stream I could find on the map. I was down to my last bottle of water and finding a good creek had been difficult. But luck was with me. Although the stream smelled of peat, the water flowed cool and clear out of the hillside. I was also delighted to find a flat gravel bar large enough to set up my tent. It, I thought, was the perfect time for the Kraft Dinner.

But the sky soon darkened almost to black. The smoke was so thick and acrid it must have been from a forest fire, and it was headed my way. Any thoughts of staying put and eating supper were dashed as two cawing ravens announced the arrival of something coming down the hill toward me. Through binoculars, I saw a bear that had caught wind of my cooking. Whether it was a black bear or a grizzly, I could not tell, but I didn't waste a moment. I shoved a mouthful of macaroni into my mouth and dumped the rest in the river. Then, I loaded up and pushed off into the swell of water, just as the animal burst through the tall willows toward me.

Once again, I was thankful for bringing a kayak instead of a canoe. In a canoe, I would have had no chance of escaping. The water was just too rough. Luckily, a shift in the wind blew the smoke from the forest fire away from me. An hour later, I found myself in an all-too-familiar position – feet braced against the wall of the tent trying to prevent it from collapsing. It was depressing. Between 2 a.m. and 4 a.m., I watched water pool around me as bolts of lightning thumped into the sand.

The rain never let up. Downstream toward an abandoned trading post at Thunder River, and the communities of Tsiigehtchic and Inuvik, the downpour was relentless. After four days, my tent had become so soggy that the pressure points along the seams had begun to rip apart. I was tired and dehydrated and everything from then on became routine, just like the flat terrain and uniformly grey sky. I headed toward Point Separation where the east channel of the Mackenzie River flowed a hundred ways through the delta and into Inuvik. I thought only of a hot bath and a warm bed. After 61 days on the Nahanni, Liard and Mackenzie, all the bears, monsters, giant beavers and extraordinary people I had met were behind me. With the prospects for dams, pipelines and gas wells in the future, I wondered if this great wilderness would be the same when I returned.

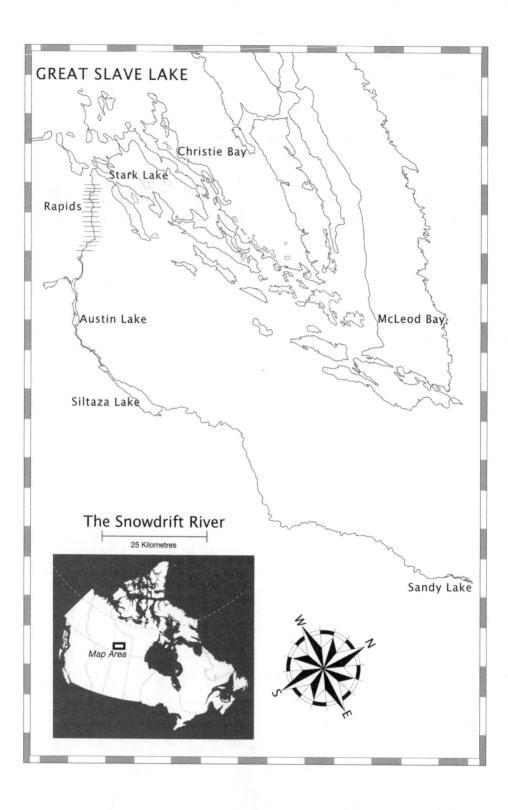

GREAT SLAVE LAKE

Christie Bay

Stark Lake

Rapids

Austin Lake

McLeod Bay

Siltaza Lake

The Snowdrift River

25 Kilometres

Map Area

Sandy Lake

Snowdrift River

River Falling Down the Mountain

I t is raining lightly when we take off from Back Bay in Yellowknife with my canoe strapped to the float of a single-engine plane. The forecast for the entire Great Slave Lake region is not promising; rain and occasional heavy showers for the Labour Day weekend, then more rain the following week. The pilot again reminds us that we may have to turn back if conditions worsen. Good thing I have a priest for a canoeing partner.

As luck or prayer would have it, we are heading southeast across Great Slave Lake for the one bright spot on the grey horizon. Nearly two hours later, when that crown of light over the rim of the world disappears in a thick drizzle, the float plane is skimming along the surface of a big tundra pond just downstream of Sandy Lake on the edge of the Barren Lands. Not quite the headwaters of the Snowdrift, the river the Dene once called "River Falling Down Mountain," but close enough.

The Snowdrift is no more than a trickle when it spills out of a treeless corner of Whitefish Lake. But then it rises quickly as it is fed by a number of unnamed creeks that flow from the Catholic Lake and Lake of Woe regions. By the time it spills over half-a-dozen boulder-strewn rapids into this pond where we are camped, it is big and deep enough to carry a canoe. This is striking sub-Arctic wilderness, an ominous transitional zone where pockets of stunted white spruce trees give way to open tundra, and where tens of thousands of barren-ground caribou take refuge during fall and winter. Here, the ground is carpeted with white and lime-green lichen, soft, spongy mosses and big clumps of blood red, low-bush cranberries whose leaves have now turned bright orange. The few birch trees are found here are along the riverbank pushing up from between the frost-fractured cracks in the pre-Cambrian Shield. Now, with their leaves in their autumnal phase, the bright yellow colours are glorious.

I am here with René Fumoleau, an Oblate missionary who has spent more than 40 years in the North photographing, filming and writing about the history, the politics and the culture of the Dene. Although it is late in the evening, 7 p.m., we paddle downstream after setting up camp to a set of rapids, which I realize are not on the map. It is a bad sign, a warning that we need to be extra vigilant in case there are more unmarked rapids ahead of us. Just above the whitewater, on a crest of small hill that has now been taken over by a fox den, René spots a Dene burial site, marked by a simple, elegantly carved wooden cross that had toppled over many years ago.

Here we sit watching a bull caribou trying unsuccessfully to cross the river and contemplating what father or mother, wife or husband might have been thinking when they said their goodbyes to this loved one. Maybe, this is why the Lake of Woe got its name. Perhaps, an elder had come here many times to sit, think or hunt. This may be where a son had to bury his father or mother in haste because he and his family had to reach the next lake before the ice came and prevented them from going any farther. Whatever happened, the power, the beauty and the cruelty of this treeline country is all here.

Despite the heavy clouds, the air is warm, 12 C, and dead quiet, except for the rain that occasionally splashes hard on the water as if handfuls of small stones are being tossed into the lake. It's not often one experiences an evening like this on the edge of the tundra — certainly not this late in summer when driving rain, sleet and gale force winds are more the norm. Back at camp, we brush our teeth and watch the shadowy figures of several foot-long trout swimming up from the depths of this lake to investigate the toothpaste we spit out. A pack of wolves howl in the distance. René turns to me just as I turn to him. Wide-eyed, neither one of us say a word. A perfect moment like this needs no commentary.

It is now dark as it can be although a full moon occasionally peaks out from between the racing black clouds. A dry wind from the west is sucking up and sweeping away the moisture that has saturated the air. This, I think, is just what I need to put me to sleep, something that never comes easy when I am in the city. It is not meant to be. René snores — the musical kind who plug their sinuses in such a way that every exhalation sounds like a tuba and a kazoo being blown at the same time. It is not unpleasant. But it isn't a lullaby either. Outside our tent, the chattering of a squirrel suggests that it isn't happy about all the noise either. But then a sharp crack of a branch makes me think that the squirrel is announcing the arrival of a visitor. Thinking bear, I grab the flashlight and look at René. He is still deep in sleep, and it will be up to me to pull out the bear spray and confront whatever is outside.

First, I resolve to make some noise so that the creature knows that it might be dealing with something bigger than a fat beaver. As I pop my head out, I see two caribou bucks bolting in a panic, smashing through the trees as if we had been the pack of howling wolves they no doubt think we are. Funny, their anxiety provides me with such great relief.

I first met René Fumoleau when he was a youthful looking 54-year-old marching purposefully out of the Dene Nation office in Yellowknife, heading toward the motorcycle that he used to get about town in those days. It was 1980 or 1981. During that time, very few non-natives could walk in and out of those offices as Fumoleau so frequently did. Dene leaders were still riding high following a successful three-year battle to stop a multibillion-dollar natural gas pipeline from cutting through the Mackenzie Valley. And George Erasmus, president of the Dene Nation, was talking about nationhood and self-government. One politician was so incensed with Fumoleau's very public solidarity with the young upstart Dene leader that he demanded that Paul Piché, the bishop of Mackenzie, stop Fumoleau from publicly supporting the Dene's right to self-government.

Piché was one of many religious and political leaders of the time who viewed the Dene as children – too young and ignorant to govern themselves. He felt that Thomas Berger, the judge who presided over the pipeline inquiry, had been duped and that Fumoleau had contributed to the deceit. But ultimately, Piché had no power over the outspoken missionary. Fumoleau was by this time not just a radical priest, but a legend-in-the-making — winning universal acclaim for documenting the plight of the Dene in the North. Berger, for one, was so impressed with Fumoleau's research in a book that made a case for Dene land ownership, he went out of his way in his report to the federal government to praise the priest.

René and I were more acquaintances than friends in those early years. United from time to time, by people we know and respect, he had once told me that he had never been on the tundra. When I invited him to come along on this canoe trip that I had originally planned to do alone, he accepted, but only after I assured him that his age — he was now 65 — and paddling skills — he's a lake paddler — would not be serious impediments.

What I did not mention was that I really did not know much about the Snowdrift. I'm sure others had paddled it before, but try as I did, I could find only two references to anyone having canoed its entire length: the geologist Guy Blanchet who canoed it in 1925 while searching for the source of the Thelon River, and Americans Peter Browning and John Blunt who did it 40 years later while paddling 1,000 kilometres from Stony Rapids in northern Saskatchewan to the shores of Great Slave Lake.

Blanchet's was the more notable journey. He set off from Fort Fitzgerald on the Slave River with three other men in a six-metre wood canvas canoe, and packing a small, collapsible boat they hoped to use when they went overland to the Barren Lands. They followed the so-called Dog River route northeast. Traditionally, the Dene had exploited this interconnected series of streams, rivers and lakes to get them on the tundra in summer and fall. But in 1925, the country was largely unmapped, and Blanchet and his colleagues had only a rough sketch of the region that had been drawn by Richard King. The naturalist/surgeon had travelled down the Back River with explorer George Back in 1837, initially in search of fellow explorer, John Ross, who had been missing on the Arctic coast for four years. So slow was the going that by the time Blanchet arrived at Eileen Lake, 60 kilometres south of where René and I started our trip, it was evident that they would not get to the headwaters of the Thelon before winter set in.

Blanchet considered the possibility of turning back. But a chance encounter with an advance guard for a Dene hunting party heading toward the treeline convinced him to return by way of what would later be called the Snowdrift River. A blind 80-year-old woman travelling with the party gave Blanchet the gumption to continue heading north. The map she had her grandson sketch for Blanchet was so similar to King's map that Blanchet was sufficiently confident in his decision to try the unknown river. There was, however, one thing that the blind woman said that concerned him. "This is a good river to travel," she warned. "But you must leave it by the portage (trail) before it falls down the mountain."

Blanchet wasn't sure what to make of the woman's advice. For the first hundred miles, the Snowdrift is a fast but gently flowing river and the rapids that break its course have to be portaged only occasionally. Only near the end of the river, before it spills into Great Slave Lake, did Blanchet come to appreciate what the old Dene woman was telling him. Ten kilometres from Great Slave Lake, which he had explored on an earlier expedition, he realized that the river would drop at least 183 metres.

Blanchet fully intended to pull out to portage the rapids and waterfalls that would present themselves. But he ran the first of them at the head of a deep canyon downstream of Austin Lake when a black bear popped its head up from above some bushes to distract the paddlers long enough for them to pass the point of no return. "Looking back, the gap in the mountains appeared as a gate closing behind us," Blanchet wrote. "We were committed to 'fall down the mountain' or to abandon the canoe and travel overland with our folding canoe."

Recalling the wild ride that followed, Blanchet was amazed that the canoe had not broken apart. He also doubted that such a descent could ever be attempted again. "Circumstances forced us to take the risk and because this was a summer of low water, we succeeded in bringing the canoe down. Ledges were exposed that would ordinarily have been flooded. We dropped 500 feet in six miles, a large part of it in three (miles)."

Once on Great Slave Lake, Blanchet's party met with some Yellowknives heading east. Among them was an old man with whom Blanchet had once travelled. "He asked where we had been, then by what road we had reached the lake," Blanchet wrote. "I told him that we had followed "the river down the mountains." He shook his head gravely and said, 'I think maybe no.'"

—

The weather did not clear as I had hoped that first night and so our second day on the Snowdrift begins with a cold rain that escalates into an icy drizzle and then a full blown gale. The long, sandy esker above our camp can not be more photogenic, however – all red and yellow with fall colours that refuse to be dulled by a leaden sky. Nor can the caribou be more friendly. They surround our camp feeding on lichen, and paying us no attention. Neither of us dares attempt a close-up photo though; it is just too wet.

We are teased from time to time by a patch of blue sky that lights up parts of the dark tundra like a spotlight. They call these sucker holes. Only suckers pack up their gear and head off believing the weather will clear. By 1 p.m., however, we abandon the possibility that the weather will improve. We have factored no down time into our tight schedule, so we put on our warmest clothes and rain gear, break camp and head downstream toward the rapid we visited the night before. Here, a boulder garden stretches 18-metres across the entire width of the Snowdrift. While the left side of the river looks to be runnable, I choose to line the canoe rather than risk filling it with water. René is incredibly spry for a man his age but a novice when it comes to river paddling. He doesn't need a soaking this early in the trip. Nor do I.

Soon after we are in the canoe, the sky begins to clear. The river, however, remains black like the lakes of Algonquin in Ontario or the Yukon's Big Salmon River. Black water has always spooked me. I always imagine that some serpent will rise up and swallow me. I am not alone. René tells me that some elders in Fort Good Hope believe that a fire-breathing monster lives in the depths of the Mackenzie where the river does not freeze. We talk about these fears for awhile, and then just like that, two enormous creatures dive into the water in front of us. René turns to grab his camera, but it is I who snap the photo of the two moose making the splash.

The next set of rapids are the first that are marked on the map and easy is to identify. We can hear them from more than a half-kilometre away. More waterfall than riffle, they are not high but neither are they runnable. Lining — using ropes to steer our boat through the rapids — doesn't appear to be an option either, so we do what all voyageurs must inevitably do in Shield country — we portage. It is no more than a 200 metre walk, but it requires three trips — two to lug our food cooler and camping gear and a third to carry our boat to the big pool of water downstream just below the cascade. By the time we are all done, there is time to carry on for an hour or two. Instead we decide that there isn't likely to be a lovelier spot to camp than here.

René is an Oblate missionary, the Roman Catholic religious order that, along with the Hudson's Bay Company, and the RCMP, was the third member of the so-called Unholy Trinity that dominated cultural, spiritual, economic, and political affairs in the Canadian North for more than a century. Founded in 1816 by French bishop Eugene de Mazènod for the purpose of evangelizing to the poor of France, the first Oblate missionaries arrived in

Canada a quarter-century later at the invitation of Ignace Bourget, the second Roman Catholic bishop of Montreal.

Initially, the Oblates set their sights on the Blackfoot, the Cree, the Sarcee and other Indian tribes of the Prairies, But taking to heart their early motto — *Peregrinari pro Christo* (March: go forward for Christ), and *Usque ad extremum terrae!* (Right to the ends of the Earth!), they turned their attention to the Dene, Métis and the Inuit of the North by the 1850s.

Many Aboriginals first encountered the soul-seeking Black Robes as the swifter runners in the religious foot race with the Anglicans. When Henri Grollier "the Frances Xavier of the frigid zone" stepped off the York boat at Fort Simpson in August, 1858 on a trip that would take him more than 1,000 kilometres to Fort McPherson where no priest or minister had gone before, he baptized 45 children and blessed six marriages within just a few days. A competing Anglican minister managed only two marriages, both involving men working for the Hudson's Bay Company. Men like Grollier, who died a wretched death at the age of 38 from asthma and malnutrition, regarded their "ministry of truth" as a "war against the ministry of error." So zealous was he in his missionary zeal that even his colleagues viewed him as a "veritable cross for his companion." The Alberta-based bishop responsible for the Mackenzie diocese at the time was well aware of this "source of torture," that Grollier inflicted on all he confronted, but he was more interested in winning souls than he was in keeping Grollier's companions happy.

In addition to the Anglicans, the Oblates also wrestled with the Dene medicine men and the Inuit shamans, the North's indigenous priests. In the eyes of the many of the missionaries, aboriginal people were children of nature who could not be civilized or Christianized until freed from a "perfect net of superstitions." Because the shamans and medicine men played upon those so-called superstitions, the Oblates would go to extremes to combat them. Dogged persuasion usually accomplished the job, but it wasn't uncommon for some to use violence in order to get the upper hand.

Although the Oblates never completely defeated the Anglicans and succeeded only in driving the shamans and medicine men underground, they frequently prevailed because of their willingness to live in the most primitive conditions. Unlike British explorers such as John Franklin who refused to adopt native ways in his travels, the Oblates readily took to dogteams and birchbark canoes. They also took great pains to learn the languages of the people they tried to convert.

Based at Caribou Lake in northern Saskatchewan, Father Alphonse Gasté was, after Samuel Hearne, one of the first non-natives to travel through the treeline country past Whitefish Lake into the Dubawnt River region. In the spring and summer of 1868, he walked more than 1,200 kilometres in freezing water and boot destroying rock in search of Inuit to convert. For seven months, he lived in a tent, often without fire — a feat that so impressed one Inuit shaman that he requested the honour of sleeping beside him one night. When they awoke the next day, the shaman referred to Father Gasté as "Number One", meaning that he considered him to be superior among men.

Not all Oblate missionaries were as triumphant. In 1913, Father Jean-Baptist Rouvière and Father Guillaume LeRoux headed down the Coppermine River hoping to spread their religion to the Inuit along the Arctic coast. After a month of hard living, they were murdered by two Inuit men who then cut out and ate their livers, and left the rest to the ravens and wolves. Father François Frapsauce and Father Pierre Fallaize, who followed in their footsteps, also suffered. Frapsauce disappeared through a hole in the ice on Great Bear Lake. Fallaize, who was then left alone to live in a decrepit little hut on the Arctic coast, spent the next nine years evangelizing and travelling with the Inuit before he converted enough to celebrate the first mass in the region.

The heroics of Gasté and Fallaize, and the sufferings of Rouvière, LeRoux and Frapsauce inspired many Oblates from France, Belgium, Holland and Quebec to follow. René, it surprises me to learn, was not one when he was ordained in 1952.

"There were 12 of us who had completed our studies at the Solignac scholasticate," he tells me after supper as we gaze at a gigantic half moon rising above the horizon. "Our Superior-General in Rome was to send our obedience — our first posting. Bishop Plumey, the leader of the new Oblate mission in Cameroon was visiting, and he was invited to preside over the ceremonies. But a few days before the great event, he had to back out. So they brought in (Father Pierre) Fallaize who was then a retired bishop living in France. Nearly blind and very frail, he agreed until he saw the obediences "Cameroon, France, Cameroon, France, Cameroon, France, Cameroon, France, Cameroon, France, Cameroon, France."

"I spent 30 years in the Canadian North and not one of these young men are going there," Fallaize told the local superior. "I'm not interested in participating in this celebration."

"It was then that the local superior pleaded with him to sleep on it for a night, suggesting that maybe things will look better the next day. Then, he phoned headquarters in Rome and asked what he should so. The Superior-General simply told him 'Fumoleau has his obedience for Cameroon. Erase that and replace it with Mackenzie in the Canadian Arctic.'"

René then shrugs, turns to me, and says. "And so here I am today."

He is the kind of short, round-eyed man with horned-rimmed glasses who might readily be recognized as a French priest were it not for his pony tail and the black leather bomber jacket that he inherited from a hitchhiker who left it in his pick-up. René's voice is soft, his manner polite, but he does not suffer fools easily. People who do not know him well find him intimidating. He does, however, love to tell stories. And I find that the farther we move down the river, the more I am struck by how he completely this Black Robe was converted by the people he came to save.

"You know when I first moved to Fort Good Hope (Radeli Ko) in 1953, I wore the long robes like the Oblates did at the time," he says. "I don't know if I was there three months when I was preaching the Ten Commandments — you know, don't kill, steal, or commit adultery. I told them that sins were rated as big and small. Then, I asked these people what they thought was the biggest sin of all. Ten or so of them gathered together and talked for some time. Then, one of them turned to me and said 'We all agree. The worst sin of all is to lock your door.' I only realized much later that it was I who was going to have change my way of thinking if I was going to connect with these people. I knew nothing about their history, their spirituality, their mythology or their social structure."

Fumoleau arrived in Fort Good Hope when there were no trucks, no telephone and no radio reception. Mail sometimes didn't come for five weeks. Most families were still living on the land for a good part of the year and the only way of getting to them was by dog team or canoe. Getting "bushed" was an occupational hazard. René recalls the bishop visiting him one year and asking him how far he had travelled that year.

"Maybe 1,000 miles," René said.

"And do you travel with anyone?" the Bishop asked.

"Sometimes, I do. Often, I go by myself," said René.

Then the bishop wondered out loud if René ever talked to his dogs on the trail. It was a test to see if he was still mentally healthy.

"Yes, sometimes," he admitted.

"And do the dogs answer you?

"No, never," René said.

"Then you can stay another year," the bishop told him.

René offers nothing after that, not a smile or commentary. I sit wondering how to respond when he turns and deadpans: "I can not tell a lie. The dogs did answer me three times."

———

Bad news this third morning on the river; René's camera batteries have died. He has no spares. The poor man is like a boy who has lost his favourite toy. Fumoleau's photographs have been published all over the world and displayed in some of the finest galleries. He tells me his best review came during a showing in Montreal some years ago. But this particular accolade was not uttered by the famous artist who described one photograph as "perfect." It came from the janitor who walked in with her pail and mop at the end of opening night, stopped, looked at one of his photos for some time and then said; "This picture, I'm telling, it's beautiful."

René bought his first camera in 1965 when he realized that before going home to France for the first time in 13 years, he had nothing to show his mother. He never intended being the artist that he is until the Dene and others started asking him for his pictures to illustrate a book, magazine or public presentation. Most of Fumoleau's photos are remarkable for their composition, style and use of light. But his most important and evocative images are portraits of elders such as Maggie Fisher of Fort Good Hope and Naedzo, the Dogrib prophet from Deline on Great Bear Lake — people who would never have allowed their photographs to be taken so intimately by anyone else.

Fumoleau only reluctantly accepts the praise that he receives for his photographs and for his writing: the most important of which was a book called *As Long as This Land Shall Last*, published in 1975, the year Berger came North with his inquiry. When a French consul in Canada asked Fumoleau many years ago for a *curriculum vitae* so he could submit his name for Les Palmes Academiques, one of the most coveted French honours, René wrote back to thank him. "I feel happy that my work also brings glory to France. But I don't see how a medal could make me a better person or a better Frenchman. Why don't you send me instead a return plane ticket from Yellowknife to France so that I can visit my mother and my brothers."

"Guess what I received?" says Fumoleau, his eyebrows raised in mock disbelief. "No medal and no plane ticket."

As Long as This Land Shall Last is, along with Justice William Morrow's 1973 decision that the Dene may not have given up their land rights by signing Treaties 8 (1899-1900) and 11 (1911), widely regarded as one of the most important milestones in the modern history of aboriginal people in the Northwest Territories. It is a thorough documentation of the events and negotiations that led to the signing of both treaties. Those treaties promised that the Dene could hunt on their ancestral lands for "as long as the sun rises from east to west, as long as the river flows downstream, as long as this land shall last."

The book grew out of concern from other like-minded Oblates who sympathized with the Dene struggle for justice. It took more than two years of delving into Church and government records, and months of interviewing more than 70 aboriginal elders to get the book written. Ultimately, it exposed the Church for inadvertently doing the dirty work for the Indian agents. Thinking that the Dene had no choice but to sign, Church leaders never anticipated that the government would not come through on its promises. The book, re-released by University of Calgary Press in 2004, continues to be an important resource for land-claim negotiators and university students.

The Snowdrift got its name from the huge drifts of white sand that line the floor of the valley downstream of Sandy Lake. Recognizing that these dunes and drifts could easily be mistaken for snow, someone — no one seems to know who — gave it this name. The name has little to do with the community of Snowdrift which recently changed its name to Lutselk'e. While Lutselk'e, is located near the mouth of the Snowdrift River, it is a relatively new community of Chipewyan people who had lived near the Lockhart River on the east arm of Great Slave Lake until the Hudson's Bay Company established a post at the present townsite in 1925.

The Chipewyan retained their traditional hunting, trapping and fishing patterns, and in the fall, they still go to the treeline by way of Pike's Portage on Great Slave rather than the Snowdrift River. (They do use their snowmobiles to hunt caribou in the Snowdrift region.) And every August, they make a pilgrimage to Parry Falls on the Lockhart, 60 kilometres north of where we are now, to pay homage to Ts'akui Thdea, the "Old Lady Who Sits in the River." To the Chipewyan, the Old Lady is a water spirit who was loved into existence by the Great Creator. Believing in her powers of regeneration, the old and the infirm come to drink and take home some of the river's water.

"You know, I was there one summer with the people of Lutselk'e taking pictures of the falls," says René. "Then one of the men who was there with us showed me a Polaroid that he had taken of me in front of the falls. It was unmistakable, right below me in the water at the bottom of the falls, you could see the eyes, ears and nose of the Old Lady. Her face was there for all of us to see."

Only a few rivers in the Northwest Territories — the Yellowknife, the Talston and the Beaulieu — can match the lake-river-waterfall character of the Snowdrift. Ever changing, it can be a taxing way to travel. And so it was on the third, fourth, fifth and now the sixth day of our journey that we are constantly in and out of the canoe, or standing up in the boat, scouting falls or whitewater that may not be marked on the map. Given how slow we are going, I now realize, as I had pretty much expected before we set off, that we will not get to Great Slave Lake in the next three days when the plane is scheduled to come in and take us home. Our best bet is to find a landing spot on either Siltaza or Austin lakes, which appear before the Snowdrift falls down the mountain. René is surprised that I was even contemplating the idea of dragging him down the canyon that Blanchet and his colleagues ran. Nevertheless, he is relieved that we no longer have to try and maintain the pace that kept us on the river for an hour or two longer than either one of us would have liked. He prefers tranquility to stress.

René spent 20 years serving as a traditional priest in Fort Good Hope and Fort Franklin (now called Deline) before moving to a cabin in Yellowknife's Rainbow Valley. While living there, he came to fully appreciate the Dene's attempt to decolonize themselves. Liturgical concerns, he realized, were secondary to the Dene struggle for self-determination. But he was not the only rebel among the group of Oblates in the North. Like-minded thinkers such as Lou Menez and Camille Piché, the nephew of the bishop, also saw the need for a new church role in the North. And somehow, they managed to sell their message to southern bishops. In 1975, the Canadian Conference of Catholic Bishops issued a statement that recognized the negative impact that the Church had had on northern native culture. In "Northern Development, At What Cost?" they called on the Canadian government to settle land claims and to consult with native northerners before giving the go-ahead to future industrial, mining or oil and gas developments. It was also the bishops who convinced Pope John Paul to come North in 1984 and again 1987.

René is proud of that and of his role in Project North, a coalition of five Canadian church groups that supported the Dene, Métis and Inuvialuit causes during the 1970s and 1980s. Now retired, he is considering new challenges such as writing more books and maybe drawing. He is also thinking seriously of moving to Lustelk'e. "I need a change," René says. "Yellowknife is too big for me. This looks like country I could really enjoy living in."

———

I wake up at midnight on what I expect will be the last day of our trip to the sound of René moaning with excitement outside the tent. At first, I can't imagine what he is doing out there. I find him in his long johns, arms outstretched, staring up at the heavens. "My God," he says over and over. "My God." Religious devotion like this I hadn't anticipated. Does he expect me, a lapsed Catholic, to go out and join him in this devotion? It's bloody cold to boot. The ground is now white with a heavy frost. We had never talked about my thoughts of God or whether I held any religious convictions at all. Is this now the time to open up the dialogue? Only when I look up at the night sky do I realize how badly I have interpreted René's moans. The Northern Lights are among the most electrifying that I have ever seen. These have no reds or purples like the classic aurora borealis. But the emerald ribbons of frosty, glimmering light from them are so powerful, I can almost feel them pulse with energy. "My God," I moan. "My God."

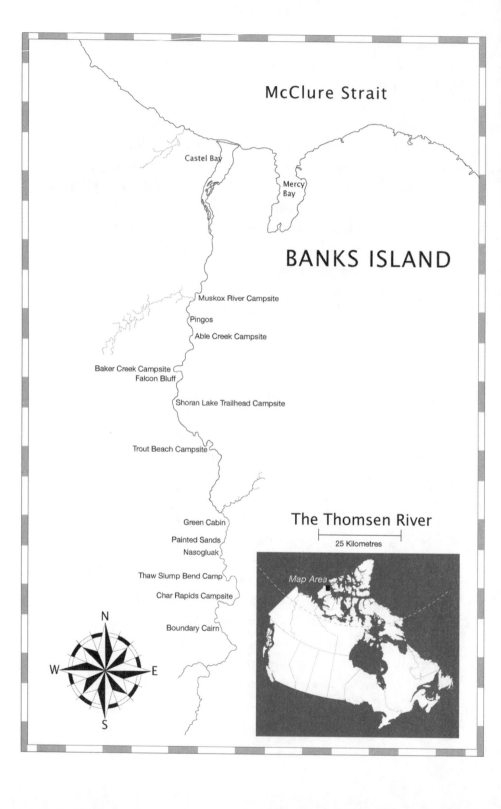

McClure Strait

Castel Bay

Mercy Bay

BANKS ISLAND

Muskox River Campsite

Pingos

Able Creek Campsite

Baker Creek Campsite
Falcon Bluff

Shoran Lake Trailhead Campsite

Trout Beach Campsite

Green Cabin

Painted Sands

Nasogluak

Thaw Slump Bend Camp

Char Rapids Campsite

Boundary Cairn

The Thomsen River

25 Kilometres

Map Area

N
W E
S

Thomsen River

Magical Mystery Tour

We were at the north end of Banks Island, high in the western end of the Arctic archipelago, drifting with the last gentle thrust of the Thomsen River before the tides in Castel Bay pulled us out to sea. It was a half-hour before midnight. The air was calm, the sky clear and the river shimmered beneath the glare of a molten sun that was slowly extinguishing below the horizon. Huge walls of ice danced in the distance. Large boulders appeared and then disappeared. Then, what looked like a sailing ship faded in and out of a fog that moved, ghost-like, across the frozen sea. Mirage. We drifted through this smoky twilight, haunted by moving shadows on the dark shore and by the glittering specks of Arctic poppies that reflected the last rays of drowning light from the hilltop.

It was August 1, the second last night of our month-long canoe trip down the continent's most northerly navigable river. And here, finally, we were on the frozen coast, where 150 years earlier, Captain Robert McClure looked daily for a sign — another ship, a sledging party, or a break in the ice that had held his ship captive for more than 18 months. McClure had sailed around the coast of Alaska in an attempt to rescue the 129 men who, under the command of Sir John Franklin, had gone missing seven years earlier while coming the other way searching for a Northwest Passage to the Orient. None survived. In the end, it was McClure who had to be rescued and forced to abandon his ship after three miserable winters. They were fortunate to be where they were. In the High Arctic archipelago of Canada, Banks Island is a tiny oasis in a forbidding polar desert.

The Thomsen flows gently out of cluster of frozen lakes on a treeless plateau in the south central region of the island. From there it trickles gently north for more than 180 kilometres through a broad valley of lush sedge meadows filled with dwarf willow, potentilla, Arctic poppies, water sedges, and various herbs. We had come, in part, to see what was left of McClure's camp. We had also hoped to witness first hand one of the great unexplained natural wonders of the world — the rise of more than 50,000 muskoxen in a region where the animal had been absent for nearly a century following McClure's return home to England.

The flying conditions were marginal at best when we landed on a small, sandy island near the headwaters of the river early in July. The pilot had aborted the attempt four times out of fear that his big tundra tires would sink in the wet sand. A numbing north wind was blowing in from the northwest as he departed and the rain, which quickly turned to sleet, and then to snow made the routine job of putting up the tents and cooking supper a nightmare. Leaning into the wind, trying to imagine how we would make progress paddling downstream, I had hoped that first night that the weather would improve shortly. It didn't.

We were an eclectic group of six adventurers. Fran and Mike were wife and husband, a doctor and engineer who had recently moved to Inuvik to pursue, in part, their love of outdoor adventure. Peter, a grizzly bear and wolf biologist, who had been an Arctic paddling partner of mine for several years. We had canoed the Burnside, the Anderson, and the Horton — all mainland tundra rivers that flow into the Arctic Ocean. This time he was paired up with Irene, a fellow biologist from the West Coast. I was with Julia, an architect-turned lawyer whom I had fallen madly in love with two years earlier during a year-long fellowship at the University of Toronto.

Many of my friends couldn't believe I had fallen so hard for someone who had never sat in a canoe let alone camped in the wilderness. Those who did accept the possibility that love could conquer all thought it unconscionable that I was introducing her to canoeing by taking her on a month-long trip down a river that flowed towards the end of the Northern Hemisphere. But I was hopelessly smitten, and although Julia was more than a little nervous about what lay ahead for us on that trip, she was willing and eager.

Covering an area of 70,000 square kilometres, Banks is a largely uninhabited island that is about the size of Ireland. The 120 Inuit who live on the southwest coast in the hamlet of Sachs Harbour refer to the Thomsen River Valley as Aulavik – "the place where people travel." Two plateaus dominate the landscape: Durham Heights, which hovers 750 metres above the south central part of the island and a larger, more rugged mesa that occupies 5,100 square kilometres between Mercy Bay and Parker Point, along the island's northern coastline.

Partially unscarred by the last ice age, Banks is an island of striking contrasts. The west coast is flat, sandy and often shrouded in fog during the short summer months when the cold air is blowing in from the west over the sea ice and colliding with the warm air on land. Much of the north, east and south coast of Banks is flanked by 250-metre-high cliffs and steep scree slopes that drop directly into the sea. This is a part of the world where summer normally begins in June with a rapid melt of snow and ice and then ends in mid-to-late August with a big blizzard. That said, summer is defined a little bit differently up here. Although temperatures can rise to 20 C, the average high in July struggles to get to 10 C; the low sits at around 3 C. It is twice as likely to snow as is to rain whenever any appreciable precipitation occurs during the summer months.

Having hiked and skied in the High Arctic numerous times, I had thought I would have been well prepared for my first river trip on the archipelago. But, in truth, there's really nothing that can acclimatize one to the kind of cold, blustery winds that blow relentlessly across this island. That first night we clocked the wind gusting at 50 knots per hour. The next night, they held steady at around 25.

There are few things on a paddling adventure that are more frustrating than being in a canoe on a slow moving tundra river when the weather is like this. It's akin to watching the hour-hand of an old grandfather clock moving forward. We made no more than 10 kilometres the first day, and it would be generous to say that we covered eight more the next. It was all we could do to keep the boats going straight instead of being spun sideways by the headwinds. It was exhilarating to get off the river and sneak up on the first large herd of muskoxen we saw grazing high up on a small hilltop towards the end of the second day.

The hump-shouldered muskox is a strange looking beast, one that appears to have stepped out from the distant past as its ancestors did crossing the Bering Land Bridge from Asia a million years ago. Much like a bison, the animal's enormous head, short legs, long, shaggy coat and sharp horns make it an imposing sight on the treeless tundra. That's why it comes as a surprise for first time observers to learn that while a typical muskox bull weighs 300 kilograms, it stands no more than 120-centimetres tall.

There were at least 30 animals in this group we were stalking. Initially, they were oblivious to our presence. But once we got within a hundred metres, they thundered off, kicking up a huge cloud of dust behind them. Like Peary caribou, the diminutive ungulate that is found only in the High Arctic of Canada, muskoxen are curious animals. So when this group sensed that it was not being chased, the herd stopped and turned to see what we were up to. In short order, one of the bigger bulls returned to have a closer look. Many others dutifully followed. Then they all stood in a perfectly straight line while we looked back in wonder.

We stood face to face there for a good half-hour as if waiting for the other to make the first move. Having been bluff-charged a couple of times on previous trips, I wasn't interested in tempting fate again. A muskox has never, as far as I knew, gored and trampled a person to death. But they have, on occasion, injured those foolish enough to get too close. The only aggression these animals showed, however, was in the occasional rubbing of heads along their legs. This is what they do when they are agitated. But all hell broke loose when one muskox head-butted another that had trespassed into its zone of security. As the offending bull quickly retreated, a sheath of qiviat — the underlying wool that the animals shed in summer — came loose in the gusting wind and wrapped around its head. With its vision obscured, the animal whirled around madly, sending the others racing around like a herd of wild horses that had been spooked by a snake. In their wake, large balls of qiviat fluttered like giant cotton balls on the ground, trapped in the gnarly branches of dwarf willow. Sensing an opportunity to warm her frozen toes, Julia gathered a pile and lined the bottom of her rubber boots. Then we all headed back to camp satisfied with the way the second day ended.

McClure and his men had seen evidence of muskoxen during their 18 months on the island. But they were no more than lifeless piles of bleached skulls and bones sitting on hilltops. The ship's records show that while the crew managed to kill 110 caribou, 169 hares, 186 grouse, 198 ducks and 29 geese, two wolves and four polar bears in order to stay alive, they were able to harvest just seven muskoxen – five of which were shot during a sledging trip toward Victoria Island to the east.

How 50,000 animals – well over half the world's population – came to be 150 years later remains a mystery. There is no evidence, for example, that the population slowly rebounded over time. On the contrary, few muskoxen were seen on the island in the century that followed McClure's departure. Travelling across Banks in 1911, explorer Vilhjamur Stefansson was looking for but did not see a single animal. When asked, the Inuit he encountered along the way told him that the animals had left the island. The intimation was that someone had broken a taboo, and taking offence, the animals simply disappeared.

Successive surveys of the island over the next half-century also produced no sign of the species. In fact, it wasn't until the fall of 1952 that anyone had seen a muskox anywhere in the area. Tom Manning and Andrew Macpherson were circumnavigating the island in a canoe powered by a five-horsepower motor that year. They were mapping the coastline and counting wildlife for the Defence Research Board of Canada. About halfway through their voyage, the two men were stopped by a massive sheet of ice that was wedged tightly to the north shore. They hunkered down at Castel Bay for ten days hoping a southern breeze would sweep the floe back into McClure Strait. But by August 29, when winter's dangerous grip was beginning to take hold, the two biologists decided to start motoring up the Thomsen River as far as they could go before hiking overland to Sachs Harbour where they were to be picked up by boat.

But 20 kilometres upstream, they found the river too low to carry their canoe. The tundra was white with snow that wasn't melting. With no other choice, they tore the thwarts from their wooden boat, built a primitive sledge and began a 320-kilometre trek southwest. It snowed hard for the first three days and it snowed intermittently every day thereafter. A foot of snow lay slightly drifted across the treeless tundra when Andrew spotted a black dot in the distance. Turning to Tom, who had become moderately snow-blind, Andrew confessed with some excitement that he couldn't believe what it was he had spotted. But there it was — a shaggy bull muskox — crisply silhouetted in the bright Arctic light.

Slowed by the deep, wet snow and unable to dry out their damp clothing in the sub-zero temperatures, Tom and Andrew had no time to investigate whether there were more muskoxen in the region. They had barely enough time to meet their boat. Finally, three days after their scheduled rendezvous, they reached their destination at Sachs Harbour fearing that maybe they had missed their ride back to the mainland. (The hamlet was still two years way from being established.) The next day, however, the pilot showed up unexpectedly. He was four days late after having got lost crossing the strait from the mainland.

While muskox sightings on Banks did rise in subsequent years, the numbers weren't especially dramatic. One hundred were counted in 1961, 800 in 1967 and 1,800 in 1971. This is the kind of growth one would expect in years when the weather is good and predators are few and far between. By the 1980s, however, scientists were scratching their heads in wonder at all the animals they were seeing. In 1982, they counted 9,393. By 1991, there were nearly 50,000.

There wasn't a day during our first week on the island when we didn't see dozens of muskoxen. We observed them grazing on the hilltops, head-butting each other on the treeless flats, and cooling themselves off in the river. Occasionally, we'd find one or two dead, uneaten and with no sign of what had killed them. It was as if a perfectly healthy animal had fallen over and died suddenly. At one point, we got to thinking that maybe there was some unworldly creature exercising its powers to punish humans for breaking some taboo. Not until the end of that first week did we see any evidence of wolves, the muskox's only predator on Banks. This wasn't entirely surprising. In an effort to conserve caribou, muskoxen and Arctic fox numbers to help the starving Inuit, the Canadian government systematically poisoned thousands of wolves throughout the High Arctic. It wasn't until the 1970s that the predator control program was phased out.

Arctic wolves (*Canis lupus arctos*) found on the Banks and other islands in the far north are a subspecies of the grey wolf (*Canis lupus*) that occur elsewhere on the continent. Apart from their white- and cream-coloured fur, and the fact that they tend to have shorter ears, muzzles and legs, they are essentially the same animal. That they survive in a land where the temperatures routinely plummet to −50 C during winter days that come with 24 hours of darkness is a testament to how hardy these animals are.

Largely unhunted, Arctic wolves tend to be less shy of humans. I have, on a number of occasions, had wolves walk right up to me like a dog looking for a handout. Once, an alpha male leading a pack, walked in, stared a bunch of us down and then almost daring us to stop him, peed on our tent and backpacks. Only the yelping of worried pups behind persuaded him to move off.

There has been some debate about the uniqueness of Banks Island's wolves. In the 1950s, Tom Manning concluded that some of the specimens that Stefansson had collected for the Canadian government were distinct from those found elsewhere in the Arctic. Banks Island's *Canus lupus bernardi*, Tom noted, was smaller and more dog-like in appearance than its modern cousins. Scientists have since cast some doubt on Manning's conclusions. But one recent study suggests that the current population is more genetically isolated than wolves found elsewhere in the Arctic. With prey so plentiful on Banks Island, there is little reason for wolves to migrate long distances, as almost all other Arctic wolves do. At the same time, open water and vast stretches of sea ice are significant enough geographic barriers to prevent mainland wolves from crossing over to Banks. So while Banks Island wolves may not at this time be a distinct subspecies, theoretically, the population could evolve into a different animal down the road if it remains geographically isolated.

I was in another zone, daydreaming, when I heard the wolf bark at us as we headed down river on the sixth day. Initially, I thought it was a dog, but then when I quickly regained my senses and looked toward the hillside, I saw two big wolves standing there looking at us. Seconds later, four perfectly white pups popped their heads up to see what was going on. A game of hide-and-seek ensued when we ferried upstream to have a closer look. The wolves would run away, then come back and sit down, and run away again. We played with each other for a good 10 minutes like this before the small pack scampered over the hill and disappeared for good. A faint howl being carried in with the wind was the last we heard from them.

It was our intention to get to the confluence of Dissection Creek and the Thomsen River where archeologists working on the island several years earlier had built a clapboard cabin. Julia was terribly ill by this point of the trip. She had come down with a bad cold on the second day and the infection was now burrowed deep into her chest. She was suffering from chills and fever, but she did not complain. Any hope of finding refuge for her, however, was dashed when we arrived at our destination, opened the cabin door and were overwhelmed by a nauseating stench. God, I thought, some poor old Inuit polar bear hunter must have died there in the spring. But it was only a weasel that had drowned in a big water barrel inside. The smell was so stomach-turning we quickly realized it would take days, if not weeks, to air the place out. So as a cold, steady rain fell from the clouds that were almost touching the ground that evening, we looked around in the mist and set up camp in a sheltered spot across from Dissection Creek.

As it turned out, we could not have settled on a more beautiful stretch of river. When the clouds lifted slightly the next morning, we were delighted to discover that Dissection Creek, fogged in the night before, flowed blue and fast out of the high, rugged badlands country in the northwest corner of the island. Bouquets of wildflowers like yellow Arctic poppies, purple saxifrage, Jacob's ladder and potentilla coloured its banks. The Thomsen was also very deep a short way downstream — just the kind of place, I thought, where big fish like to be. Before Peter had a chance to wake up and muscle in on my territory, I quickly got out my fishing rod and cast the first line.

High Arctic streams are often too cold, too shallow and nutrient-poor to sustain many fish. Only Arctic char, lake trout, cisco, and the remarkably homely fourhorn sculpin and ninespine stickleback can live in an environment so unforgiving. The Thomsen is likely the most northerly watershed on the continent to support all these fish species. Lake trout, which will eat everything from their own kind to lemmings, grow big if there is enough water to get them through a winter. That pool, I was sure, would be the perfect home for a big one, even if it was much too deep and glacial for me to see anything coming toward my line. It didn't take long to find out. Once a fish struck my lure, I knew I had one — a three-kilogram lake trout that Julia and I decided would make for a perfect breakfast.

Months before we had set off on this trip, one of the archeologists who had built the so-called Green Cabin at Dissection Creek
warned me about the winds. So while I was prepared, I had not
expected to be pounded so hard every day. Nor was I ready for the
looming gale that intensified as we fried up our fish that morning.
Peter and Irene bore the worst of it. Just seconds after they stepped
outside that morning to see what I had caught, their tent took off
like a hot-air balloon. Around and around it whirled for several
seconds while sleeping bags and clothes spilled out and spiraled into
the river. Peter and I raced to shore and jumped into one of the
canoes, hoping to get to it before it sank. We got there just in time
to save the tent, but not before one of Irene's boots and wildflower
books had been given up to the river.

With rare exceptions, every long, bad-weather canoe trip has a turning point. Ours arrived on the 10th day when we were all so wet,
cold and miserable that even the toilet paper we had tucked into the
pockets of our rainjackets had been reduced to mush. The sudden
burst of bright light that broke through that day literally transformed the landscape around us. What had been drab and grey was
then soft and green. And the air that had made us so wet, cold and
clammy was suddenly radiating with soothing warmth. Almost in
unison, each one us put down our paddles, lay back in the canoes
and let the gentle current and calming breeze set the pace.

There is also a saying in the Arctic that if you wait five minutes,
the weather will change. And so it was the next day when we were
paddling for the first time in our shirts instead of our jackets and
raincoats. We were in the midst of the White Sand Hills, a part of the
Thomsen River valley where the lush meadows give way to patches of
desert. It was a treat to have the wind at our backs for once and it
seemed, if only for a fleeting moment, that the sand around us was
of a semi-tropical origin. But within an hour or so of our departure
from a lunch break that day, the bright blue sky turned to a dull grey
once again. Overhead, a rough-legged hawk — the first one we

had seen — pierced the air with a descending trill, a warning, it seemed, that something was about to happen. Then in the distance, the rumbling of thunder announced the arrival of a blast of wind and some big, fat raindrops. Suddenly, everything — the river and the sand on the hills — were swirling in chaotic motion. Even the muskoxen on the hilltop bolted — first this way, and then that — with each strike of lightning and clap of thunder that followed the rain. It was as if they had never experienced an electrical storm as violent as this one.

As the rain fell harder, we paddled to shore and hunkered down under the splash covers of our canoes. Julia and I were fine with our cheap rubber raincoats, but the others were getting seriously chilled in their expensive breathable suits. The fabric had not stood up well to all the rubbing that comes with paddling. Sitting in their boats, heads buried into their chests and arms tucked into their spray covers, our four companions looked like sleeping ducks in a rainstorm. "Perhaps we need to modify that saying about the weather," Julia quipped. "Maybe for Banks Island it should be: 'wait five minutes and the weather will get worse.'"

———

E. O. Wilson, the great Harvard biologist, once noted that nothing in the natural world makes sense without theory. It is human nature, he noted, to put knowledge into context in order to tell a story and recreate the world that surrounds it. But the problem with theories, he cautioned, is that they are almost always hobbled by multiple meanings. And so it is with theories about the mysterious fall and rise of muskoxen on Banks Island.

Stefansson was convinced that he had figured out the first part of the equation after he returned from his five years in the Arctic. One clue came to him while he was camped on Melville Island to the north. Sitting there one night, looking all around at the muskoxen he was seeing, he wondered how it was that Melville, with just a fraction of the vegetation found on Banks, could support this healthy population when the other could not sustain one animal.

Another clue came in May 1911, when he was visiting the Inuit at Prince Albert Sound on neighbouring Victoria Island. Having had virtually no contact with the outside world at this time, these people were still living a primitive lifestyle, one without guns, fossil fuel or modern tools. In order to survive, they had to migrate long distances, hunting seals on the coast in spring before crossing over the sea ice to Banks Island to look for caribou and muskoxen in the summer.

Stefansson was intrigued to learn that while on Banks Island some of these people had discovered McClure's ship abandoned on the north coast. "She was to them, naturally, a treasure house, especially for her iron," he reasoned. Stefansson assumed that news of the abandoned ship spread quickly to Eskimo communities as far south as Coronation Gulf and east towards King William Island, and Mercy Bay for 20 or 30 years. Northern Banks, he believed, "became a place of pilgrimage for perhaps a thousand Eskimos. They made long trips there to get material for knives, arrow points, and the like, certain families making the trip one year and other families another year."

It was only inevitable then, Stefansson believed, that the muskox population would have declined dramatically as a result of all of those people hunting the animals in order to stay alive. Unlike caribou, most muskoxen do not flee long distances when being chased. When the animals stopped to form their defensive circles, as they would normally do when pursued by wolves, the Inuit would slaughter them en mass.

———

We were at the top of Head Hill, a 450-metre plateau overlooking the confluence of the Thomsen and Muskox Rivers, when we saw first hand what Stefansson was getting at. There, sprawled about, were the remains of 581 muskox skulls, 20 food caches, and 17 tent rings — all left from a time long ago when the Inuit, presumably, were migrating up toward the coast to scavenge from McClure's ship.

There is a temptation to liken Head Hill and hundreds of other sites like it on Banks Island to the buffalo jumps of the Prairies, where the Blackfoot and other Plains Indians developed a strategy of driving the animals off steep cliffsides while another group waited down below to spear the injured animals. On Banks Island, however, the Inuit would have driven the muskoxen up hill – a direction the antelope-like animals instinctively followed when threatened. Waiting for the muskoxen would have been another group of hunters, perhaps accompanied by dogs. Trapped, the muskoxen would have huddled in their defensive posture, then fallen one by one with each pierce of spear or arrow.

Stefansson's theory was so elegant and reasonable that no one questioned its veracity for more than 70 years. But in 1974, when scientist Chris Shank and his colleagues investigated Head Hill and other sites, the first seeds of doubt were sewn. Given that Banks is as big as Ireland, Shank wondered how it was possible for such a primitive people with such rudimentary weapons to kill so many animals in 20 or 30 years. It seemed to him implausible that every corner of the island would be hunted out.

Several years later, Shank returned and collected some bone fragments for radiocarbon dating. Neither he nor anyone else were prepared for the results. They indicated that 11 of the 12 bones were deposited long before McClure's ship, *Investigator*, had arrived in the region. The radiocarbon dating seemed to suggest that whoever, or whatever killed those muskoxen, did so some time in the 17th century.

Shank's one and only attempt to get the results published was greeted by fierce opposition from those who felt that either the radio-carbon dating was unreliable or the sample size was too small. To this day, Shank believes that Stefansson's theory, although correct in the sense that McClure's ship did result in an extraordinary concentration of people travelling to the north end of Banks Island, does not adequately explain the extirpation of muskoxen from Banks Island.

Andrew Macpherson was a biologist who believed that all things could be explained by science. But before he died recently, he confessed that the fall and rise of muskoxen on Banks Island might endure as one of the great unsolved mysteries of the Arctic. Theoretically, there may have always been a remnant population somewhere on the island that no one had ever spotted. Or it may well be that a herd had migrated across the sea ice from either Melville Island to the north or Victoria Island to the east. Ideal conditions created by extremely favourable weather and the absence of predators and disease could have resulted in a remarkably successful rate of reproduction that produced so many animals. But the fact is nothing quite like this has been seen anywhere in the polar world. And without nature reproducing similar results in a different environment, Macpherson's prediction may prove to be true. The debate could go on for some time.

—

It was hot and humid when we left our camp near Head Hill. The skies were a deep blue and there wasn't a cloud anywhere to suggest that the weather, which had been warm and balmy for several days, was going to change. It was lovely paddling in the placid river. Neither Julia nor I thought anything of it when the gap between us and our more energetic partners widened. But then when an eerie moaning of wind began funnelling hot, dry air up the valley toward us, we began looking ahead with some concern. Weighing just a little over a hundred pounds, Julia was not the anchor we needed to keep the bow from getting lifted out of the water. Each time we crested one of the big waves coming toward us with the wind, the canoe would be hurdled sideways. It was all I could do to steer it back on track.

We kept on like this for some time hoping that perseverance would ultimately get us to where we needed to go. But it was futile. So we hopped out, and tried dragging our canoe along the shallow shoreline. This was also a losing proposition. Three times, Julia was knocked over by the winds and the waves trying to help me haul the canoe in the storm. It was only a matter of time, I thought, before she would succumb to exhaustion or hypothermia.

We had only our tent and sleeping bags and a nearly empty barrel of dry food with us that afternoon. Neither one of us was looking forward to spending the night alone on the coast without a stove or gun to ward off polar bears. We had, however, no choice. But we needed to find a spot along the riverbank that was sheltered enough to allow us to put up a tent.

As it turned out, the perfect spot was no more than a few hundreds yards away. But it seemed like 10 kilometres of hard effort getting there. Sinking in the soft sand on the river bottom, pressing into the wind with pull ropes over our shoulders, we lost a step with every two or three that we put forward.

We were resigned to the fact that we would end up eating hard biscuits and drinking cold water while we waited out this windstorm. But just around the corner of the river where we found the spot we were looking for, was Fran and Mike sitting in their tent boiling up some tea. Like us, they had also come to the conclusion that there was no point trying to keep up with Peter who, as always, was a brute for punishment. In time, we would catch up with them. In the meantime, we played cards, fried up some bannock and drank copious amounts of hot tea.

———

It is an 18-kilometre hike walking a straight line from Castel Bay to Investigator Point, the rise of land on the northwest coast of Mercy Bay where McClure would routinely go to look for his rescuers. Taking into consideration that the terrain would likely be a lot more rugged on the northern part of the island, we had planned on doing the trip in six hours. It took us almost nine. There were a lot more streams to cross, wetland to go around and hills to climb than we had anticipated.

The air, however, was dead calm when we finally arrived at our destination later that day. A rolling thunder could be heard in the distance and the sky was covered with wild looking clouds that swirled in nearly every direction. It was sublime, as terrible as it was beautiful. Scanning the horizon with my binoculars I looked for, but did not see the polar bear that had left its tracks back at our camp at Castel Bay. Nor did I see any sign of caribou or other wildlife that the crew of the *Investigator* were always on the look for. With the exception of a snowy owl perched on a big rock, pivoting its head in search of lemmings, there was almost no life at all.

McClure had the *Investigator* anchored several kilometres down the coast at a spot he called Providence Point. By the spring of 1853, after three winters in the Arctic, his men had been reduced to insufficient rations. Many crewmen, by then suffering from physical or mental illnesses, had been confined to their beds. Those still fit enough to move rummaged almost daily through the garbage that had been tossed out weeks and months before. At one point, Lieutenant Robert Wyniatt became so crazed and despondent that he began to howl throughout night, despite the protestations of his shipmates. When he threatened to murder the captain, not once, but three times, McClure had him lowered down to the sea ice to try to calm him down.

The plight of the crew had become so desperate by the spring of 1853 that McClure concluded that their only chance of survival was to escape on foot. His was a Darwinian scheme, worthy of a Machiavelli. The idea was to send two parties out in different directions. Lieutenant William Haswell would lead the first group, taking with him poor Wynniat and 12 of the sickest men. They were to walk 800 kilometres east across the sea ice to Port Leopold where, in 1848, the explorer James Clark Ross had cached some food and clothing as well as a small steamboat. Once there, they were instructed to wait on the off chance — a miracle, really — that a whaling boat would find them.

The second party would be led by Lieutenant Samuel Creswell, the expedition's artist. He was to take 10 men overland to the Princess Royal Islands in Prince of Wales Strait. From there, they would go past Victoria Island by boat, then across Dolphin and Union Strait and up the Mackenzie River to Fort Good Hope.

Once at Fort Good Hope, they would solicit the support of the Hareskin Indians to help them return to Fort Edmonton and eventually to Montreal.

McClure, in the meantime, would remain with the ship along with the doctor and the rest of the healthy men. They would stay put for another winter in the hopes that the ice might finally break loose and set them free.

It would have been suicidal for the departing expeditions to leave the ship. The hardiest of men would have had a tough time making such journeys. Even Johann Miertsching, the Moravian missionary who remained loyal to McClure throughout the ordeal, thought the idea to be insane. "Twenty men are now in hospital, and in six weeks, we must, with those judged unfit to remain longer with the ship, harness ourselves to the sledges laden with supplies, and drag them through snow and ice for hundreds of miles. How many of us will in this way see Europe again. The answer is 'No one.'"

McClure, however, never had a chance to carry out his scheme. A few days before the two groups were to set off on their separate ways, an event comparable to Stanley's famous encounter with Livingstone unfolded. On deck, McClure was telling Miertsching that if they didn't see each other the following year, he could be assured that he would be dead and unburied in this desolate part of the world. Before he could finish, McClure spotted a black dot on the sea ice. Initially, he thought it to be a muskox. In time, however, McClure was surprised to find himself confronted by a man "whose face was black as ebony." An Inuk, he thought. But then when, in typical British naval fashion, the heavily tanned man politely introduced himself as Lieutenant Bedford Pim, McClure realized that they were being rescued.

Under the command of Henry Kellett, Pim and his fellow sailors had overwintered at Dealy Island some 250 kilometres to the east in the ship *Resolute*. He had been sent out to search for the *Investigator* after the crew of the *Resolute* found a note that McClure's men had left in a cairn on Victoria Island the previous autumn.

Pim's arrival, however, did not do much to alter McClure's sadistic ways. Still convinced that the *Investigator* would ultimately be freed that summer, McClure sent a small party of men to Kellett's ship informing the superior officer that he planned to stay with his frozen ship. Upon seeing the decrepit condition of McClure's men, Kellett stopped short of ordering him to scrap his crazy plan. Instead, he sent his surgeon to see if any of the remaining men, if willing to stay on, were fit to serve on board for another winter. Only four —all officers bound to duty - offered their services. Informed of the sorry state of the crew, Kellett ordered the *Investigator* abandoned immediately.

The crew spent one more winter in the Arctic in the relative comfort of a well-supplied ship. Back home, McClure claimed the £10,000 prize for being the first to traverse the Northwest Passage. When asked by a select committee of the British House of Commons whether he would be willing to share it with his rescuers, McClure declined noting that he did not willingly abandon his ship.

What happened to the *Investigator* after she was left behind is a mystery. Inuit scavenging certainly took place. At various sites on the island, Archeologists Richard Will, Cliff Hickey, Peter Schlederman and others have found mahogany, glass crockery, oak, a metal button, lead and copper that almost certainly had come from the *Investigator*. Some believe that under the crushing pressure of the ice, the ship eventually sank. Others suggest it was finally freed and sent sailing, ghost-like, into the Arctic Ocean.

———

We headed back to our camp at Castel Bay that evening after reluctantly forfeiting our plan to hike down to Providence Point. Time had run out on us by this point, and with no food or tent to get us through the night, it was only prudent that we head back before the storm that appeared to be building over the Arctic came our way. As it turned out, it was the right thing to do. All the way back, a thick, smoky fog followed us with such spooky stealth that we didn't dare stop for a break. So close was it on our tails that we didn't even bother removing our boots while fording the streams. All told, we hiked 23 hours that day. By the time we got back to our camp, it was all we could do to collapse on sleeping bags and fall asleep.

Early the next morning, Julia and I woke up to the staccato, bugle-like call of two sandhill cranes. The mist was then so thick that we could barely see the other tents six metres away. It was still warm so we strolled along the shore of Castel Bay, marvelling at the soft luminous light of the thinning fog that had chased us back to camp the night before. There was no need to run now, even if the tracks of the polar bear in the sand still seemed too fresh for our comfort. The plane was going to pick us up in 24 hours. In that dream-like hour, we were happily lost in this lonely primeval world of sedge meadows, desert flats, and badlands in which muskoxen, Peary caribou and wolf numbers rise and fall with the slightest shifts of nature. And unlike the last few days of the trip, we were no longer longing to go home.

HADLEY
BAY

Rapids
Canyon

N
W   E
S

The Nanook River

22 Kilometres

Map Area

NAMAYCUSH LAKE

SANDSTONE DESERT

Nanook River
Into the World of the Great White Wanderer

ll I really knew about the river when we landed near its headwaters was that it was called the "Nanook," Inuktituk for polar bear. Actually, I wasn't even sure of that, for the river carries no name at all on most of the more detailed maps of Canada, including the topographical ones we were hoping would guide us down its length. Perhaps that's why, when I first spotted it on a map back in elementary school, threading its way across the central plain of Victoria Island in the western Arctic archipelago, I became obsessed with it, developing an urge that could only be satisfied by me paddling its waters and exploring its shores.

Not the least among the rewards, if I succeeded, would be the sight of the Arctic Ocean at a place that had defeated many of my childhood heroes: William Edward Parry, Leopold M'Clintock, and other 19th-century Northwest Passage explorers. Who was I to think the trip was even possible? As a young adult, I had developed a passion for canoeing northern rivers, and during the past 25 years, I have been lucky to run some three dozen of the better known. Still, no one, as far as I knew, had ever descended the Nanook. Not even the few Inuit who live on the south and west side

of this island venture here. The closest they come is during the
spring polar bear hunt, when the Nanook is a frozen wasteland, and
when Hadley Bay — into which the river flows — is overrun with
the great white wanderers. The question really was: who was I to
deny the mystery and adventure evoked by that anonymous blue line
snaking across Victoria Island?

Pertinent to the undertaking was the knowledge that most
rivers in the High Arctic are little more than dry gravel beds or
muddy streams. This part of the world, after all, is classified as
desert. Winters pass in almost complete darkness. And while snow
may come anytime of the year, no more than 200 millimeters of
precipitation falls over 12 months. At best, I speculated there would
be five or six weeks in midsummer — as the scant snow that falls
each year melts and the upper layer of permafrost thaws and perco-
lates to the surface — when the river would have sufficient volume
to float a canoe. There are no glaciers to feed the river as there are
on nearby Melville Island. But even if there were sufficient flow,
there was no guarantee that the numerous lakes on the river route
would be ice-free or safe from the river's namesake. Polar bears, I
knew, usually remain on the coast but they do wander inland from
time to time.

Such possibilities, however, were not foremost on my mind. I
had convinced a small group of friends that this would be the trip
of a lifetime, and my wife Julia that it would be a romantic setting
in which to start the family we had been dreaming about. Their
ready acceptance hinged on my idyllic recollections of earlier trips
that my friend Peter, Julia and I had done: a gentle paddle down the
picturesque Natla in the Mackenzie Mountains on a warm summer
day; a nose-to-nose encounter with a white wolf that we surprised
on a hilltop after scaling a cliff along the Burnside in the central
Arctic: the mirage of a ghostly ship floating on the sea ice while we
were canoeing down the Thomsen at the north end of Banks Island.
What I did not mention were the summer blizzards, the dense
clouds of blackflies and mosquitoes, the torrents of water sluicing
through dark canyons, the damp sleeping bags – the standard litany

of arctic river dangers and displeasures that is forgotten as each new season arrives and another river presents itself.

It was not until we were on route from Edmonton to Cambridge Bay at the south end of Victoria Island that I had the first inkling that I might have deceived not only my friends, but also myself. Summer 1992, it appeared, was going to be late coming to northern Canada. It should not have been a surprise, given the fickle nature of the Arctic climate even in normal times. I have experienced summers where it is warm and dry for weeks on end and others where summer barely shows up at all. But this year was anything but normal. The sulphurous plume that followed the eruption of Mount Pinatubo in early 1991 (average hemispheric temperatures dropped by 0.2 C to 0.5 C for a period of one to three years) and the shifting of the El Niño current in the South Pacific were playing havoc with the planet's meteorology. Although it was already near the end of July, I could see from the window of the plane that lakes hundreds of kilometres south of our intended destination were still fast with ice.

But it was the two-hour long flight in the Twin Otter from Cambridge Bay to the Nanook River that really rattled me. Everywhere we looked, we saw bare soil and gravel, black tundra melt ponds, cold, grey sky and curtains of thick Siberian fog undulating in the wind. It was the Arctic at its most desolate, and it was all I could do not to imagine our group of eight down there for the next two weeks, dragging canoes over ice and mud by day, and shivering along the river's edge at night.

"Great idea, Eddie," someone shouted over the drone of the small plane's engines. It was not meant as a compliment. I was already mulling over maps, making contingency plans and feeling a little queasy when the cover of thick cloud unfolded and the verdant hue of a fertile river valley came into view. True, there was not much water below, but there was enough to float a loaded canoe and at least one spot on shore that was flat and firm enough for the pilot to feel comfortable enough to land on big tundra tires. If this wasn't precisely the headwaters of the Nanook, it was close enough. At least this way, I reasoned, it would be less of a rush to get to Hadley Bay where the pilot was scheduled to pick us up in two weeks.

With one problem solved, of course, another surfaced. After years of paddling in the North, you learn — with luck — to be circumspect when choosing your companions. To travel together successfully for weeks in a remote, unfamiliar landscape with no chance of retreat or rescue, requires from all who would try a rare combination of experience, patience and like-mindedness. Finding the right mix is not easy. Although many are intrigued by the possibility of paddling in the Arctic, few Canadians are willing to participate in a summer holiday if they suspect it may mean experiencing winter all over again or not having hot water to wash with at the end of a day. And more importantly, not everyone sees wilderness in the same light.

We were, truth be known, an odd company, with varying levels of outdoor experience and — as would become painfully evident — fundamentally different outlooks on life and on wilderness. Dawn and Brian are professional photographers who variously call home a one-room schoolhouse in Manitoba or the back of a Volkswagen camper parked wherever they find themselves in the backwoods of North America. Brian's biting wit, Dawn's gentle grace and their shared appreciation for food, adventure and nature make them two of our favourite people. With Peter, a bear biologist working in the Northwest Territories, I have enjoyed another kind of friendship. We first met nearly a decade earlier on the shores of Hudson Bay where he had been assigned the formidable task of detecting and deterring polar bears before it became necessary to kill them. I was there to write about the project for *Equinox* magazine. We had developed a friendship ever since and enjoyed paddling many northern rivers together. He is one of the most capable outdoor people I have ever had the privilege of travelling with.

In truth, Peter's paddling partner, Jim, and the two Americans he had invited along to share the cost of the charter, were another story — last minute surprises, in fact. Jim, who had accompanied Peter, my friend Ian and me on a trip down the Hornaday River the

previous summer, was a wealthy veterinarian — a businessman really
— who, as I had learned on that first trip, was prone to dramatic
mood swings. On the Hornaday, he never accepted the possibility
that the people he was travelling with would object to being treated
like the people who worked for him. Although I never did warm to
him, I felt there was no reason why things couldn't be better on this
trip. On the other hand, the Americans Bob and Dave — blue-collar
workers from Washington — were a study in personality and
circumstance. In theory, they were supposed to be heading off on
their own once we landed. They had been invited simply to fill out
the plane. Maybe it was the extremity of our isolation that changed
their minds. Whatever it was, they set up camp 20 metres from us
that first night with their boom box blaring country and western
music, and leaving the four of us to wonder what lay ahead.

Still, there was nothing to suggest that we couldn't get along.
During those first hours we were all absorbed by the novelty of the
terrain, the brilliance of the midnight sun and the peaceful face of
the Nanook. Taking stock of the river that lay before us, all looked
as it should be.

It was difficult to believe that this was the same stark island we
had flown over. All around us were wooly lousewarts, yellow Arctic
poppies, white-and-lemon-coloured avens, green sedges and tawny
tufts of qiviat —the downy underside of the muskox's guard hairs
— which was blowing all around us and getting caught in low lying
willow branches. There was so much of this qiviat, Peter went about
gathering it industriously, vowing to collect enough to have a
sweater knitted by his mother in Alberta.

It was midnight, just as we were about to turn in for the night,
when Brian pointed to a cluster of black specks on a distant hillside.
The specks were several female muskoxen with two newborn calves
and a yearling. The animals did not run as we approached. Nor did
they budge when we set up our tripods four metres from them. Instead,
they pressed together in a defensive formation, rump to rump, with
the younger animals squeezed between. The posture is effective pro-
tection against wolves, their main predator, but offered little against

human hunters with rifles who decimated their numbers between 1880 and 1917. Once the buffalo were all gone on the prairies, the Hudson's Bay Company turned to muskoxen to satisfy European demand for warm robes. And entire herds were shot so that hunters could capture the calves that would be sold to zoos. So many animals were killed in the North that the Canadian government was forced to put a ban on hunting in 1917 to save what few animals were left.

That first hike — a leisurely exploration of no more than four kilometres — set the pace for the early days of the trip. The Nanook was, as it looked — a slow, meandering river that was so clear, there was rarely any point where we couldn't see its gravel bottom. We happily adjusted to its rhythm. There was little wind to fight, and when we put our shoulders into the paddle, it was only to race each other through moments of exuberance. Mostly though, we surrendered to the current, and allowed it to carry us deep into a primeval world of golden light, gurgling whirlpools and gently rolling tundra.

The one marked rapid on the map was a bit of a dud when we ran it on the third day. Here, the river braided into several channels before tumbling over a small drop into Namaycush Lake, the first of several lakes on the river. The channels were so shallow that the canoes bumped and ground over a bed of stones before settling into a deep dark pool. I couldn't blame the map entirely. The constantly changing force of some rivers flowing over unstable permafrost can shift tons of gravel from the bottom, turning a small waterfall into an inconsequential riffle or a riffle into a fulminating cascade.

We camped near this rapid for a few days feasting on monster trout that we pulled from the lake below, sleeping unconscionably long hours, and ridding ourselves of the last vestiges of the nervous energy that governs urban life. The conditions were ideal: blue skies, a balmy breeze, and best of all, no bugs. Only two or three varieties of mosquitoes are found this far north, none as aggressive as their southern cousins.

From our camp at Namaycush Lake, we could see what appeared to be sandstone pillars far in the distance, beckoning us to come see them. We set off the second evening at the lake hoping to reach them around midnight when the sun is at its magical best. But there were, as there are in all northern adventures, a number of diversions along the way that slowed us down: snowy owls gliding effortlessly across the tundra; an enormous, solitary muskox bull that reluctantly posed for our cameras before challenging our advance with a bluff charge and a handful of fearless Arctic fox puppies playing near their den. For a while, it was easy to imagine that we had stumbled into a Garden of Eden where wolves and humans, caribou and muskox, fox and owls, coexist. Then we came upon a litter of newborn lemmings recently evicted by their mother. Tiny puncture wounds on their bodies were caked with blood. It was the first case of animal infanticide that I'd ever seen. The Arctic, I was reminded, and was to soon learn again on this and other trips, is not often the friendly place that Canadian-born explorer Vilhjalmur Stefansson — the so-called "Prophet of the North" — described after he spent five years exploring this part of the world between 1913 and 1918.

With each kilometre, the sandstone hoodoos we headed for became more imposing. Even through binoculars, they seemed an apparition. We scoffed at someone's suggestion that they were 10-storeys high. Most of us believed they were much taller.

Three or four hours into the hike, we noticed heavy clouds on the horizon, so Jim, Peter and I picked up the pace, determined to reach the hoodoos before we lost the rich evening light. What followed was surreal. The more we advanced, the less sure we were about what we were confronting. Like ghosts, the hoodoos seemed to recede with our every step, as if they were spooked by our human forms and uncertain of our intentions. After an hour we finally stood in front of them, scratching our heads in bewilderment. The giant monoliths had inexplicably shrunk. The tallest was no more than a four-metre tall sentinel standing on the edge of a great sandy desert. Perched atop one of them, a lone rough-legged hawk nervously flapped its wings, seemingly warning us with its eerie trill that we did not belong there. We had been duped by eyes untrained at navigating through a flat, treeless world in which there are few reference points with which to measure.

—◢◣—

Back at camp early the next morning, Bob and Dave listened enviously as we described our adventure the night before. They would not be deterred. So unwisely, we thought, they set off early the next morning when the heavy clouds we had seen the night before were moving in. Damp, bone-chilling Arctic weather descended shortly after their departure. The clouds, at times, were nearly touching the ground. When an icy rain started falling, we began to worry that they might not return. Not only would they be cold and wet, they would have no means of finding their way back through the fog if they didn't have a compass. After several hours of waiting and watching out for them, we anticipated that possibility. So, Peter fired off a couple of shot gun blasts in the hopes that it would lead them in the right direction. We listened for a whistle or a cracker shell to respond, but none were issued.

In the meantime, we hunkered down in Peter's big tent, drank tea and took turns reading stories out loud. Julia read us a Stephen Leacock tale about the eternal optimist who smiles in the face of adversity in the dentist's chair. Then I followed with an excerpt from Edward Abbey's *Desert Solitarie*, hoping that its poetic descriptions of the arid canyon lands in Utah would warm up everyone. Then, curiously, Jim followed with the *Tao of Leadership*, a distinctly Western interpretation on ancient Far East wisdom, which was aimed at those seeking self-improvement. Dressed in khaki, military-style garb, Jim read out solemnly "A good leader is one who sits in silence and lets the rest do their thing. A good leader is one who. . ." On and on it went but no one, judging by the expressions, understood why he had chosen this militaristic piece of literature to read.

As it turned out, the more time we spent together, the more nervous and uncommunicative Jim became, particularly with Julia and Dawn. Even Peter's dog became the object of his occasional hostility whenever Peter was not around. Each time he gave the poor beast a whack, he would go and furiously wash his hands. When someone suggested this was odd behaviour for a veterinarian, he explained: "I've handled so many sick animals over the years, I can't stand touching them any more."

For the first eight days, we let Jim's silent rages and mood swings pass, but the night when he announced to Dawn and Julia that the two things he hated most were cats and women, it was clear that we were on the brink of a culture war. In fact, the lines were drawn not an hour later when Jim took out his hunting knife after dinner inside the tent and began to sharpen it on a whetstone, as he had been constantly doing, unnecessarily we all agreed, throughout the trip. When it was clear that the big knife was giving Dawn the creeps, Jim asked in a sinister way whether if what he was doing was bothering her. Dawn confirmed that, yes, it was, and then left the tent to blow off some steam when Jim smiled with satisfaction and went back to his sharpening. "Someone ought to give that man a good shake," she hissed. Always laid-back, Brian shrugged it off and offered his own unique perspective. "He's just like any other jerk on the 401 (highway) who whizzes by and gives you the finger in heavy traffic. He's not worth getting upset over."

It was a good 12 hours before we finally spotted our American friends slowly making their way toward our camp. Without a rain-coat, Big Dave didn't even bother to take off his boots or pants to cross the river that was thigh-high to waist-deep. Once across, he made straight for his tent barely able to speak. Pale, blue-lipped and shivering, he climbed into his sleeping bag without removing his wet clothing. All he could mutter was: "I've never been so cold in my life."

The safe return of Bob and Dave, however, didn't turn out to be cause for optimism about the remainder of the journey. Most of us realized that a parting of ways was inevitable. It wasn't just Jim's bizarre behaviour that was solely the issue; it was also his insistence on keeping to a nine-to-five city schedule that made the situation impossible. Dawn and Brian, professional photographers, favoured paddling late into the night when the light was at its buttery best and the wind was calm. So did Julia and I. There was also a matter of perspective. While our main reason for stopping on the river was usually to gaze on a scene or to investigate wildlife, Jim's was to go angling for fish that we didn't need.

The following night – Day 11 of the trip – Julia, Dawn, Brian and I lingered behind in the canoes for most of the day discussing how we were going to break the news that four of us were hoping to finish the trip on our own. The possibility had been discussed so it shouldn't have come as a surprise to the rest when we informed them of our decision to push on for a ways that night. But as we would discover later, it had. Maybe we hadn't made our point clear enough. But unbeknownst to us at the time, the decision to do go it alone would come back to haunt us in a most unpleasant manner.

It was the right decision, however. Notwithstanding Jim's behaviour, there was simply too many personalities and therefore not enough opportunity for quiet contemplation and full immersion in the rhythm of the river. The enthusiasm we had brought with us and the expectation of camaraderie and joyful exploration, was in danger of disappearing. It was better to go it alone than allow the growing tension, not to mention the country and western tunes, to develop into an ugly confrontation.

The tacit understanding from then on was that we would tag up from time to time to ensure that all was well. This was more than courtesy; it is one of the commandments of wilderness travel. We had expected that they would never be more than a couple of hours away from us.

There was, however, no sign of the others two days later when we woke up. Initially, I thought little of it. A fierce wind was blowing in from the north, directly in our line of travel. It would have been difficult, if not futile trying to make headway that day. I assumed that, like us, they were waiting for the weather to blow through. But when the wind subsided by late afternoon and the others had still not paddled by, we suspected that they must have moved on before we had woken up. That they had not stopped or shouted to indicate their intention of forging ahead towards the coast was more than a little troubling. The days had been ticking by, and now with only 48 hours left in our two-week trip, there was no time remaining for mind games. We had to get to the coast quickly if we were going to meet the plane that was coming in to pick us up from Cambridge Bay.

We had to move, but it was with an uncertainty that was taking on shades of panic by the time we arrived at the last of several lakes that the Nanook runs through before spilling into the ocean. The last and biggest one was still frozen. Nearly 10-kilometres long and seven-kilometres wide, the only way to avoid a two or three day portage around it — time we didn't have — was to walk across. Yet we all agreed that would be too dangerous. We now had serious doubts the others had moved ahead of us. Had they paddled by, they would have waited here or left a sign signaling what they had done.

We paddled back upstream and made camp at the first piece of flat ground we found. We waited there for hours and hours but no one came. By the time we made the decision to strike out on our own and risk crossing the frozen lake, Dawn suddenly announced that she had been stricken by a plague that was forcing her to involuntarily purge her intestines. She couldn't go 10 minutes without having to crouch.

It was a bad scene. The terrain around us was wet and spongy. Great for loons and geese, but too soft for a plane to land should a pilot come searching. It was also fairly clear that if the others were not ahead of us, one or more of them was probably injured or too ill to travel. Without means of communication, we had no way of knowing what was going on.

By 7 p.m., that night, Dawn bravely announced that she felt strong enough to carry on. While we had our doubts, there was really no choice. We had to get to the plane. So life jackets secured, we paddled back toward that sheet of ice with a plan to haul our boats and gear across it.

Taking the loaded boats out of the water and onto the ice turned out to be simpler than it looked. After an initial unsuccessful try, we discovered that if we paddled full steam, the canoes would lift themselves up over the lip of the ice rather than crash through. Once on the ice, we harnessed ourselves to the boats with ropes and paddles and, like mules, dragged them fully loaded, always aware that at any moment we might plunge through.

It was tough going, but exhilarating. The weather, dead calm and less than 10 degrees, meant that there was little threat of the ice shifting and breaking as it does in the wind and heat. When sections of open water stopped us, we either used the canoes as bridges or hopped back into them and paddled to the other side. It took about five hours to make the crossing and that included a 90-minute stop to catch a trout and cook it.

When open water greeted us on the other side of the lake, Brian suggested that we take a few minutes to lie back in the boats. There would probably not be another time on this trip to enjoy the river. No one argued. There can't be more than three or four days in an entire summer this far north when it is as calm, and warm, and bug-free past midnight as it was this early morning. I don't know that I've ever seen light so holy.

We must have floated for a good half-hour, swirling ever so slightly with the current as it picked up speed heading toward the entrance of the river. Mesmerized by the idyllic ease of it all, I stared up at the kaleidoscope of oranges, yellows and pinks radiating from the cool glow of the sun lying low on the horizon. The gentle lapping of the water against the boat and the call of unidentified birds from the willow thickets along the shore were hypnotic.

This glorious trance, however, was broken by Dawn who asked in all innocence, "Do you hear a waterfall?" Snapping out of my lethargy, I looked at the map and assured her that it was not possible, though I too wondered where the rushing sound of water was coming from. When she repeated her concern, I looked again and jabbed my finger at the map to reinforce my claim. "There are no rapids or falls marked here, Dawn." But even as I spoke, I could see that we were passing a stationary herd of muskoxen on shore as quickly as if we were aboard a train. Swept on by the unexpected current, we suddenly found ourselves slicing through a shallow canyon. Again, I confidently predicted that this was just a riffle, only to find myself staring into the maw of a most unfriendly, kilometre-long rapid.

Julia and I picked through the boulder-strewn rapids before landing our boat in an eddy downstream. In the meantime, Dawn and Brian decided it would be safer to pull into shore. Standing there, waiting for them to line their boats along the river bank, I looked down into the clear waters of the Nanook and spotted a can of chewing tobacco bobbing in the shallows. It was the brand that big Dave favoured.

It was 3 a.m by the time we crawled back into our boats. We figured that at best we had nine hours to make it to the coast. Still plenty of time, we assured ourselves, even if by chance there was a rapid or two along the way. My heart sank, however, when I scouted the landscape ahead. A distinct downward slope in the course of the river suggested that there was more rough water to come. It didn't take long to find out. A couple of minutes later, we were bouncing up and down, heading into a canyon that was deeper and darker than the last one. My stomach churned at the sight of the white-capped waves rolling over a maze of boulders at its entrance. There was no choice but to head to shore and signal Brian and Dawn to follow.

To scout what lay downstream we scrambled up the canyon cliffs. Once on top, we could see the shores of Hadley Bay no more than four or five kilometres away. We could also see two tiny dots on the spit of land where the pilot had planned on landing. With binoculars in hand, I could see that they were tents. It was no surprise after seeing the can of chewing tobacco in the river, but still disappointing finally to confirm our darkest suspicions. They had breezed by early that stormy morning without telling us that they were passing. They hadn't offered the courtesy and concern that we showed by waiting for them back at the lake. It seemed like such an obvious thing to do given the dangerous nature of the situation.

More to the point, and more depressing yet, was the sight of more rapids ahead, the last of which would be more appropriately classified as a waterfall. The river was not going to yield to the ocean without a fight. I could see that after taking a slight turn, it narrowed, picked up speed and dropped five or six metres over a huge altar of studded, naked rock.

To portage, I figured, meant five kilometres of honest effort, a good part of it up hill, the rest of it over rough ground. To transport our canoes and gear would require three round trips. That meant we would have to trek a total of 30 kilometres in six hours.

Knowing that would be impossible, I suggested that we cut the long portage short by walking a couple of kilometres past the worst part of the whitewater where we could lower our boats down the side of the cliff, and then line whatever dangerous river followed. But the others had had enough by this point. "That might be OK if we were all wide awake and fresh and not in a rush," said Julia. "But we're all exhausted and we could easily make mistakes and get injured. We've been up for nearly 24 hours. This is not the time to take chances."

Perhaps because I had enough energy to propose the plan, I was the one conscripted to take the shotgun and hike to the coast to inform the others of our whereabouts. It would be important to let the pilot know where he could find us now that it was clear we wouldn't make it to the coast on time. Still, there was a possibility that he might be delayed coming into get us, so as I made my way to the coast Julia, Dawn and Brian began portaging our canoes and equipment just in case there was time to carry on.

I don't remember anything about the first kilometre or two of my hike. My mind was lost in a fog of fatigue. But then the sight of something white moving slowly along the top of a hill ahead of me startled me. Frozen with fear, it was all I could do to unstrap the shotgun from my shoulder and release the safety. Unsure of whether to retreat or stay still, I scanned the hillside, certain that a polar bear would pop out at any moment. For the next 10 minutes I remained paralyzed, wondering if what I saw was indeed a bear, an oversized Arctic hare or just a hallucination. Knowing that I could not stand there indefinitely, I gingerly moved on, only to realize in short order that with all of the hills and twists and turns in the river, it would be a full day before I could reach the others. Knowing too that if it was a bear I had seen, my companions would be defenceless. And so I headed back.

What I found when I returned was not a pretty sight. My companions had barely transported the first load one-tenth of the distance I had covered in an hour. Julia was so tired and disoriented that she was stumbling over every rock and tuft of grass. Dawn and Brian weren't doing much better.

Obviously, we needed a new plan. We simplified our approach: if we couldn't get to the plane, we could at least make it easier for the plane to get to us. So we consolidated our gear and laid out the brightly coloured spray covers of canoes on the flattest strip of land we could find, presuming that the pilot would easily spot them when he came searching. Then we laid down our weary, aching heads, and covered ourselves with the tent fly. I did not whisper a word about the polar bear that had been occupying my thoughts at the time. Nor did I contemplate the field day it would have if it found us lying there like that.

Two hours later, I woke up, stirred the others, and fired the stove up to make tea. It wasn't enough to get any one of them on their feet, but the drone of a plane was. Our plan, it seemed, was working. The plane circled a couple of times then headed off to the coast and landing where the others were camped, presumably to pick them up first.

In the meantime, we pulled our gear together in a pile and waited. Within the hour, the plane returned. This time, it circled just once, long enough for the pilot to drop a black leather glove out the window of the cockpit. Our hearts sunk when the plane disappeared into the distant sky a couple of minutes later.

Inside the glove we found a note and a hand-drawn map: the pilot would return the next day, weather permitting, and meet us on the spot of the coast marked on the map. The map also warned us of the rapids and waterfalls that we had already seen.

"Return tomorrow, weather permitting." What would happen if the weather did not permit? We were virtually out of food and not looking forward to hunkering down on the polar bear-infested coastline if a heavy fog rolled in. What was this second flight going to cost us? Another four hours of Twin Otter time would add $5,000 to our already very pricey bill.

In the end, we surrendered ourselves to the situation, realizing that there was nothing we could do but try and make this last day or two as pleasant as possible. Dawn and Brian pulled out a vegetarian chili lunch they had been saving, and we heated it up by a small waterfall that I had spotted on my hike.

At the waterfall, basking in the radiance of the midday heat, protected from the wind, we rediscovered our appetite for this wilderness adventure. The skies were clear, the wind was calm and there wasn't a hint of a storm or fog rolling in. After lunch, we showered in the surprisingly warm spray of the waterfall and returned to sleep, this time without worrying about planes or even polar bears. Somehow, we would get back home. As we snoozed in that soothing sun, it crossed my mind that if this was not the Garden of Eden, then it was surely as close to paradise as I would get on Earth.

When we woke up to the gentle nudge of a stiff breeze blowing towards the ocean, we descended once again into the shadows and coolness of the canyon. Carefully lining around the rapids, we let the current carry us out to sea, above the milling schools of Arctic char that we could see in the clear salt water, and toward the narrow spit where the plane was to land. Nanook, the white bear we had thought might greet us on the coast, was no where to be seen, but it did leave a few fresh prints in the sand where we had camped on.

———

Some months later, Peter came to visit us in Edmonton. Time had not entirely resolved the issue of who was to blame for what had happened on those last days on the Nanook. But by this point, it didn't matter. We had been friends too long to let this episode threaten the relationship. As Peter was leaving, amid talks of rivers we had yet to run, he produced a toque he had his mother make from the muskox qiviat that he had collected on that trip. He asked that we pass it to Brian so that his balding head would be warm in winter.

It was then that I no longer looked at this trip as one of troubled or tested friendships, but one that gave us what city life can never provide: a link with the natural world that is normally beyond human reach and an understanding of human nature that does not come easily, but is always forgiving. The Nanook had satisfied that irresistible urge that I had had as a child when I first spotted its name on a map of Canada. I was no longer obsessed with that anonymous blue line snaking across Victoria Island. I had found mystery and adventure and I was content. The Nanook also gave us a son who we named after Jacob's Ladder, the fragile Arctic flower that retains its bloom even after a summer blizzard. Our Jacob was as small as babies come into the world but more spirited than doctors normally see. Spirited, Julia and I like to think, like the Nanook.

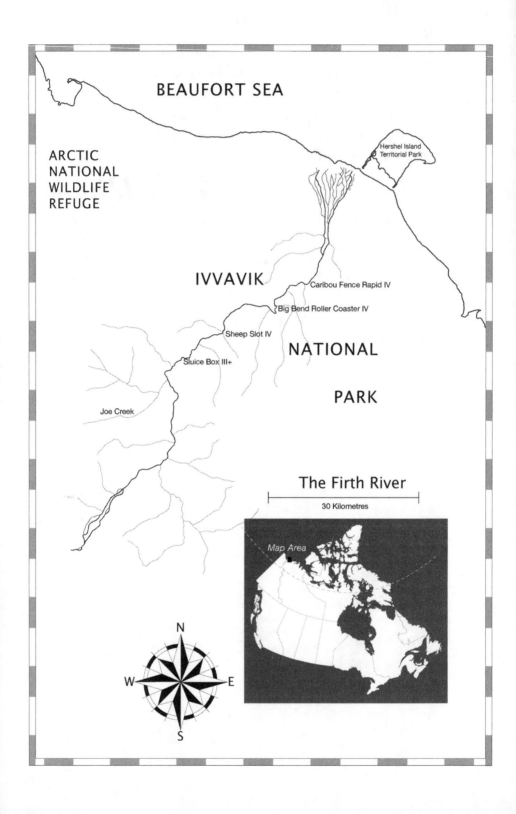

BEAUFORT SEA

ARCTIC
NATIONAL
WILDLIFE
REFUGE

Hershel Island
Territorial Park

IVVAVIK

Caribou Fence Rapid IV

Big Bend Roller Coaster IV

Sheep Slot IV

NATIONAL

Sluice Box III+

PARK

Joe Creek

The Firth River

30 Kilometres

Map Area

N
W   E
S

Firth River

Land of the Barren Ground Grizzly

I was standing on the banks of the Firth River along the Alaska/Yukon border watching intently as a grizzly bear was feeding on thick clumps of late-summer blueberries. The bear — 270 to 320 kilograms — was big by Arctic standards. It gave no indication that it was troubled by my presence on the other side of the river, or by the park wardens who were eating their lunch in the raft a short distance away. But something set it off. It whirled around, stood up, and then charged towards us. I was mid-air, jumping into the boat by the time the wardens were pushing off and propelling the raft downstream. But no matter how hard they rowed in the shallow water, it was clear there was no way we could have outrun this animal if it had really wanted to get us. It stopped short of the riverbank, however, leaving us breathless, but relieved as we continued our trip downstream.

The Firth River flows out of the Arctic National Wildlife Refuge in Alaska near the Yukon border. A little more than a 150-kilometres long, it is no more than trickle of water high in the alpine country where the verdant rolling hills are dotted with small pockets of spindly spruce trees. But it picks up speed and volume quickly as it carves a path through the V-shaped valleys of the

British Mountains, which rise to heights of 1,680 metres in Ivvavik National Park.

There are few crags and turrets dominating this range; the scarring advance of the last ice age of glaciers never had a chance to chew up this country. So there's a sweet virginal aspect to this wilderness that would enchant even the most discriminating backpacker. The weather, however, is one of the things that dissuades many hikers from coming here. A summer morning on the Firth might begin with the soothing warmth of sunshine and end under a blanket of snow and a shroud of icy fog.

The Firth would be the perfect whitewater river to canoe if it weren't for a 45-kilometre stretch of water along the heart of the river on the Yukon side of the border. Here the river races through a series of boiling rapids — Sheep Slot, Sheep Horn, Ram Rapids, Big Bend Roller, Surprise Rapids and Caribou Fence — each one of which might be runnable by an expert. There is, however, few ways of getting out of the 55-metre-high rock-walled canyon that you have to pass through to get to the Arctic coast. So, a lost or capsized boat would likely result in disaster.

A potentially bigger threat in paddling the Firth, however, is the water levels that can rise and drop dramatically depending on the amount of rain or snow that is falling upstream. Ivvavik warden Steve Travis and his colleagues learned this the hard way one summer when they tied their raft to the canyon rim at Sheep Creek one night and found it tangling nine metres down at the end of the rope the next morning.

The Firth River valley is best known for its caribou. There are 129,000 in the Porcupine herd. Most of them migrate onto the coastal plains of the Yukon and Arctic National Wildlife Refuge in spring to calve and feed before retreating to the treeline in autumn. But this is also the part of the Arctic where grizzly bears and polar bears meet, and where some grizzlies act more like polar bears than like their southern cousins.

This was the fourth time I had been charged by a grizzly while travelling in the Arctic. I had had close calls with bears while hiking in the Burwash Uplands in the Yukon and while paddling down the Anderson and Hornaday rivers along the western Arctic coast. I have no doubt that the Hornaday bear would have ended up in our boat had it not been for my partner, Ian MacLaren, who set off a blow horn just as the bear was bounding through the water towards us. The animal was running so hard when the horn went off, it literally skidded to a standing stop before losing its balance, falling over backwards and retreating.

Nearly all grizzly bear attacks fall under two categories: a female protecting her cubs, or a young bear trying to stake out new territory after it has been separated from or lost its mother. But every once in a very rare while, you get an otherwise mature, healthy animal that, for whatever reason, attacks without provocation or warning. It is this wide degree of variation in behaviour that makes grizzlies so unpredictable.

Over the years I have often wondered whether grizzlies in the Arctic tend to be more aggressive than they are down south. Although some biologists would disagree, I am not alone in thinking that way. In the south, most of the more aggressive bears have been selected out of the population by wildlife management practices that have turned aggressive bears into dead ones. Many of those that remain may be the shyer, gentler bears that avoid humans at all costs, even when it comes to feeding. Most Arctic grizzlies have also evolved in a largely treeless world in which there is no avenue of escape. So aggression — a bluff charge, for example — may well be the way some bears react when they feel threatened.

Arctic grizzlies are by almost every measure the same animal that roams the Rockies in southern Canada, the interior and coastal regions of British Columbia as well as Montana, Wyoming, North Idaho and the North Cascades of Washington state — the only remaining places they are found in the Lower 48. But there is another environmental constraint that might make Arctic grizzlies more intolerant of humans. Because of the cold climate, they must den for one or two months longer. With less time to put on the fat reserves they need to reproduce or to get them through a winter, it may well be that they are more stressed and less accepting of anything invading their territory. No one really knows for sure if this is the case. But on the southern coast of Hudson Bay where polar bears gather in late fall waiting for the sea ice to form, it is the thin bears that tend to get into trouble with humans, not the fat ones.

Liz Gordon, a Parks Canada patrol person on the river trip with us, was so rattled by the bluff charge that day she couldn't sleep the next night at our camp at the confluence of Joe Creek and the Firth. No one believed her in the morning when she insisted that she had heard something splashing across the stream shortly before dawn. But the doubting stopped when we spotted the fresh tracks of a lone grizzly walking along Joe Creek, and then those of two wolves following it. Judging by the pattern of the bear prints, the grizzly had no interest in crossing over to our camp. The wolves, however, were curious enough to walk right up and around Liz's tent that night, leaving their scent mark on the ground a foot away from her door. That was the last night Liz slept alone.

I had come along with Liz, and wardens Steve Travis and Merv Joe for the final patrol of the river that summer. After a blustery start at Margaret Lake near the Alaska border, we were blessed with unusually warm late-summer weather on the first five days of the trip. Apart from the early morning frost that iced up our tents in the morning, there wasn't even a hint of snow in the air.

The practice of patrolling the backcountry of national parks has been part of the warden's job since the parks branch was first established in 1911. Keeping track of what's going on in an extremely remote park like Ivvavik, however, presents some unique challenges. Since, there is no permanent warden station in Ivvavik, park officials must either fly in from the community of Inuvik more than 200 kilometres away. Then they must raft the river to the coast and get flown out from there.

The standard for campers in Ivvavik is higher than in any other park in the country. Not only are paddlers prohibited from lighting a campfire at night (unless there is an emergency), large groups must also carry out all of their human waste. Any sign that ground squirrels have become habituated to a particular campsite warrants closure of the area. No one is allowed to carry a gun.

We were hiking up Joe Creek on the fifth day of the trip when the sight of another bear feeding on a big stand of blueberries stopped us dead in our tracks. The animal was just a tiny dot in the distance when Merv spotted it through his binoculars. But as it moved closer, we could see that it was as big as the animal that had bluff-charged us upstream.

A number of people have mistakenly suggested that the Arctic grizzlies are bigger than their cousins down south are. This may be true of the Kodiak, a subspecies of brown bear in Alaska, which lives in a very productive, salmon-rich environment. But out on the Arctic coast in northern Canada and Alaska, the farther away a grizzly bear is from trees, the smaller it is likely to be. The two bears we had seen on the first part of out trip were exceptions. On average, an Arctic grizzly is two-thirds the size of those found in the southern Canada and the northwestern part of the United States.

That doesn't mean Arctic grizzlies are less of a force to be reckoned with. In the spring of 2003, I was in the the tundra region west of the Firth River flying with Canadian scientist Andrew Derocher and his PhD student Mark Edwards searching for bears that they were hoping to radio-collar and track over the long term. The behaviour of two bears in particular was a sobering reminder of how powerful these animals can be. One had dragged a good-sized caribou across the snow for two kilometres, perhaps to find a spot to hide it. The other had killed a bull caribou before digging a hole in the snow and burying it. It then stripped the branches off several nearby spruce trees and meticulously covered the carcass before putting another layer of snow and dirt on top of it. Standing over the icy grave and seeing the legs and nose of the caribou sticking out, I couldn't help thinking what it would have been like had it been me who had been mauled to death and then dumped into that shallow grave as a future meal.

As small as the bears are in the far north of Canada and Alaska, the Firth River country of Ivvavik and the Arctic National

Wildlife Refuge may well be the best grizzly bear habitat north of the Arctic Circle. Not only is there an abundance of wild berries and vegetation for the bears to feed on, there are also caribou in large numbers. Bears primarily prey on newborn calves and sick animals. They just aren't fast enough to run down a healthy adult caribou. But that doesn't mean they don't try. Grant MacHutchon, a biologist who conducted one of the first studies of bears in this area, recalls vividly the day he was on the upper part of the Firth watching a grizzly walking into the middle of a herd of some 30,000 animals. The herd gave the bear a wide enough berth to allow it to walk through. The bear did not charge. It was, recalls MacHutchon, akin to Moses parting the Red Sea.

Downstream of Joe Creek, the soft verdant hillsides along the Firth gave rise to steep slopes of grey talus and bedrock outcrops that rose 914-metres above the shoreline. Dall's sheep feeding on the shoreline seemed unconcerned as we raced by. Heading toward the warden's cabin at Sheep Creek, I found myself gripping the side of the raft as we picked up speed and plunged through a series of rapids, dodging a group of some 20 caribou that were swimming against the current trying to get to the other side.

Caribou are strong swimmers, but they are not always the best judges when it comes to finding a place to cross a river. In the fall of 1984, some 10,000 animals drowned in the Caniapiscau River in northern Quebec in waters that had been swollen by heavy rainfall and the floodgates of a dam that had been opened upstream. Nothing nearly as tragic has ever happened on the Firth so far as anyone can recall. The river really isn't big enough to produce that kind of carnage. But in the summer of 2002, some two dozen caribou were swept away to their deaths while trying to cross the Firth just above the canyon at Sheep Creek.

Steve Travis was one of the wardens patrolling the river at the time. Neither he nor his colleagues thought much of the first carcasses that they had spotted along the way. But then when they nearly bumped into three grizzlies feeding on a drowned caribou just downstream, and then 16 more on their way to the coast, they realized that something had to be done to ensure the safety of other people on the river. "It was crazy," he said. "It seemed like there were bears around every corner. It quickly became clear that this was a public safety issue. We couldn't have every raft group come through here, and be forced to clear off the bears with bangers. You have to figure that at some point one or more of the bears were going to get mad and retaliate."

In the end, one of the rafting parties on the river sat at Sheep Creek for three days waiting for the bears to clear out of the canyon. Trippers that didn't have the luxury of spending extra time on the river, were flown out by Parks Canada to meet their plane on the Arctic coast.

Created in 1986, Ivvavik is a relatively new national park, and one that few people get a chance to visit. No more than 150 people paddle the Firth in a given year either because it is too difficult to run, too expensive to get to, or too wild and stormy for most people's comfort. Inevitably, people get in trouble on the river. One year, an American rafter had to be pulled off Nunaluk Spit on the Arctic coast when a storm surge sent big waves washing over the spot where a plane was supposed to pick him up. Another year, a helicopter had to be brought in to sling some canoes over the canyon after a group of paddlers mistakenly thought they could run this part of the river.

So far none of those lucky enough to get to this part of the world have been mauled by a grizzly. Biologists Dave Jones and Debbie Wellwood, however, had a close call several years ago when they were attempting to follow and observe grizzlies that had been radio-collared by Grant MacHutchon. The aim was to get a 24-hour insight into how these bears were behaving. It was hard, frustrating work. Most of the time, the bears would simply bolt off, never to be seen again after the pair were dropped off by helicopter. The bears weren't necessarily going out of their way to avoid them. They were more likely doing what bears normally do, which is to travel long distances to hunt for food. But then one day, they had a bear come upstream to a spot where it would have been able to see or smell them.

Jones recalls going down the steep riverbank to get a better look at what the animal was up to. He had expected the bear to run off once he approached. But when Jones sat down, so did the bear. When the two made eye contact, Jones realized that it was time to pick up and move camp. This bear was showing no fear.

That night, however, the bear caught up with them at around 3 a.m. when they were sleeping in their tent high up on slope away from the Firth River. At one point, it was no more than a metre from their tent door, sniffing around, and looking in at them. Thunderous explosions from a couple of bear bangers failed to frighten it off. It was only when Jones – a big man – picked up a rock and showed the bear the full frame of his size – that it grudgingly left the area.

We were high up in the British Mountains, hiking back to the Sheep Creek warden station when Steve Travis and I spotted our third bear in a valley that we had to pass through. Arctic grizzlies will feed on alpine hedysarum in spring, horsetail and bearflower in summer and berries in fall. They will also expend a considerable amount of energy digging up ground squirrels, as this animal was doing. Sitting there with binoculars, watching it from a safe distance, we were amazed by the amount of hard dirt and gravel that was flying through the air. For the morsel of food that the bear might or might not have gotten, it was hard to figure why it was going to so much trouble for the effort.

While squirrels and other smaller mammals are an important part of the grizzly's diet, caribou may well be the one thing that compensates for the constraints that the animal faces at the northern edge of its range. Biologists have found that the more a bear population feeds on caribou, the higher the densities are likely to be, and the more successful the bear will be in reproducing. That's why MacHutchon wasn't all that surprised to find that some of the grizzlies he tracked on the Firth River spent a great deal of time hunting for caribou, even bypassing berry and vegetation patches along the way. Those bears, which fed primarily on caribou, he discovered, had more time to travel and rest than those animals that relied primarily on plants for food.

MacHutchon had a hunch that bears along the Firth might use the long daylight hours to compensate for the extra time denning. But he found no evidence of that. Nor did he find animals feeding for longer periods of time in the fall when the berries were ripe and more digestible. This suggests that as long as Firth River bears have caribou, they don't have trouble building up the energy reserves they need to get them through the winter.

The future of the Porcupine caribou herd in Canada and Alaska, however, is in doubt. In 1989, there were 178,000 animals in the population. In 2005, when the U.S. Senate passed a bill that would allow for oil and gas drilling in and around the environmentally sensitive calving range of the herd, there were no more than 123,000. No one knows why the population has been in this free fall, but it may have something to do with climate change. One explanation connects the declines to an acceleration of thawing episodes in northern Yukon and Alaska. Warmer spring days that are typically followed by cold snaps make it harder for the caribou to crater through the hard snow. Desperate for food, the animals are driven into the wind-swept hills where they are more vulnerable to wolves, bears and the debilitating effects of malnutrition.

It's not surprising then that in the absence of caribou in springtime, when there is nothing but snow greeting the animals as they emerge from their winter dens, some grizzlies occasionally venture out onto the sea ice. The scent of a seal, dead or alive, is all that would be required to get them to take that first step away from land. Over the years, a few coastal bears have been known to cross over to Banks and Victoria Island in the High Arctic and out onto the sea ice in Hudson Bay. No one read too much into this phenomenon until the spring of 1991 when polar bear biologist Mitch Taylor, flying across Melville Sound 640 kilometres north of the mainland, spotted something dark moving in the distance. Thinking the light was playing tricks on him, he signaled the pilot to fly the helicopter in for a closer look. Instead of running away, as most polar bears do when they hear the sound of an engine, this animal abruptly turned and ran toward the machine in an aggressive manner. That's when Taylor, scarcely believing what he was seeing, realized that it was a grizzly bear.

That was not the only surprise Taylor got that day. After tranquilizing the bear, and determining that it was in good health, he instructed the pilot to follow the grizzly tracks to see what it had been up to. Not long after, they found the remains of two seals, and what was left of the carcass of a young polar bear. It was pretty clear to Taylor that this bear had been hunting seals when it got into a scrap with a polar bear doing the same thing.

What Arctic grizzlies are doing out there in the kingdom of their great white cousins is not clearly understood. No one, for example, has ever seen a grizzly kill a seal. (The seals that Taylor saw may have been killed by the polar bear). But in this vast world of snow and ice in which few people venture, scientists like Ian Stirling, who has studied polar bears and other marine mammals longer than anyone else, suspects that some of them may have always been doing this, and that what we're witnessing today is similar behaviour to the first evolutionary process that originally resulted in grizzlies filling a rich but vacant niche as supreme predator of the sea ice.

Humans, in comparison to bears, are late comers to this part of the world. Archeological evidence found at the Bluefish Caves in the northern Yukon suggests that the initial migration may have occurred 30,000 years ago. Buried in the dirt there are the bones of wooly mammoth, steppe bison, horses, caribou, sheep and lions, some of which show signs of human butchering.

The Arctic lion, the mammoth, horses and many other ice age animals were all gone by the time humans started camping at Engigstciak, a rise of land jutting from the lowlands along the coastal plains of the Firth. Here the remains of nine cultures that used this site during a 5,000 year period, tell a powerful tale of what it was like to live in this part of the world.

The premonition of our first stretch of bad weather on the Firth arrived early in the evening on the second last day of trip when an icy finger of fog reached out from the Beaufort Sea, grabbing at our heals as we hiked along the coastal plains towards Engigstciak. Once on top, we could see how these early people could be attracted to the panoramic view that allows for an unobstructed view in all directions. All around were the bones of animals like the now extinct steppe bison that had been killed in the area.

How these stone age people dealt with polar bears and grizzlies is unclear. Traditionally, however, the Inuit and the Inuvialuit view Aklak (grizzly bear) and Nanook (polar bear) as two very different creatures. That's reflected in both folklore and in real life. Tales of polar bears almost always portray the animals as powerful, keen-witted and worthy of great esteem. The grizzly, on the other hand, is viewed as a more sinister animal. The grizzly, for example, is unpredictable. One minute it ignores you, the next minute it turns around and chases you.

Scientists also recognize the differences between grizzly bears and polar bears to be significant enough to warrant separate species status of the same genus of carnivores. These differences are obvious from a physical point of view. Polar bears, for example, are white rather than brown and better camouflaged from their prey on the sea ice. They are also generally larger, and have heads and bodies that are much more elongated, and therefore better adapted to penetrate seal lairs. Their larger, sharper teeth allow them to tear up seals efficiently, and their shorter claws and larger feet make it easier for them to travel on the sea ice and swim across a great expanse of water.

In some cases, however, the evolutionary distinctions are incomplete. Most female polar bears, for example, have four nipples instead of the grizzly's six, which makes it more difficult for them to feed triplets. But every once in a while, scientists come across a female polar bear with five or six nipples — possibly a throwback to an earlier period of evolution.

Not all scientists are convinced that the polar bear has evolved far enough away from the grizzly to warrant separate species status.

By one definition, different species of the same genus, are unable to produce fertile offspring. That's not the case with the polar bear and the grizzly. Interbreeding between the two at several zoos have produced fertile hybrids that become bluish brown or yellowish white as they grow older. Recent DNA studies, in fact, suggest the polar bear and the grizzly are basically the same animal no matter which part of the world they are found. Canadian scientist David Paetkau points out that for two species like the grizzly bear and the polar bear to develop significant genetic differences, they would have to have been geographically isolated from each other for a long period of time for the genetic mutations to be come imbedded in the populations.

Like all animals, both polar bears and grizzly bears will continue to adapt and evolve. But just how successful they will be in the future is unclear because the habitat for both animals is shrinking. Those warmer temperatures that are apparently hitting caribou so hard in the Yukon and Alaska are also melting the Arctic sea ice. As those temperatures continue to rise as forecasted, more and more polar bears will have to make due with less time hunting seals in order to put on the fat reserves they need to reproduce. Ultimately, polar bears may find themselves grounded on the territory from which they evolved.

Stirling and Derocher doubt that the polar bear will ever be able to turn back the clock. The ecological niche they left behind so long ago is now occupied by grizzlies. And being at the very edge of their range, Arctic grizzlies are just barely hanging in there as it is. The decline of caribou in the North and/or the development of oil and gas reserves could ultimately tip the scales against them. Like the Arctic lions, the wooly mammoth and the small horses that once thrived along the Firth, they could disappear altogether,

———

We saw one more grizzly on our trip down the Firth River, and the tracks of either a grizzly bear or a polar bear on Nunaluk Spit where we camped and waited for our plane to pick us up. The imprint in the sand was too wind-swept to tell for sure. There was a huge sheet of ice in the distance, which had likely blown in after breaking off from the permanent pack farther north in the Beaufort Sea. I took my binoculars out to see if I could detect anything on it — the yellow telltale sign of a polar bear or perhaps the dark dot of a grizzly. The ice, however, was too far away. So it was left up to me to imagine the possibility of one or the other heading into land or floating out to sea. That it could happen was at least reassuring, as was the notion that in the Arctic, there are still a number of natural mysteries yet to be solved.

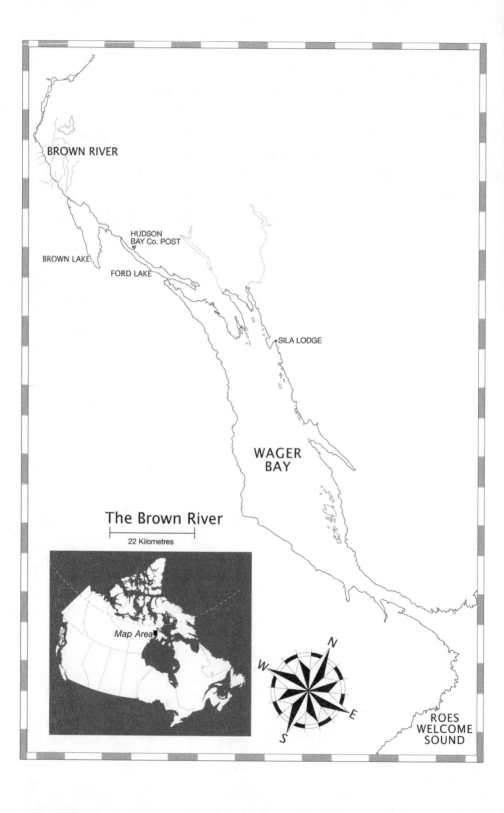

BROWN RIVER

HUDSON
BAY Co. POST

BROWN LAKE

FORD LAKE

SILA LODGE

WAGER
BAY

The Brown River

22 Kilometres

Map Area

ROES
WELCOME
SOUND

Author Ed Struzik.

Rabbitkettle Lake on the Nahanni River. Ndambadezha, "protector of the people," is believed to be living in one of the vents in the giant tufa mounds located near here.

The highest cliffs in Canada, higher than those found in Grand Canyon, are found along the Nahanni River.

For paddlers going down the Nahanni, it has become a tradition to carve your own paddle and drop it off at the old forestry cabin in Deadmen Valley.

Also known as Figure of Eight (Hell's Gate) Rapids. American Fenley Hunter described the Nahanni as a "heartbreaker." The Nahanni is unknown and will remain so until another age brings a change in the con-formation of these mountains," he wrote. "It is an impossible stream, and a stiff rapid is met on average every mile, and they seem countless."

Parks Canada biologist Doug Tate taking in the view from the top of Tlogotsho Plateau in Nahanni National Park.

The 117-metre plunge of water at Virginia Falls is twice the height of Niagara Falls, and is split in two by a towering spire.

Hell's Gate has claimed its share of victims over the years. Travelling upstream in the 1920s, Raymond Patterson described the rapids as the "queerest piece of water that I ever did see."

Paddling through "The Gate."

Sluicebox Rapids, just above Virginia Falls.

Mackenzie River in between Fort Good Hope and Tsiigehtchic.

Summer snowstorm in the Mackenzie Valley.

*The Natla River flows out of the Mackenzie Mountains
into the Keele and Mackenzie Rivers.*

*Saw-whet owl – The Southern Mackenzie Valley
is a haven for a large variety of birds.*

Bern Will Brown's plane docked at Colville Lake.

Boat dock at Colville Lake.

Midnight on the Mackenzie River
near Great Bear River.

The Church of Our Lady of Fort Good Hope was designated a National Historic Site in 1977.

The Chipewyan used to call the Snowdrift, "River Falling Down Mountain."

The Snowdrift River carves a path through the Canadian Shield on course from the Barren Lands to the boreal forest around Great Slave Lake.

A Barren Land caribou near the treeline on the upper reaches of the Snowdrift River.

Photographer, filmmaker, historian, storyteller, René Fumoleau is a retired Oblate missionary who now lives in Lutselk'e near the mouth of the Snowdrift River on Great Slave Lake. His book As Long as This Land Shall Last *is widely regarded as one of the most important historical documents relating to the history of the Dene and Métis in the North.*

The Snowdrift rises out of the Barren Lands, then quickly passes through a boreal forest filled with swamps, muskeg, sandy desert, and huge rock outcrops.

One of a number of cascades along the Snowdrift River.

Sun sets on a small lake near the upper reaches of the Snowdrift River.

In 1927, Norwegian Helge Ingstead and his partner poled and paddled up the Snowdrift to the Barren Lands and spent four years trapping. His time with the Chipewyan of that country is described in the book *Land of Feast and Famine*.

The Thomsen is a slow, gently moving river with no rapids. Gale force winds, which routinely blow across Banks Island, can make paddling difficult, if not impossible.

The fall and phenomenal rise of muskoxen on Banks Island is one of the great unsolved mysteries of the Arctic.

Muskox skull on Head Hill along the Muskox and Thomsen rivers. The remains of 581 muskox skulls, 20 food caches, and 17 tent rings – all left from a time long ago – can be found here.

Peregrine falcon nest on a cliffside at the north end of Banks Island.

The Thomsen is arguably the most northerly navigable river of appreciable length in North America.

The view from Head Hill overlooking the Thomsen and Muskox Rivers.

The lush vegetation found along the Thomsen River valley is unlike anything in the Arctic archipelago. More than 150 species of flowering plants have been identified.

Peary caribou populations in the Arctic have plummeted in recent decades from a high of 26,000 in 1961 to fewer than 3,000 today.

Remains of the Investigator, the British ship that got locked in ice at Mercy Bay while searching for the lost Franklin expedition.

Biologist Peter Clarkson sneaking up on a herd of muskox along the banks of the Thomsen River.

Arctic fox dens lined the entire length of the Nanook River.

Julia Parker paddles the last stretch of the Nanook River into the polar bear infested region around Hadley Bay.

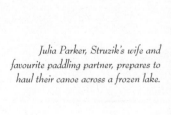

Julia Parker, Struzik's wife and favourite paddling partner, prepares to haul their canoe across a frozen lake.

Photographer Brian Milne carefully sneaks up on a muskox.

Brian Milne and Dawn Goss drag their canoe across an icy lake on the Nanook River.

Midnight hike across the treeless tundra along the Nanook River.

From a distance, we estimated the
sandstone formation to be more than
15- or 20-storeys high. It wasn't until we
got to within a few hundred metres that
we realized how easily our eyes had been
tricked by this alien landscape.

Victoria Island has one of the largest populations of muskox
in the Arctic outside of Banks Island. This one didn't
appreciate the intrusion.

Midnight paddle on the Nanook River.

A Barren Land grizzly cub waking up after it had been tranquilized.

University of Alberta scientist Andrew Derocher transports a tranquilized cub back to its mother so that it will not be overly stressed when it wakes up.

Caribou along the Alaska/Yukon border near the upper reaches of the Firth River. The Porcupine caribou herd, which Canada and the United States share, has been on a steady decline.

The Firth River valley is home to Canada's most northerly population of Dall's sheep.

Sluice Box rapids on the Firth River.

The headwaters of the Firth are located in the Arctic National Wildlife Refuge in Alaska.

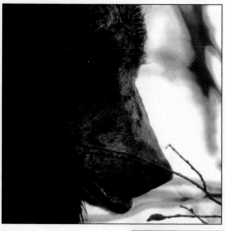

Among Arctic mammals, the Barren Land grizzly is one of the least understood and most enigmatic.

Biologist Mark Edwards prepares to remove a tooth from a Barren Land grizzly. The extraction of the small tooth is a means of measuring the animal's health. The removal of the small tooth does not debilitate the bear in any way.

The Firth River flows out of Alaska into the Yukon before spilling into the Beaufort Sea.

North Yukon; Parks Canada warden James McCormick sets up camp in Ivvavik National Park in the northern Yukon.

Parks Canada warden Steve Travis looks over towards the Arctic National Wildlife Refuge in Alaska from this rocky perch in Ivvavik National Park.

Water levels in the Firth River canyon can rise by more than five metres after a rainstorm.

There may be as many as 150 polar bears in Wager Bay.

Low tide on Wager Bay. Tidal flows in Wager Bay are powerful enough to cause the waterfall at Brown Lake to reverse.

Sunset over the mouth of the Sila River at Wager Bay.

Trapped in the ice along the coast of Hudson Bay heading towards Wager Bay.

Polar bears can often be seen swimming in Wager Bay, cooling off, hunting for seals or travelling from one side to the other.

Boating along the Hudson Bay coast towards Wager Bay.

Nineteenth-century whalers called belugas sea canaries. At Cunningham Inlet, the sound of belugas whistling, screaming, and blowing "raspberries" make them sound very much like a playground of romping children.

Biologist Tom Smith sitting on a beluga whale as he and Tony Martin of the British Anatarctic Survey prepare to attach a satellite transmitter to its back.

Satellite data has shown that beluga whales travel farther and dive much deeper than scientists previously thought.

Lush tundra meadow of cottongrass near the banks of the Taggart River.

Paleontologist Dick Harington and his associate John Tener have excavated the remains of three-toed horses, ancestral bears, miniature beavers and other animals from this site in the High Arctic.

The Beaver Pond site was first discovered in 1961 when geologist John Fyles flew up to Ellesmere Island to do some research for the Geological Survey of Canada.

The Taggart River flows out of the icefields on Ellesmere Island into Strathcona Fiord.

Paleontologist Dick Harington sorting through peat and dirt that he and John Tener have excavated from the 4.5-million-year-old beaver pond site on Ellesmere Island.

Not much was made of the beaver pond site until 1988 when John Fyles returned as a semi-retired chief geologist of the Geological Survey of Canada. With him was paleobotanist Jane Francis who discovered the partial skeleton of a beaver. The animal turned out not to be Castoroides, the giant beaver, but Dipoides, a beaver two-thirds the size of its modern-day relative.

Strathcona Fiord on Ellesmere Island has been a gold mine for ancient fossil finds in the High Arctic.

Brian Milne portaging around one of 83 rapids and waterfalls that occur along the Back River.

The Back River is one of the longest and most remote rivers in the Canadian North.

Paddling on Clinton-Colden Lake heading upstream towards the headwaters of the Back River. A. W. F. Banfield, one of Canada's great pioneering wildlife biologists, paddled from Clinton-Colden to the Back River in 1948.

Midnight on the shores of Aylmer Lake. In 1907, artist/naturalist Ernest Thompson Seton canoed from Great Slave Lake to Aylmer Lake in the hopes of finding muskoxen.

Pike's Portage is a string of 10 lakes that travellers use to get them from Great Slave Lake to Artillery Lake near the treeline.

A recent study of the Bathurst Caribou herd shows the size of the herd to be 186,000.
That suggests a decline of five per cent for the past decade.

Brian Milne surveys one of the many rapids along the Back River.

All that remains of George Back's winter quarters at Fort Reliance at the mouth of the Lockhart River are the remnants of stone chimneys.

"There were some 15 or 20 canoes concealed in the bushes" when George Back arrived at the Hoarfrost River in 1833. He speculated that they belonged to his old friend Akaitcho and his party of Yellowknife Indians.

"The boat was lightened of her cargo, and I stood high on a rock, with an anxious heart, to see her run it. . . . Away they went, with the speed of an arrow, and in a moment the foam and rocks hid them from view." George Back, as he watched his steersman descend Malley Rapids.

In 1833, George Back and a small group of men hauled their canoe and gear up the Hoarfrost River in the hopes of finding the river that now bears his name.

Brown River

Part One — Shipwrecks, Ghosts and the Inuit Garden of Eden

We headed out of Rankin Inlet hoping the passing three-day gale that had grounded us on the shores of northwestern Hudson Bay might be the end of the horrid July weather. But the early morning calm was swept away by a gust of wind that suddenly brought in two-metre-high swells and a thick soupy fog. Abandoning the security of the small cove that we had taken refuge in, Jack Anawak decided to head out toward the open sea for a short, but risky ride toward the Barrier Islands.

The west coast of Hudson Bay is a wondrous place when the weather is fair. But most of the time, the hand of God is against it. Ice and rough water are constantly battering the shoreline and terrorizing ships' captains. This is where Henry Hudson's mutinous crew tossed him, his son and several other "poor, sick lame men" into a small boat with only a musket, a kettle and tools before sailing back to England in 1611. It is where 11 years later, Jens Munk buried 13 of his 16 men on a lonely hilltop, and this is also where all 40 of James Knight's men died a long, slow death after their two ships were damaged while running aground in a shallow harbour near Marble Island.

There was seven of us in the open, eight-metre long aluminum boat: Jack, the 58-year-old Interim Commissioner of the new

territory of Nunavut, his wife Caroline, and four of their 17 natural and adopted children; Stacy, 20, Robin, 15 as well as 10-year-
old Tommy and nine-year-old Joel. It was a tense moment watching
the mainland fade from view. There was nothing ahead but a ghostly
grey sky that was the same colour as the rolling sea. The occasional
rogue wave washed over the starboard bow, leaving us ankle deep in
icy water. At times, it seemed like we were going to sink and
disappear. With a mischievous smile, Jack turned from the steering
wheel and scolded me for looking so worried, "Trust me," he shouted over the drone of the moaning wind. "Do you really think I would
do this if I wasn't sure we'd make it?"

It was a question I would ask myself many times in the days
that followed as wind, ice, fog and our own mistakes turned what
should have been a leisurely trip up the coast to Wager Bay into an
eight day, 650-kilometre misadventure that landed us on the wrong
side of Roes Welcome Sound, an ice-infested region renowned for
chewing up ships. Not only did we fail to get even remotely close to
the Brown River that I was hoping to scout out for a future canoe
trip, we also didn't get to see the inland polar bears, narwhal, and
reversing waterfalls that make Wager Bay such a legendary place
among the Inuit. Instead, we very nearly ended up like Henry
Hudson who was never seen again.

Wager Bay is a huge inland body of saltwater — 160 kilometres
long and 50 kilometres wide — that stretches west from the shores
of Hudson Bay to the mouth of the Brown River. The entrance to
the bay is deceptively narrow and can easily be mistaken for a big
river or an ocean strait — as British explorer Christopher
Middleton did in 1742, while searching for the Northwest Passage
to the Orient. The tidal currents in the narrows of the bay are so
powerful, they cause waterfalls to reverse and patches of sea to
remain open year-round. These open water polynyas attract the
scores of beluga, narwhal, walrus and seals that, in turn, sustain an
estimated 130 polar bears in this part of the Arctic.

"You're going to Wager Bay?" an old, gap-toothed Inuk from Rankin Inlet had asked me shortly before I set off on this trip with Jack. "You are a lucky man," he said wagging his finger at me. "For the Inuit, it is our Garden of Eden. It is the last place left in the world that has not yet been spoiled by man."

Peter Irniq, a cultural teacher and one of the first Inuit members of the legislative assembly to sit in the Northwest Territories legislature, convinced me years ago that for those who grew up in the region, Wager Bay was, indeed, a kind of "Heaven on Earth." So it didn't take much persuading when Jack called me out of the blue one spring and asked if I would be interested in spending a week to 10 days exploring the area. Jack had just been given the job of Interim Commissioner. And before he settled down to the job in Ottawa, he wanted to visit the old Hudson's Bay Company post at Wager Bay that, in 1932, his great-grandfather, Iqungajuq, had taken over and made profitable when it was abandoned as a losing cause. Having descended the Nanook River a few years earlier, I was itching to find another navigable Arctic stream that had not yet been run by anyone other than a Thule or Inuit kayaker. While the Brown had been high on my list of possibilities, it was simply too remote and expensive a proposition until Jack's offer came along.

Jack and I had first met 22 years earlier in the tiny Inuit hamlet of Salliq (Coral Harbour) on Southampton Island. He was just 36-years-old, and already head of the Inuit land claims organization. He was on the remote island in the northwest corner of Hudson Bay attending a strategy meeting. I was there with photographer Mike Beedell, doing a story on polar bears for *Equinox* magazine. When Jack learned that we were heading off to observe a traditional hunt with two men he knew from Salliq, he asked if he could tag along on the floe-edge journey. Since that trip, which saw a lot of ugly weather and many conversations about life and politics, we had kept in touch.

The Barriers are a string of low-lying islands that stretch out like a necklace from Rankin Inlet into Hudson Bay. Like barrier islands found in other coastal areas of the world, these are shaped by the wind, tides, waves, currents, as well as the isostatic rebound that has been occurring along the entire west coast of Hudson Bay since the last ice age depressed the landscape with heavy sheets of ice. Not only do the islands buffer the mainland from the erosive forces of the weather and the sea, they also provide boaters like us shelter from dangerous gales.

Jack's plan that stormy July day was to pass through these islands on the first part of our journey north from Rankin Inlet. Along the way we would stop at the tiny Inuit community of Chesterfield Inlet to pick up his sister, Elizabeth, her husband, Cyril Kusugak and Harry and Roland Aggark.

Once we got to water buffeted by the Barriers, the going got much smoother. It was, however, still too slow for Jack's speed, which I quickly realized, is always in overdrive. It soon became apparent to him that something on the boat would have to go if we were to make better time in the stormy waters that awaited us beyond the protective shell of the islands. First, Jack beached the shuttle boat we were pulling. Then he ditched the spare engine that had been riding heavy on the front deck. Jack didn't seem to mind that some of what was being tossed might leave us vulnerable later on. "We'll pick these up on our way back," he reassured me." If we break down, or lose an anchor, so be it. Someone will find us sooner than later."

The less burdened boat, however, was still no match for the storm that rose to another level once got beyond the Barriers into the open sea. Exposed as we now were to the full force of the weather, the wind literally took my breath away. It was wild out there. Loose plastic bags and other light objects in the boat were zipping past my head as we rode into the waves. The youngest of our small crew were getting tossed back and forth as if they were on a wild carnival ride. Usually calm and reserved, I saw and heard Caroline tapping Jack on the shoulder and telling him she had a bad feeling about this. Jack didn't respond. But I could tell by the way he was fighting the steering wheel, and frowning at the three-metre high waves that were battering us that he was worried about losing control of the boat. Faced with this growing danger, Jack, to my great relief, steered us back toward the mainland, past the boulders that booby-trapped the shoreline, then onto a safe stretch of land where we skidded to a stop on a sandbar.

We were no more than 50 kilometres north of the Rankin Inlet, but it may well have been the end of the world — a more bleak or desolate place could not have been found. Jack, however, was philosophical, at least for a moment: "I like to think that Nunavut is the land that God saved for Abel." He looked out through the fog and rain at the slimy cobblestone beach before us. "But I think that this is the part he saved for Cain."

Resigned that we were going to spend the night there, we headed toward an old plywood hunting shack that had seen better times. I opened the rickety door and looked into the tiny, cold damp room that had been rotting from age, neglect and moisture. There were vole and weasel droppings and piles of dead flies littered everywhere. I saw this as an opportunity to see how my fancy new, single-walled tent would fare in the storm. Jack and Caroline, however, saw only sanctuary. "Let's go find a caribou for supper," Jack said to me as he waved goodbye to Caroline and the children, leaving them to deal with the business of cleaning up. "I'm hungry."

———

When Danish ethnologist Knud Rasmussen explored the northwest coast of Hudson Bay in the 1920s, an Inuit woman by the name of Kibkarjuk told him the legend of how the barren ground caribou of the north came to be. The story, as Rasmussen translates it in his "Report of the Fifth Thule Expedition, 1921-1924", tells of a time when there were no caribou in the world, when the animals came into being only because of the desire and hard work of a single man. This man cut an enormous hole into the ground that allowed the animals to rise up in numbers so great that they covered the tundra. Once there were enough caribou to feed all of mankind, the man closed up the hole.

The caribou have lived in this treeless world ever since. There are now some two million animals amongst several herds dwelling in various distinct regions across the Canadian North and Alaska, more than enough to feed the Inuit and Dene who still rely on them for food. The Qamanirjuaq herd that moves across this part of the Hudson Bay region is one of the largest. During the early 1970s, when scientists suggested the Qamanirjuaq population had been reduced by more than half — to 50,000 adults — there were emotional debates about whether the Inuit could continue to hunt. The hunters never believed the scientists. They were convinced that the herd was increasing. But the debate was never really settled until 1982 and 1985 when aerial surveys done in those two years estimated the numbers at 200,000 and then 500,000. The hunters seemed to be vindicated.

Still, the issue was not so simple. Aerial surveys were fairly crude in the '70s. The area the Qamanirjuaq cover is also vast, spanning 965 kilometres north to south and more than 480 kilometres east to west. Furthermore, there's no guarantee that the herd will follow the same migration from year to year. So the scientists may be forgiven for missing so many animals.

No one knows why a herd strays from the beaten path. Weather is likely a big factor. Bugs and predators may be as well. Even in the good years, some Inuit communities have occasionally had trouble getting enough meat to carry them through the winter as migrations veer into different directions.

These days, people get by if the caribou don't come. Social programs guarantee that no Inuk starves in the Canadian North. But as author Farley Mowat noted in several books, the Caribou Inuit who inhabited the interior of this tundra more than 50 years ago suffered miserably when the herd went off their traditional track. Hundreds starved to death in those days waiting for the animals to come.

In 1958, Jack was eight-years-old and living in a canvas-and-caribou skin tent when the last great famine in northern Canada left dozens dead near Ennadai Lake, and in the Garry Lakes region northwest of Wager Bay. Walking with him on the tundra that night looking for these caribou, I found it remarkable that from such humble and tough beginnings, he had grown up to become a mayor, a key land claims negotiator, a two-term Member of Parliament and now the Commissioner of a new territory. "My first wife, Guita, survived that famine," Jack told me. "But she never forgot it. She was just a kid at the time and most everyone she knew was lost to her. All she remembers is that she had a hard time keeping up with the adults and older children who walked for hundreds of miles trying to find food. Many of them didn't make it."

Jack considers himself fortunate to have escaped that famine, but he has had his share of heartbreaking tragedies. Shortly after he was born, he was given away, in a common Inuit tradition, to a childless couple. He always considered Phillipa Piova and Lionel Angotingoar to be his true parents. But Phillipa was diagnosed with cancer when he was just five years old and taken away to a hospital down south. Jack vividly recalls standing on shore the day she left, crying, waving goodbye, and wondering why it was happening. He never did see her again. But a friend who did get a chance to visit Phillipa on her deathbed recalled her saying something Jack will never forget. "The last thing she told this woman," Jack told me, "'was to take care of my Jacky.'"

Phillipa's death left Lionel with many difficult decisions. He could have put Jack in the care of another family while he continued hunting, trapping and whaling. Instead, he chose to take the five-year-old with him. It could be a lonely life, Jack admitted. The only time he saw anyone his age was a few times each year when he and his father got together with the Irniqs, the Kusugaks, and the Airuts who lived in or around Repulse Bay. Until that night, I hadn't known that the children's story *Baseball Bats for Christmas*, a book I had read to my son, was based on the true-life escapades of Jack, Peter Irniq, Yvo Airut, one of the most successful businessmen in Nunavut today, and author Michael Kusugak.

—

After nearly three hours of hiking inland from the coast looking for caribou that night, Jack and I finally arrived at the top of the one high point of land in the area. Below us, to the east, was an expanse of treeless tundra that rivals Tanzania's Serengeti Plain in its breadth. Everything was a lush green because of all the rain and wet snow that had fallen the week before. But through our binoculars, we were only able to see a single white gyrfalcon gracefully riding a thermal updraft against a spray of rain – shining in a momentary glow of sunlight. Nothing else moved. It looked like every other living thing had been swallowed back into that mythical hole in the ground. "Looks like there will be no caribou for supper tonight," said Jack as he turned and started heading back toward the shack.

By the time we returned, Caroline and the kids had somehow transformed the miserable shack into a warm cosy shelter. We ate Palaugaq (fried bannock) and a Kraft Dinner while the wind and the rain rattled the walls and the door. Jack ate a steak he had barely singed on the Coleman stove and the kids were playing a noisy game of cards on the floor when suddenly, a telephone rang from somewhere within the bowels of the enclosure. Everything went silent. How could a cell phone possibly find us in the midst of a gale on the coast of Hudson Bay? Then Jack pulled out a satellite phone, and I was reminded that there were some perks to being the Commissioner of a new territory.

On the line was someone from the CBC news, hoping to get Jack to comment on the controversial bowhead whale hunt, the third in the Canadian Arctic since the lifting of a hunting ban in 1997, that was going on in Hudson Bay that summer.

The bowhead is one of three whales that lives exclusively in the Arctic. It grows to more than 18-metres long and can weigh up to 72 tonnes. Had it not been for the signing of an international treaty in 1937 that banned all harvesting of the mammal, it may well have been hunted to extinction. This hunt in Hudson Bay was stirring a great deal of controversy from around the world. While the bowhead appeared to be recovering in the Bering, Chukchi and

Beaufort seas in the western Arctic, the population in the eastern Arctic had not been recovering as quickly as hoped.

The first Inuit hunt off the coast of Baffin Island was also disaster. The one whale that the Inuit were allowed to kill sank after being strafed with bullets from high-powered rifles. By the time it surfaced two days later and was hauled to shore, it had begun to rot. Most of the carcass was burned, nearly all of the kill wasted.

After he was finished with the interview, Jack bristled when I asked him how he felt about the controversy. "Who are they to tell us what to do?" he asked. "What would they rather have us do, eat the cows that people get from grocery stores down south? Do they really think that a cow is not a living being as well? That it just comes wrapped in plastic for their convenience? We are a hunting culture. The world has to accept that. That is how we've been able to survive for thousands of years in this part of the world."

We spent two days in our camp — me in my tent and the Anawaks in the shack — before the winds calmed long enough to allow the sun time to burn a hole through the thick fog. Heading back out into Hudson Bay to resume our trip up the coast, we could see the white quartzite contours of Marble Island heaving into view like a castle lit up with artificial lights. "Some people believe it's haunted with the ghosts of all the kabloonas (white people) that died there," said Jack. "I'm not so sure, but I have to admit that you do get the sense that you're not alone when you go there."

Marble Island is a wind-scarred outcrop of rock that rises 90-metres above sea level. Legend has it that long ago a family of four led by a man named Uanik decided to move away from this region because the caribou had all gone. The old woman of the family refused to go, professing instead her desire to live on a rough part of the sea ice that looked like land. Reluctantly, the family set off without her. All alone, the old woman sat on a rock on shore, repeating over and over again a wish that the ice be turned into an island.

When Uanik returned a few years later with his family, he could find no trace of the old woman. But one day while out hunting he heard her voice say, "Uanik, don't worry. I have got my wish. My spirit lives on this marble island." It was then that Uanik saw that the ice had turned to stone. Believing that the old woman's spirit lives on the island to this day, some Inuit who go to Marble Island crawl the first few feet out of respect for this spirit.

The European connection to Marble Island is not nearly as spiritually satisfying. There, in 1719, two ships, the *Albany* and the *Discovery*, were damaged beyond repair when their captains, James Knight and David Vaughan, tried to find a safe harbour during their search for gold and copper and a route to the Orient. Only five of the 40 crew members reportedly made it through to the second summer. Those five men, according to the Inuit whose story was conveyed to explorer Samuel Hearne a half-century later, "were in such distress for provisions that they eagerly (ate) the seal's flesh and whale's blubber as they purchased it from the natives."

The men, however, were too far gone by that point. Unable to keep the oily meat down, three of them died soon after, leaving the other two, already in a very weakened state, the sad chore of burying them. Left alone in this desolate part of the world, the pair walked daily to the high point of land on the island, looking earnestly for a boat to come and save them. But none did. The Inuit recall one particularly melancholy moment when the two men sat down in despair, huddled together and wept bitterly. When one finally died, the other did his best to give him a proper burial. But the effort so exhausted him that he ended up lying down and dying as well.

No one knows whether Knight or Vaughn were among the last survivors. And up until very recently, there was little else but Hearne's narrative to indicate how the crew got itself in such a miserable situation. But then an archeological survey of Marble and three other nearby islands in 1989-91 took a closer look at Knight's winter house and the surrounding area. Found were part of one of Knight's frigates, some graves, humans bones, a leather boot, coins, brass dividers, a musket ball and such. The survey has added to the knowledge of what happened to Knight and his men three centuries ago, but it has also, as archeologist Owen Beattie and author John Geiger have noted in their book *Dead Silence*, resulted in many more unanswered questions. Were the survivors attacked and killed by the Inuit? Or did they simply all die slow, miserable deaths from scurvy and starvation? If hunger was a factor, why wouldn't they have crossed over the ice to land, which was in sight, and then walked the four or five days to the closest Hudson's Bay trading post?

Looking towards the shores of Marble Island that night as we headed up the coast, I could see the shape of a human standing on top of that high point of land. It was, in all likelihood, just an inuk-shuk, the stone marker the Inuit build to guide them on journeys. But like Jack, I couldn't get over this spooky feeling that someone or something on that island was staring at us.

To hear Jack, Cyril and Harry describe it, the entire northwest coast of Hudson Bay is haunted by some ghost or other spirit. At Daly Bay, Jack told me how his father had once heard music coming from some sod huts that had long been abandoned. When he went in to see who it was that was playing the instruments, he found the huts cold and empty as they had been for hundreds of years. "My father left the area as fast as he could and vowed never to come back," said Jack.

Farther on at Fullerton Harbour, Harry told me how one dark day in the dead of winter, his father was travelling by dog team with an Oblate missionary when they saw lights on in the abandoned RCMP station. When the two approached to see who it was that was in the remote outpost, the lights mysteriously dimmed to darkness. "They couldn't find a footprint in the snow anywhere," Harry said. "It was very cold that day and they could have used the post for shelter. But the missionary insisted on leaving right away. He believed an evil spirit was living there."

The wind was veering from north to east as we headed up the coast towards these two sites — a good sign that the weather was finally improving. The water was so black and creamy, it looked as if we were floating on oil. All around, seals and the occasional walrus popped up to see what was making all the noise. Once past the islands of Pikiuliaqjuk, Nanujumaaq and Qikiqtaarjuk, where the Inuit at Chesterfield Inlet traditionally collect the eggs of various migratory birds in spring, we headed into Fish Bay. There we looked for pods of beluga and narwhal that are occasionally seen. Not far into a small cove where the tiny hamlet of Chesterfield Inlet lies, our boat's engine sputtered, smoked and then died. Jack stared into the empty gas tank and then looked at me, wide-eyed and concerned, as I must have been from his perspective, and offered some advice; "Remember, into each life a little rain must fall," he said trying to reassure me. "That's what I tell my staff when they occasionally get down in their spirits."

We bobbed in Fish Bay for nearly an hour before Jack managed to tap into a satellite that enabled him to call Harry Aggark's tiny seaside home less than a kilometre away. It would have been funny to see Harry, phone in hand, doing a double take when he looked out his window to see us floating in the bay. But we were all so seasick by that point that no one was in the mood for a laugh until well after Harry and Roland had motored out to us with a can of gas.

Philip Dormer, an 18th-century British aristocrat, once noted that "whatever is worth doing is worth doing well." It is unclear what Dormer, as the Fourth Earl of Chesterfield, did so well to earn him the honour of having this beautiful place on the coast of Hudson Bay named after him. Even though the Inuit occasionally call it Igluligaarjuk, "place with few houses," Chesterfield is the name that sticks.

Jack had mixed feelings about being in the community. Seeing old friends was a treat, but revisiting the place where he was sent to school at the age of nine still opened old wounds. Here at Turquetil Hall and Joseph Bernier school, Jack and many other Inuit children were abused physically, and in some cases sexually, by some of the nuns, brothers, priests and lay people who worked or taught there.

Jack was taken directly from the trapline to live at this residential school. Once in, there was no way out until the end of the year. "You know there was just one teacher, Sister Arcand, who really seemed to be human," recalled Jack. "She was a Cree woman from somewhere out on the Prairies. I remember her because she was the one nun who showed us that she had hair under that big black and white habit. The others, especially the brothers . . . to do what they did to a child, and to one who is so alone and vulnerable . . . I still have to get counselling to help me with my sense of shame and rage."

We spent a good part of the day at Chesterfield helping Harry and Roland and Elizabeth and Cyril pack their boats for the trip to Wager Bay. Fortunately, fair weather had prevailed by the time we headed out. It was exhilarating to be on the move again, with nothing above but clear blue skies and a soft breeze blowing in from the southwest. For the first time, everyone was optimistic that our troubles were now behind us. But a half-day into the trip up the coast of Hudson Bay, all eyes were drawn to a long ribbon of white on the eastern horizon. Words of concern in Inuktituk were muttered back and forth before Jack spoke the one word I needed to understand:

"Ice," he said. "Lots of it."

For more than five centuries, ice prevented explorers from the finding a northwest passage to the Orient. It also hindered them in their search for a mythical open polar sea. From the time John Cabot first set off from Bristol in 1497 to the moment, almost 350 years later, when all 129 crew members of the Franklin expedition disappeared, more than 140 ships had failed to find a way through the ice pack. By the time Roald Amundsen finally made it through Arctic Canada in his ship Gjoa between 1903 and 1906, most of the world was no longer interested in a route that held little or no economic promise.

Hudson Bay was an especially pitiless place to search for a route to the Orient. It was here in 1611 when Henry Hudson, the most famous of the regions' explorers, was set adrift in a small boat with eight other men after his crew refused to spend another year searching for the passage. Perhaps it was it intended simply as a reminder of how badly they desired to go home. But when Hudson managed to use a tow rope to pull up to the ship, someone among the mutinous crew cut the line. The rest watched silently as Hudson and his fellow outcasts faded from view.

It was Hudson himself who summed up the futility of trying to find a route to the Orient through these icy waters: "If the passage be found," he said before he disappeared forever that fateful day, "I confess there is something gained in the distance, but nothing in the navigation. For allow that this passage falls into the South sea; if it does, little good is likely to ensue of it because of the hazard of cold, of ice, and unknown seas which experience must teach us."

Johann Miertsching, the Moravian missionary who was aboard the *Investigator* with Captain Robert McClure searching for the lost Franklin expedition between 1850 and 1852, wrote that "no one can form a conception of the perils of Arctic sea ice" without actually seeing it. "To describe it," he wrote, "one must write archives full — and then those who have seen only European ice in rivers, ponds, and the sea would find it unimaginable and beyond belief."

I had skied and snowmobiled on the Arctic sea ice, kayaked and sailed through it on a Canadian Coast Guard vessel, but nothing made me appreciate what Miertsching was trying to convey until that night on Hudson Bay when we saw that ribbon of white advancing towards us. It really did seem like the hand of God was against us. Initially, Jack's plan was to get out of harm's way as quickly as possible and find a place on shore to land the boats. The tides, however, moved in much too quickly for us to do anything but hope that there would be wide enough ledes through which we could escape.

It was both exhausting and nerve-racking seeing this big sheet of white building around us. Jack thrust the engines both backwards and forwards trying to bore a path through it. But all he succeeded in doing was tilting the boat at crazy angles. Each time it appeared as if we might get rolled over, a lede would open up just long enough for Jack to gun the engines and get us out and for the other two boats to follow. Twice, Robin and I had to hop out to push the boat back in after the ice lifted the bow out of the water. Each time, I fully expected that one or both of us would go crashing through the floe.

It was nearly three hours before we finally bumped our way safely to shore. But even on land, our troubles were far from over. As the tides continued to move in, we had to use ropes to manoeuver the boats back and forth in the shallow water so that the house-sized blocks of ice that were being hurdled our way could do no harm. Then as the tides retreated, it was all we could do to keep the boats from being torn up on the sharp rocks.

It was early the next morning when the winds finally calmed and the danger passed. Completed enervated, I sat there on a rock staring at the ragged icescape, waxing and waning with the tide, refusing to yield gracefully to the annual summer collapse. The scene was daunting. Some of the crystalline sculptures that had formed overnight looked so real in the alpenglow radiating through the thin haze, I had to take out my binoculars to confirm that the preternatural shapes were not alive. Staring into this icy labyrinth, I told Jack that I now understood why the Inuit have a reputation for being superstitious.

Jack offered no argument. "We are a superstitious people, no doubt about it," he said, handing me a cup of coffee that Caroline had made, kept hot and topped-up throughout the night while we were busy with the boats. "You learn to be that way early on in life up here. When I was young, I was told to look out for the Ijirac. They're little people who suddenly appear on the sea ice or on the land, and then disappear the moment you take your eyes off them. When you were a kid, you were told never to go with an Ijirac because they were so good at hiding, no one would ever find you."

Having finished the story, Jack gave me a long, icy stare before telling me there was a reason why his middle name was Ijirac.

———

We spent most of the next day close to camp waiting to see if a west wind might rise up and blow the ice back into Hudson Bay. In the meantime, Robin went off and shot a caribou that Roland subsequently skinned and butchered in the middle of our camp. Jack sliced off several strips of raw meat and devoured them with the greatest pleasure. "You Alberta boys can have your beef. I'll take our caribou any day," he said. "The government once tried to get us to change our ways, but they will never convince us that anything is better than caribou."

The Canadian government, in fact, did try to wean the Hudson Bay Inuit off caribou when it first appeared that the Qamanirjuaq herd was being over-hunted. Jack remembered the plan vividly because he was one of the people hired to feed the pigs and chickens that were brought up to Rankin Inlet. The experimental farm, however, was a spectacular failure.

"When it came time to roast the first pig, the *kabloonas* (non-natives who ran the farm) were horrified to find that it tasted of the fish and seals that we were adding to their diet," said Jack. "In the end, they closed it down after someone came in and slit the throats of all of the chickens. But I doubt that anyone will ever forget that crazy plan. People in Rankin Inlet still call the spit of land where the farm was located "Pork Peninsula."

During the time we waited for the ice to clear, I slept, read about Henry Hudson and James Knight, took notes and worried about how much longer my kidneys could sustain a diet of raw seal, caribou meat and the briny sea water we had been forced to drink. There were no freshwater streams nearby to replenish our supply. I was dozing off when Harry and Roland came to visit me in the tent that I had set up far away and upwind of the dead caribou.

At first I thought they wanted to know how I could manage with such a tiny tent. Like most Inuit, they were used to the big canvas-walled shelters in which you could stand up and walk around. But while I explained to them the genius of the high-tech design and how it was tested at high altitudes, I could see that wasn't what had interested them.

"Where's your gun?" Roland finally said, cutting to the chase. He looked over my shoulder to see whether I might have had one tucked inside. "Aren't you afraid that a polar bear might come in when you're sleeping?" I had thought of that, especially with the carcasses of a partially butchered caribou and seal lying in a pool of blood so close by. Not having a gun, I had just hoped that any bear that did show up would go for the caribou or seal before it came for me.

———

It was at the end of that third day when Jack, Harry and Roland finally decided to bust out with the first sign of open water — and once again it was a harrowing experience. At one point in our struggle to bore a path through the ice, I thought for sure that Harry's wooden *Winnipeg* schooner was going to collapse under the strain of being squeezed so hard by the massive sheets of ice that closed in on him. I could hear the wooden hull of his boat crack or buckle under the strain. And once again, I was amazed to see how calmly everyone reacted to this drama. The only show of emotion was the cheer that was given out when we finally got to the open water.

The celebration, however did not last long. Although we were finally free of the ice that imprisoned us, it was clear by that point in our journey, there would have to be a change of plan. We had lost six days to bad weather and ice. Now there was not enough time to get to Wager Bay and back, even if, somehow, nothing slowed us down in the coming days. So the decision was made to go straight up the coast past Wager Bay to the hamlet of Repulse Bay. From there, Jack and the rest of the gang would spend a couple of days narwhal hunting while I, hopefully, hitched a plane ride heading south.

On our way north, the lowlands of Hudson Bay gave way to rolling hills and the sea got noticeably deeper. Although the fair weather persisted, it also got much colder. Even Jack, immune as he seemed to be to the freezing temperatures, reluctantly agreed to stop and fry up some food so that everyone could warm up. We were still 8 kilometres from shore. Neither Caroline nor I were very

happy about the idea of cooking underneath the plastic tarp that
Jack and Robin had wrapped around the boat to keep the wind out.
It didn't seem like such a good idea to light a match when we could
smell vapours coming from the 45 gallon fuel drum on board. Jack
shrugged off the possibility of an explosion. When Robin went to
flick on his lighter, I moved to the back of the boat. But then I
stopped after realizing that the alternative to a quick, fiery death
was a slow, cold one at sea.

Once the food started to sizzle, I was never so glad to be wrong
about the potential for a fiery end. For the next hour, we drank sug-
ary tea to help wash down the seal meat that had been cooked with
a can of meatballs. And we stuffed our mouths with pilot biscuits.
Sitting there in the boat at the north end of Hudson Bay, I gazed
out at the shadows of seals and walrus that were rising and diving in
the dark beneath the bright stars and full moon. Just as I was thinking that there was nothing I would do for rest of my life that would
be as strange and surreal as this, someone yelled "Ulinguyuq!" The
tide, I was told, was bringing in more ice from the open sea.
Determined not to get trapped again, Jack fired up the engine of the
boat while the rest of us wiped up what was left of the food. Then,
as the temperature dropped to well below the freezing point, all four
children stuffed themselves headfirst into the cargo hold, leaving
me, Jack and Caroline to fend for ourselves in the cold as we raced
up the coast of Hudson Bay.

Throughout that long night on the water I fought hard to stay
awake. I feared that I might nod off and never recover from my
hypothermic state. I had never been as cold as I was in my clammy
survival suit with just a layer of fleece underneath for extra insula-
tion. All I can recall about the night was Jack pointing to a narrow
body of water that had opened up along the distant shore, and
yelling "Wager Bay," and me giving him the thumb's up, acknowl-
edging that we had, at least, seen the gateway to the fabled water
body. The next thing I recall was waking up in the morning and
shivering uncontrollably. There was a thick, icy fog all around us,
but through it all, I could see Jack, Cyril, Harry and Roland on the

deck of the *Winnipeg* schooner, poring over a map. The more they studied the maps, the more animated they became. Then looking over at the gravel shoreline to the east of us, Harry broke, for a moment, from speaking in Inuktituk. "Southampton Island?" he asked in disbelief. I sat upright and had a look for myself.

Hard as it was for anyone of us to believe, we had strayed far from our intended course and landed on the wrong side of Roes Welcome Sound. I really shouldn't have been all that surprised. Jack had not slept for at least 72 hours. Sometime during the night, he must have lost his bearings and led the other two boats northeast when we should have been heading due north. No one realized how far we had gone off course until someone spotted land to the east where no land should have been.

I thought the drama had finally ended after we made the necessary navigational adjustments and resumed our journey to Repulse Bay. With only a few hours left to the journey, Jack decided to let the others boats pass while he showed me the landscape of his youth. Along the way we passed Fort Hope on the North Pole River where explorer John Rae and 10 others spent a winter in 1846-47. A little farther on, Jack pointed to the spot where he and his father often camped. It didn't bother me that both Cyril and Harry had passed us while I was getting this tour of the region. But then when the engine sputtered and smoked and went silent once again, I had to reconsider. Looking into the fuel drum, Jack confirmed what we had all feared. We were out of fuel. Jack looked over at me and gave me a smile that was by now all too familiar to me. "Remember, into each life a little rain must fall," he said as he pressed the numbers on his satellite phone, hoping to get hold of someone in Repulse Bay to rescue us. "Trust me, there's nothing to worry about."

And so for the first time on the journey, I did just what Jack had suggested. I was no longer nervous about what was going to happen next or whether anyone would find us. Nor was I disappointed that we had not made it to Wager Bay or got a glimpse of the Brown River. Instead I sat back in the rocking boat soaking up the heat of the sun, thinking about caribou rising out of a hole in the ground, about the ghosts of men and one old woman haunting Marble Island, about music coming from empty sod huts on the tundra, and of Ijirac, the mythical creature that plays a deadly game of hide-and-seek with Inuit children. This weird, magical journey to Wager Bay would continue, I promised myself, but it would have to wait for another time.

Brown River

Part Two — Belugas, Narwhals and Reversing Waterfalls

S hortly before midnight, the sound of someone yelling "polar bear" rousted me from my sleeping bag. It was late July in Ukkusiksalik, the second day of our journey to the new national park at Wager Bay. Outside our Parks Canada base camp on the banks of the Sila River, Chesley Ford, our Inuit guide, was pointing toward the big animal lumbering across the rocky tundra beneath the faint glow of a gibbous moon.

A flock of cranky gulls noisily objected, but failed to deter the predator from plunging past their perch into the river. Swimming effortlessly toward us, the bear rose up from the bankside, and like a giant Labrador retriever, shook itself dry. Instead of going for us, as we had expected it to do, the bear went straight for the boat that had been hauled on to shore for repairs. Finding nothing worthwhile there, the animal swung back our way, not making a sound as it moved. With its head up high, it sniffed the air, padded back and forth while trying to determine what we might have offered by way of a meal.

Before it got too close, Chesley got out his shotgun and fired off a couple of harmless cracker shells that exploded in a flash of smoke over the animal. Startled, the bear bolted toward the river; layers of fat rippled around its belly as it ran off. But it didn't go far. Realizing perhaps that the loud crack could do it no harm, the animal once again focused its attention on us. That was enough for Chesley. He had seen enough bears during a lifetime in the Arctic to know that this one was up to no good. He hopped on the all-terrain vehicle, kick-started the engine, then chased the animal across the tundra into the river. The bear seemed to take it all in stride. Back on the opposite bank, it briefly looked at us. Then it sauntered off and faded, chimera-like, into the darkness from which it had emerged.

Minutes later, it was left to Elizabeth Seale, the Nunavut field superintendent of Ukkusiksalik (oo-koo-sik-sah-lik) National Park and leader of our expedition, to interpret what this meant for me and her small crew's plans for exploring the area the next day. "Tomorrow's hike to the site where the coffin of the mystery man is located?" she said, pointing in the direction of the now long-gone bear. "It's cancelled."

It had been four years since I had set out on that journey with Jack Anawak in the hopes of getting to this part of the world. Now that I had finally arrived with a Parks Canada crew that was scouting out the region for the first time since Ukkusiksalik was established in 2003, I was itching to see the narwhal, the beluga, the reversing waterfalls, and the Brown River that I hoped to canoe or kayak some day. I also wanted to find out more about the person that lay buried beneath a pile of rocks on Tinittuktuq Flats, a desolate stretch of saltwater lowland five kilometres from our Sila River basecamp.

So was Margaret Bertulli, a national park archaeologist who had come along for a quick look-see of the 20,500 square kilometre protected area. There were more than 500 sites in and around Wager Bay for her to choose from, but the grave at Tinittuktuq Flats was one of handful that really intrigued her. In 1994, a cursory analysis of some bleached bones scattered around a partially destroyed casket suggested that they were not the remains of an Inuk, but those of a tall male of European origin.

Just how this man died and what he was doing in this remote part of the world has remained a mystery. It's been suggested, based on the length of the long bones, he might have been one of the 129 men who went missing after British explorer John Franklin set sail in 1845 to search for a northwest passage through the Arctic; the skulls and bones of some expedition members were discovered at Chantrey Inlet near the mouth of the Back River nearly two decades later. Theoretically, some of the longest living survivors may have got this far trying to get to whalers hunting in Hudson Bay. Others believe that if, in fact, the bones are those of a Caucasian, they probably belonged to a 19th-century whaler, a trapper, a policeman, missionary or a Hudson's Bay Company employee who was associated in some way with the small trading post built at Wager Bay in 1925. Eric Tatty, a native of Rankin Inlet who once lived at Wager Bay, believes the bones may, in fact, belong to an Inuk who was thought to be buried here.

"I personally doubt the grave has anything to do with Franklin," Margaret told me the next morning as we set off on a short hike to another archeological site; this one in the opposite direction our bear was last seen heading. "But I can't see it being that of a whaler, either. I don't think any of their ships got this far inland. At least there doesn't appear to be any record of it. Nor is there any indication that anyone from the Hudson's Bay Company post at Wager Bay died and was buried here. That's why I would have liked to have got there to have a good look."

Ukkusiksalik is as the Inuktituk word suggests — "the place where you find stone suitable for carving pots and oil lamps." The landscape is strewn with so many varying types of rocks and boulders, it looks as if a massive glacier had only recently made a sudden and hasty retreat. There is no refuge-like aspect to the wilderness here as there is in the verdant valleys of the Thomsen and Firth rivers. The few far-flung plants that rise up from the dirt, rock and gravel are mainly sedges, grasses and plants with hairy leaves that insulate them from the cold. Plants such as the lovely purple saxifrage literally huddle together in small clumps to keep themselves warm and to exploit the very few places where there is enough fertilized soil for them to grow. (Spots like this are often found where a caribou or muskox has lain down and died.) And still, as stark and repelling as the place can be, it is also bewitching country. The long days, the sky and sea that are bigger than the land, the rocks that gleam or change colour in the sunlight – the absence of so many things familiar, including humans – all make it the kind of imposing, dreamlike place that has so enchanted and horrified generations of Arctic explorers.

There were six of us on the hike that day: Margaret, me, Elizabeth, ecosystem scientist Jane Chisolm, Nancy Anilniliak, manager of Ukkusiksalik, and Paula Hughson, an Inuk from Baker Lake who was on education leave from the government agency. Up on top of the hill behind our camp, we found a tent ring composed of two concentric circles of large rocks. The inner circle was just big enough for a small person to lie down in. The Thule that once inhabited the circle's interior would cover this space with the skins of caribou, seals and other animals.

The Thule were the ancestors of the modern Inuit. These Alaskan whalers began migrating into the Canadian Arctic some time around A.D. 1000. No one knows what triggered the migration, but for a long time archaeologists believed that the same kind of temperatures that are now warming the Arctic may have melted so much ice in Alaskan waters that it became too difficult for them to hunt whales from the floe edge. More open water in Arctic Canada may have also allowed these early mariners to move east into areas that had previously been impossible to get to. In search of better hunting conditions, the Alaskans got as far as Thule in northern Greenland (hence the name "Thule") before fanning out to other parts of the Arctic.

Robert McGhee, the curator of Arctic archaeology at the Canadian Museum of Civilization, also believed this to be true until he came to the conclusion recently that humans do not behave in such a deterministic manner. In a wonderful book, *The Last Imaginary Place, A Human History of the Arctic World*,[1] he notes that

---

[1] Robert McGhee, *The Last Imaginary Place, A Human History of the Arctic World*, Key Porter, 2004.

the warming climate of 1,000 years ago did not affect all places in the Arctic and that the climate began to deteriorate well before the Thule appeared in areas east of Alaska. Even in the most benign conditions, McGhee argues, the sea ice of the Central Arctic would have formed a 1,000 kilometre barrier to bowhead whales and other sea mammals.

McGhee now suspects the migration was tied to a much more simple motive – the discovery that iron and metal was available in the Eastern Arctic where it was being used for carving and tool-making purposes by a people who had migrated from Siberia thousands of years earlier. The so-called Tuniit would have exploited the copper reserves along the Coppermine River in the central Arctic and obtained meteoric iron and native copper from the Greenlandic Norse to the east.

The Tuniit, according to modern Inuit legend, were a tall and gentle people. Archaeological evidence suggests they were not as technologically advanced as the Thule. They had neither the tools nor the skills to build the boats that the newcomers had brought with them. Nor did they have the weapons or the numbers to fend off the newcomers who saw that metals as theirs' for the taking. In fairly short order, it seems, the Tuniit were either driven off or assimilated by the newcomers.

No one knows when the first Thule arrived on the shores of Wager Bay. But looking out at the huge inland sea where the calm, blue waters blended so seamlessly with the sky that the horizon could not be detected, Margaret speculated that this particular place must have been a welcoming site. Out in the bay, she noted, there were more than enough whales, walrus, and seals for them to hunt. And upstream in the char-filled river, a series of rapids and waterfalls plunging down towards the bay did so with such velocity that a herd of caribou passing through would have either been stopped or slowed down long enough for hunters to throw their spears.

Sites like this one could tell us more about the Thule. But up until this point they have only been mapped, not excavated. The complex nature of some of the larger sites, like Aktungiktautalik, a

rocky isthmus that juts into Wager Bay, suggest multiple generations of thriving cultures. There, west of where we were camped,
hundreds of rocks and enormous boulders have been arranged in
various ways to form hearths, tent rings, fox traps, food caches and
game structures. "The Thule really liked to move big rocks,"
explained Margaret. "I think it was Robert McGhee who once noted
that their modification of the Arctic landscape as a geological event
was second only to the last continental glaciation."

Early European insights into the Thule presence at Wager Bay
are even more scanty. Christopher Middleton, the first European to
sail into these waters, reported seeing no one when he entered the
bay in 1742 only to get trapped in ice.[2] He, however, did deduce
from the strong tides that it was not a route to the Orient. Other
than naming the waterway after Sir Charles Wager, a member of the
British Admiralty who had never been to the Arctic, Middleton
accomplished little on this, the second of two trips from the newly
constructed Prince of Wales fort at Churchill.

Nothing seemed to have gone well on those voyages. James
Isham, the governor of the Hudson's Bay Company, was an old
friend and colleague who admired Middleton's seamanship and
navigational skills. But in Middleton's crew he saw only a "set of
rogues, most of whom deserved hanging." Middleton didn't help his
own cause either by distributing copious amounts of alcohol that
robbed the crew of their health. Of the 13 men who died that first
winter, 11 succumbed to scurvy.

Back in England, Middleton had a difficult time getting sym-
pathy from those that organized and financed the expedition.
Arthur Dobbs, the Irish-Anglo entrepreneur who had worked tire-
lessly to end the Hudson's Bay Company's trading monopoly in the
New World, was incredulous when he read Middleton's report. He
was convinced that Middleton had taken a bribe from his former

---

[2.] William Barr and Glyndwyr Williams eds., *Voyages in Search of a Northwest
Passage 1741-47, Volume One* and *The Voyage of Christopher Middleton, 1741-42*,
Hakluyt Society, 1994.

employers (the Hudson's Bay Company) "to return to their Service and not to go the Voyage (in search of a northwest passage)."

It was, of course, an absurd accusation, but one that caused so much public controversy that British Parliamentarians put up a £20,000 reward to any person other than a naval officer who discovered the waterway to the Orient. That kept alive the search for a northwest passage through northern Hudson Bay. Twenty years later, John Bean and William Christopher were also thwarted in their effort to find a northwest passage leading out of Hudson Bay. Their sighting of numerous whales off Marble Island, however, did convince Company officials to develop a whaling industry in the region in 1765.

Their sighting of numerous whales off Marble Island, however, did convince company officials to develop a whaling industry in the region — a venture that ultimately proved unsuccessful. Company traders ventured into the Wager Bay off and on from that point. But it wasn't until the 1920s that officials finally made the decision to set up a permanent trading post in the area. Ford Lake at the west end of the inland sea was the site chosen. It was established not so much for trading with the local Inuit, few and far between as they were at the time, as it was for keeping their coastal neighbours at Chantrey Inlet from establishing a relationship with the Revillon Frères Trading Co. Ltd. The rival fur trading group had set up shop at Baker Lake in the heart of the Barren Lands and was threatening to undermine the Company's monopoly in the Arctic.

A man by the name of Buster Brown was initially given the task of managing the remote outpost. According to written accounts he sent back to Company officials, it was a formidable challenge getting things up and running in 1925. Construction of the wooden buildings that first autumn was repeatedly hampered by frigid temperatures and fierce winds. Efforts to harvest food and fur were also sabotaged by wolves and wolverines that routinely raided their traplines.

In one letter to the district manager at Fort Prince of Wales, Brown described a particularly troublesome wolf as a "huge white

Grandfather, and cunning as they make them." Despite being shot in the jaw, the wolf kept coming back. On one particularly cold January night, Brown noted how the wolf "carefully pulled away the snow pan and laid the trap bare so that he could inspect the mechanism."

"After this was done, he gave a loud laugh and devoured the bait at his leisure, and in a most casual manner wandered off to the next trap where he ate the bait only if it pleased him. (Then) he pounded the snow all around with his big pads so as to frighten off any fox that might come along. He did not miss a single trap. . . There is no need to mention that the staff don't feel friendly toward him," Brown ruefully added, "though they are compelled to admire him."

It's hard to know what Jack Anawak's great grandfather, or Iqungajuq — Wager Dick — thought of these white men as they sat around a radio at night trying to tune into hockey games that were being broadcast out of Winnipeg. They never could get the radio to work properly. All they got most nights was a lot of hissing and whistling. No amount of playing with the antenna outside seemed to help.

Iqungajuq, his family and friends were even more astounded the following year when a tractor was brought in with the supply boat. Brown had been given instructions to drive the specially designed contraption to the Arctic coast in order to make contact with the Inuit. In reality, this was just your average farm tractor equipped with two barrel/corkscrew wheels designed to carry the crew and supplies effortlessly over the tundra. But it proved to be a disaster. After the first run, Brown wrote to his boss, noting that he was "trying to be optimistic about it. . . but a more futile and pathetic thing I never saw. Tried to cross this snowdrift about eighteen inches deep and about eight feet wide ...It merely wallowed into it like a pig in mire, dug itself in, with its drums revolving impotently." Brown ended the letter by dismissing the design as "the offspring of a weak mind and a distorted intellect."

In the end, Brown did make it to the Arctic coast, but with an altogether different machine. The 320-kilometre round trip took 20 days and 1,200 litres of gas. No doubt, it was a great adventure.

But as for its usefulness, it was left to one of the participants to note that it took the tractor two and a half days to travel the distance a dog team could cover in five hours.

After a few fruitless years, the Hudson's Bay Company gave up on the Ford Lake outpost. It never did make a profit, and with the Great Depression driving down the price of furs, the conclusion was made that neither the Company nor the Revillon Frères group ever would. Iqungajuq, however, saw it differently. He had worked closely with Buster Brown and the other managers who followed him at Ford Lake. Knowing what it took to get local furs to market, he picked up where the Company left off and made the post a winner.

———

Summer took its time getting to Wager Bay that August. When it finally did, halfway through our trip, the bugs came out with a vengeance. Even the caribou that routinely passed through our basecamp at Sila River seemed to be having a hard time coping. Each time they settled down to feed on lichen, the bugs would send them galloping upwind in a desperate effort to find relief.

I got up early to exploit the morning light that day. But the bugs drove me back to camp sooner than I had intended. The preparation of breakfast hadn't even begun when I walked in. Chesley was busy looking through his binoculars and suggested I look out at the mouth of the Sila River. It was high tide. Thinking that it was a pod of belugas, or better still, a narwhal, the so-called unicorn of the sea, I scanned the surface of the bay for several minutes but saw nothing. Shrugging my shoulders, I handed the glasses back to Chesley.

"Look," he insisted. "Out there, past the river."

Again I tried finding what it was he had spied. But all I could see was a chunk of ice floating in the water and what looked like pieces of wood bobbing up and down around it. And that's when it hit me. There is no wood in this part of the world. The dark dots that were bobbing up and down were seals and the piece of ice that they were paying so much attention to was a polar bear.

"I saw him doing the same thing last night before I went to bed," Chesley told me. "He hasn't caught one yet, I don't think, but he's not giving up either. He's been out there for hours."

———

The following day a Single Otter flew in from Baker Lake with the parts that were required to fix the boat. On board was Eric Tatty, his father John and Roger Pilakapsi. While the pilot of the plane waited for the necessary work to be done, Elizabeth Seale arranged for him to fly us around Wager Bay for the day. It was exhilarating seeing pods of narwhal swimming down in the water below. It was also frustrating trying to make sense of the country that rose up around the bay. There the high plateau seemed, like a giant pancake, to stretch for hundreds of kilometres in all directions.

Looking down at this landscape, I was reminded of something American historian Stephen J. Pyne once said about the Antarctic. The landscape there, he noted, poses special problems for the wordsmith because it is more underload than overload. The ice has reduced the landscape to its simplest form. Abstracted, conceptual, invariant – these and other words that Pyne used, I thought, could also describe what we were flying over. There was uniformity to it all that prevented my imagination from doing anything with it on paper. "Tints of brown and white, bleached blue sky, boulderstrewn" – the landscape was so raw and primitive and stripped of sensory impression that in the end. I knew that if I was on the ground, I would discover that there was a lot more to it. So I put down my pen and paper and just gazed out at the tundra. I had failed miserably as a viewer trying to paint a compelling picture. But I would not be denied the pleasure of taking in a landscape that challenges the limits of human consciousness.

———

We were boating from Sila River to the Ford Lake outpost when I discovered that it was Chesley's great grandfather, Sam Ford, who had constructed the Hudson's Bay Company buildings there. With us that day was Roger Pilakapsi and Eric Tatty, the two Inuit men who had flown in with the boat parts. As it turned out, Eric also had a special connection to the outpost. In the early 1960s, his grand-father, Robert Tatty, the son of Iqungajuq or Wager Dick, brought the family back to Ford Lake in the hopes of returning to a more traditional lifestyle than the one they were practicing at Repulse Bay. They lived there for two years before the homesick children persuaded the patriarch to give up on the experiment. The family, however, never did abandon the area entirely. Eric's father John, Roger's late-father Louis and John Hickes eventually started up a tiny lodge at Wager Bay. The three were also instrumental in per-suading the federal government to turn 22,500 square kilometres in and around Wager Bay into a national park.

The 60-kilometre ride from Sila River to the Hudson's Bay Company outpost is a potentially dangerous one. At high tide, the water that previously cascaded out of Ford Lake into Wager Bay starts flowing backwards. This is just one of three reversing water-falls in Canada. The other two are located on the Saint John River in the Bay of Fundy and at Barrier Inlet on Hudson Bay. Timing is everything when it comes to getting through this narrow waterway. Too soon or too late and a small boat like ours could easily be swal-lowed up by the treacherous whirlpools and rip tides that form when the current changes direction.

We, however, passed through safely that night before turning into the inlet where the remnants of the Hudson's Bay Company post can still be found. On first impression, it struck me as a lone-ly, melancholy place. The buildings were leaning away from the pre-vailing winds, and the white paint that once coloured them was now grey and peeling. A setting sun reflecting off a window pane gave the false and spooky impression that someone was there inside.

Looking at the site from the perspective of the traders, on the other hand, it wasn't difficult to imagine why they were willing to risk passing through the reversing falls to get to this spot. The high rugged hills that surround the inlet would have provided the inhabitants with the shelter they needed from the gale-force winds that routinely whip through here in fall and winter. There is also a stream flowing into the far end of the inlet that would have been a good source of freshwater for the inhabitants. "See up there on those hills," Eric told me as we disembarked from the boat. "In the fall, they're often filled with thousands of caribou. It's a great place to be a hunter."

It was dead calm that night. The water was so clear that even in the fading light we could see enormous schools of Arctic char swimming away from the prow of the boat. Scanning the dark hillsides, Eric picked out a couple of wolves stalking a small herd of caribou. Judging by the way the animals were moving, the wolves were not going to be successful catching their prey.

On watch as we were that night and the next morning, we saw no sign of the polar bears that had thwarted us from exploring the country so many times in the previous days. The great white wanderers seemed to be everywhere. We saw several of them swimming in the open sea, eight kilometres from shore in some places. We also saw them high up on cliffsides trying to sneak up on a bird colony, and on the banks of the Piksimanik River where one refused to budge from its seal hunting perch when we boated in, trying to get to an archeological site. Elizabeth Seale was so freaked by the number of bears we had spotted on this trip, she openly wondered how she could, in good conscience, allow wilderness adventurers to come here without a gun. Parks Canada regulations prohibit anyone other than their trained staff or the Inuit from carrying a firearm in a national park.

Elizabeth, in fact, had gotten so nervous about going ahead with the hike that we had planned for the next day that she considered cancelling it. Nor was she keen anymore about letting Jane and me hike upstream along the Brown River to western edge of the national park the day after that. Jane wanted to get a feel for the country; I wanted to scout out the river for paddling potential. Having both been boat, airplane and basecamp-bound for so many days, we were also desperate for a good long hike.

As it turned out, we did get to hike the next day and Jane and I got our chance to see the Brown. The river doesn't flow gently into

Wager Bay as I had expected after I had seen it from the air. Like most tundra streams of this size, its final plunge into seawater is violent, impressive enough, in fact, that it attracted the Canadian government's hydroelectric power hunters several years ago. At first sight, I was skeptical about the prospects of paddling this river some day. But up on top of a high point of land farther on into our hike, Jane and I could see it flowing more gently upstream, winding its way through the tundra in much the same way that parts of the Back River do.

Looking through my binoculars, I assured myself that the river could be paddled. Just how, however, was the question. If Parks Canada was going to insist, as Elizabeth Seale was contemplating at the time, that future adventurers be accompanied by Inuit guides, then I was stuck. The Thule may have been quintessential kayakers, but the modern Inuit aren't known for their paddling skills. Most of them would rather use a motorized boat, quad or snowmobile to get around.

And then I thought of Jack Anawak. What better way to pay homage to his great grandfather – Iqungajuq – than by kayaking into the country that his ancestors settled hundreds of years ago. I would, I decided, call him when the timing was right. Some day, I would be back.

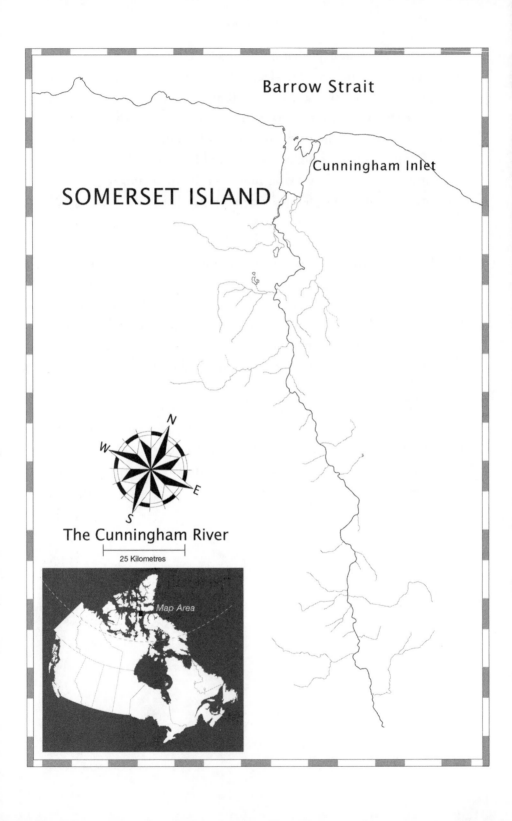

Barrow Strait

Cunningham Inlet

SOMERSET ISLAND

The Cunningham River

25 Kilometres

Map Area

Cunningham River
Sea Canaries of the High Arctic

W e were in our wet suits sitting on the shores of Cunningham Inlet at the north end of Somerset Island in the High Arctic archipelago of northern Nunavut waiting patiently for the whales to come in from Barrow Strait. The grey clouds were touching the hilltops, and it seemed like the stormy weather that was being called for during the early morning radio report was heading our way. It was no more than 8 C. I was cold and clammy wrapped in neoprene. And after a couple of days of waiting, not at all that optimistic about seeing one beluga whale let alone 2,000 that sometimes come into this High Arctic river estuary in July and August. Just as I was about to take refuge in the tiny hut behind us, Canadian scientist Tom Smith patted me on the shoulder and pointed to a line of white heading our way. "Here they come," said his partner Tony Martin, a vertebrate ecologist with the British Antarctic Survey. "It looks like there may be 200 or 300 of them out there."

The Cunningham River spills crystal clear out of the rugged hills of northern Somerset before branching out onto a broad coastal tidal flat. It is stark, rocky country largely devoid of vegetation save for the occasional patch of moss, ground willow and purple saxifrage on which the Peary caribou feed through the early summer months. Anchored on both sides by partially snow-covered bluffs, the blue-green waters of the inlet are strikingly beautiful in a way that is quintessentially Arctic. The whales come in here to rub off their old skin on the gravelly river bottom and to maybe give their newborn calves a chance to build up their fat reserves in the warmish waters. Smith suspects that they may be playing, or getting to know each other as well. Neither he nor anyone else knows for sure. But after more than 30 years of working in the polar world, Smith knows there is no better place to observe such large numbers of whales interacting.

We were there to catch a whale. Smith's plan was to attach a satellite transmitter to one so that he and Martin could track it for six to eight months. Up until the mid-1990s, scientists knew more about Mars than they did about the movement of belugas, but the satellite technology that Smith and Martin have adapted to function underwater on whales and other marine mammals has changed all that.

Belugas, long considered shallow-water mammals, routinely venture vast distances into the deep waters found below the heavy ice pack hundreds of miles north of the Arctic mainland. Those that gather along the north coast of Alaska in the early summer months, for example, move far offshore into the multi-year ice pack in August. No one knows for certain, but presumably these mysterious frigid zones are hotspots for fish and other creatures that the belugas feed on. If they are, then it suggests that the Arctic marine environment is much more complex and productive than scientists have assumed.

No one spoke, as this pod slowly moved in. Out in front, and swimming along the perimeters were the big males, some of them spyhopping — holding their heads and shoulders out of the water — to look for signs of an Inuit hunting party, or a polar bear lurking on shore. In the middle of the inlet were several nursing females with calves that were getting a helpful tow in their wake. "Hear that?" said Tom as we listened to the whales whistle, scream, and blow "raspberries," sounding much like a playground of romping children. "That's why the whalers called them sea canaries. They knew the belugas were around when the sounds they made reverberated through the hull of the ship. Some nights, when the winds are calm, it gets so loud around here, you can't sleep."

Smith was not surprised to see a squarish head rise up from the water once he fired up the engine on the Zodiac. This was evidently the kind of look-see the spyhoppers do before they dive back down to let the rest know that they might be in danger. He, however, wasn't dismayed when they all started racing back to sea. "All we need is to intercept one," he said as we motored out towards the middle of the inlet.

Belugas are not the sleekest of sea mammals. Their heads are big and square, and their mid-sections are more comparable to a barrel-chested weightlifter. After a particularly good feed, a fold of fat that protrudes from their sides can slow them. In some places like Cook Inlet, Alaska, this makes them particularly vulnerable to attacks by killer whales.

What belugas lack in speed, they make up with their ability to dive deep. While tracking some of these whales at Cunningham Inlet, coastal Alaska, northern Russia and other Arctic hotspots, scientists have discovered they can dive to depths of more than 1,000 metres, and stay under water for as long as 23 minutes. Smith suspects they may be able to dive even deeper, and for longer. "All that's stopping them, I figure, is the bottom of the ocean."

For a while, it looked as if we were not going to catch one. By the time we got to the middle of the inlet, we could see that most of the whales were already well on their way to the open sea. But then Smith spotted a perfectly still, milk-white form hiding beneath a mass of ice. The chase was on. For a good five minutes, we played a game of hide-and-seek trying to guide the whale into the shallows of the estuary. Suddenly, the whale turned around, lunged and sunk its pin-like teeth into the rubber raft.

"Jump," Smith shouted. "Jump in and put the net around her." Veins were literally bulging out of his forehead. With hoop net in

hand, Martin calmly looked at Smith, then at me, and then down
into the clear water, which was at least eight feet deep. "Fuck you,"
he said politely, as only an Englishman can. "I'm not jumping in
there."

Smith didn't take it personally. But neither was he was going
to be denied. He finally manoeuvered the whale into a shallow spot
and handed me control of the Zodiac while he and Martin plunged
into the icy waters and slipped the hoop net around her head. Half
expecting that one of them might be dragged out to sea or knocked
out by the flap of a fluke, I was more than relieved to see the whale
calm down completely once Smith mounted her as a cowboy would
a horse.

———

The word beluga or belukha is a derivation of *beloye*, the Russian
word for white. The Inuit of Canada and the Inupiat of Alaska call
them *qilalugaq* and *siqsuaq*. Whalers called them white whales; (bow-
heads were black whales). There are 16 different stocks of belugas
in Alaska, Canada, Greenland, Norway and Russia. At least three,
possibly four stocks, migrate in and out of Alaskan, Canadian and
Greenlandic waters. No one is certain because both satellite data
and genetic testing have yet to determine conclusively where all the
animals are year-round and if mixing takes place among stocks.

What is known is that the St. Lawrence, the Ungava stocks and
the belugas of Cook Inlet, Alaska are diminishing. The St.
Lawrence population has been hard hit by pollution; the Ungava
beluga has been virtually wiped out or driven away by overhunting
and boat noise. And Cook Inlet numbers appear to be suffering as
a result of killer whale predation, shallow water strandings and over
hunting. Heavily harvested as well, the West Greenland population
also appears to be threatened. The Eastern High Arctic population,
however, which includes the whales of Cunningham Inlet, appears
to be stronger.

Belugas may be small compared to the 15-metre-long bowhead,
which they sometimes follow along ice edges, (scientists have seen

the beluga playfully nipping at the flukes of the bigger mammal), and the eight-metre killer whales that prey on them, but they are still a formidable creature when you're sitting on top of one as I did while Smith and Martin prepared to attach the satellite collar to its back. "Keep your knife handy, in case she bolts and you end up getting caught in the rope," Smith advised. "If she does, and you do get wrapped up, all you have to do is stay calm and cut."

The advice was appreciated. A big male can weigh up to two tonnes and measure five metres. Females are generally two-thirds the size. Smith estimated this female we captured was more than three metres long and maybe 550 kilograms. In other words, she was a lot bigger and more powerful than I am.

Not all belugas are created equal. Those in northern Quebec are significantly smaller than those in Cunningham Inlet and the Mackenzie Delta. The Inuit from some Greenland communities believe they can tell the differences between their whales and the ones that swim over from Canada. The Canadian whales, they say, are longer and have an elongated caudal peduncle that allows them to swim through strong currents. Some Inuit swear that they have seen the occasional beluga with a hairy head. Puzzled by these reports, Smith thought he found the answer to the mystery several years ago when he spotted a female in Cunningham Inlet caressing what turned out to be the carcass of her fetus. The hairy-looking head was actually the result of the decomposition that had taken place over a period of weeks. "If they lose the fetus, they'll often substitute something else for it," said Smith. "They'll pick up boards or rocks and hang on to things like that until they more or less overcome their grief, if you want to be put it into more anthropomorphic terms. This can sometimes take a whole summer. One of the weirdest things I saw at Cunningham was a beluga swimming around with the entire front end of a dead caribou, antlers and all."

Female belugas begin reproducing between four and seven years of age; the males become sexually mature between six and nine. Calves, which are a light to dark mottled grey when born, often swim on their mother's back during the first month of life.

They nurse for up to two years. Jack Orr, a Canadian Ministry of Fisheries and Oceans biologist, is one of the few people in the world to have ever witnessed the birth of a beluga in the wild. He was taking turns with his colleagues counting whales swimming along the shores of Cumberland Sound off the coast of Baffin Island. One group in particular caught Orr's eye. He remembers it vividly because he saw a group of six or seven whales not moving and then suddenly they got very excited. Looking through a spotting scope, Orr then saw the whales piling on top of each other before lifting a newborn calf out of the water, giving it a chance to catch its first breaths. The whales, he believes, were all females, members of a distinct nursing group that aids in the birth and nurturing of newborns.

While the bond between females and calves is strong, no one is certain just how long it lasts. But here at Cunningham Inlet, Smith and Martin once tagged a mother and son, which they estimated was five or six years old. He was already longer than she. The pair was tracked travelling together for 900 more kilometres before returning to the Inlet.

⁓

The beluga's earliest known ancestor is the now-extinct *Denbola brachycephala* that lived 10 million years ago in more temperate waters off the coast of the Baja Peninsula. Ice has been the key to the evolution of this particular species. The formation of thick ice in late fall drives these whales into the winter polynyas that are kept open year round by the combined forces of wind, currents, tides and upwellings. The thinning of the ice in late spring lures them back into more shallow waters to feed on cod, herring and squid that swim in the nutrient-rich waters under and along the floe edge.

Since very little light penetrates the Arctic's thick ice, especially during the dark months of winter when there is barely any light at all for five months of the year, belugas use a means of sounding to find prey and detect killer whales. Not only do they listen for the sounds that travel clearly through water, they also emit sounds hoping they return with the information needed to interpret if a predator, a school of cod, or a fisherman's net is nearby.

The beluga is well designed to deal with ice. It has no back fin to get in the way and the fibrous tissue around its dorsal ridge is tough enough to pound through eight centimetres of ice if the whale finds that it needs oxygen. A sudden change in weather can turn these predators into prey for polar bears. So-called *savsaats* are traps that occur when the ice around a small polynya, a lede or breathing hole is too thick or extensive to break through or swim under. Crowded into a hole that becomes progressively smaller and smaller, belugas can live for weeks by smashing away at the edges. But if the scent of their distress attracts polar bears, they're doomed.

This is what happened in the summer of 1999 when dozens of belugas got trapped in two *savsaats* that formed in Canadian Arctic waters. The Inuit of Grise Fiord of southern Ellesmere Island managed to rescue several whales that got trapped in Jones Sound by driving off the bears that swatted at the whales every time they came up for air and by using augers to drill small breathing holes. But whales trapped farther south in Lancaster Sound weren't as fortunate. Malcolm Ramsey, a Canadian polar bear scientist, who was tragically killed in a helicopter crash in 2002, stumbled upon the kill site in Lancaster Sound by chance. The bears, he recalled, had gorged themselves to the point they could hardly walk.

Bears will also prey on belugas that are beached or trapped in a tidal pool. Smith recalled being at Cunningham Inlet one summer when he received a radio call from an outfitter who had spotted a polar bear on top of several beached belugas at nearby Cape Ann. By the time Smith arrived, the bear had fled. But three belugas were dead and one was breathing its last breaths. After dissecting and examining the heads of the carcasses, Smith could see that the bear had initially focused on the blowhole, slashing at it until the whales were having difficulty breathing. Critically disabled as the whales were, the bear ripped into the flesh literally eating the whales alive.

Gruesome as this all evidently was, it was nothing compared to what went on when whalers sailed into Elwin Bay on the northeast corner of Somerset. The killing field there is massive. Tens of thousands of bones lie along a kilometre-long stretch of rock and gravel beach. Here, and at Creswell Bay and other spots on the island, the whalers would drive the big pods of belugas into the shallows of the bay and make as much noise possible to prevent them from going out with the tide. Beached or stranded in the tidal pools, the whales were easy pickings for slaughter. According to James Savelle, a Canadian archeologist who was studying this and other sites while I was on the island, as many as 820 had been killed in one day. Between 1874 and 1898, an estimated 10,000 belugas were slaughtered here. Whalers in general were a tough bunch. But at least one Scottish whaling captain was suitably appalled by the work of his men. "This is terrible work," he wrote. "I have not been in my bed for 17 days and our ship is in great danger of being driven ashore. The Black whaling is bad enough, but this is a thousand times worse."

There are now serious restrictions on the harvest of belugas and other whales in the polar world. Belugas, however, are still hunted by the Inuit of Canada, Greenland, Alaska and Russia. There are an estimated 23,000 whales in the Eastern High Arctic population. The hundred that are taken by hunters each year is far too small to have an impact on the overall health of the population, but Inuit harvests have been a contentious issue in both Canada and Alaska where subsistence hunting for belugas at Cook Inlet has been greatly restricted. Only a few years ago when Fisheries and Oceans scientists were not welcome in the community of Pangnirtung. The Inuit there did not appreciate them suggesting that the harvest of 35 to 50 belugas each year might not be sustainable. Now that the hunt is being co-managed by the Inuit and the Fisheries and Oceans department, the situation has dramatically improved. Satellite tracking and genetic testing has also confirmed that the belugas hunted in Cumberland Sound are distinct from those that are hunted near the Baffin Island communities of Iqaluit and Kimmirut.

Satellite tracking technology hasn't answered the questions that make belugas, narwhal and the bowhead such an Arctic mystery. But some of the information gleaned thus far has left more than a few scientists breathless. Migration, for example, is the key to survival for most living things in the Arctic. A female wolf on the Barren Lands was recently tracked travelling 341 kilometres in just two weeks. The straight line from her den to her farthest point of travel was 103 kilometres. And an inconnu caught and tagged in the Liard River in northern British Columbia in 2001 was recaptured the following year near Inuvik 1,800 kilometres away in the Northwest Territories. Belugas, however, may well be the greatest long distance runners in the Arctic world. Having tagged dozens in the Mackenzie River delta in the western Arctic, Jack Orr and his associates have tracked a group of males heading north into the Beaufort Sea from the delta, west into McClure Strait before stopping to feed in the ice-choked waters of Viscount Melville Sound. The whales hung out there for several weeks before moving north into an environment which is 99 per cent permanent ice pack. Then as winter began to set in, the belugas migrated south towards the coast of Alaska and over to Wrangel Island in Russia. One of Orr's whales traveled more than 1,900 kilometres in just one month.

Being a creature that has adapted to the Arctic marine environment, belugas are particularly vulnerable to changes in ice patterns and movements that could disrupt or alter the timing of prey distribution. In light of predictions that much of the Arctic sea ice will disappear as the climate continues to change, scientists from across the circumpolar world are planning to catch 100 belugas each year for three years starting in 2007, the International Polar Year. The belugas in the waters of Greenland, Svalbard, Canada, Alaska and Russia will be equipped with satellite transmitters that will send out information for up to a year.

It was towards the end of my stay at Cunningham Inlet when Smith and I took a hike up the Cunningham River. It is rare, but not unusual for belugas to travel long distances upstream of an estuary.

Back in 1982, several belugas were spotted at Tanana, 1,200 kilometres upstream from the coast on the Yukon River in Alaska.
Another was seen near Rampart, a community located 80 kilometres
farther away. The Cunningham, however, is too shallow and fast for
any of these mammals to swim too far inland. And so our attention
shifted to the muskoxen, the caribou and other wildlife in the area.

During my time at Cunningham Inlet, I had been wondering
whether this river might be able to float a kayak. But by the time we
got to a high point of land to see what lay ahead and behind us, I
wasn't altogether hopeful about the prospects of a future kayak or
canoe trip. By the looks of what appeared to be the remains of a raft
we had found along the way, it seemed that someone had already
tried unsuccessfully to do what I had hoped to do some day, albeit
in a different way.

On the way back down, we stopped to have a closer look at
what appeared to be another pod of whales heading toward the estuary. Spying them through his binoculars, Smith estimated that there
were maybe two or three hundred out there. "It truly is an amazing
place," he said. "But you know, try as I did to get someone in
government interested in setting this aside as a marine reserve or
protected area, I couldn't get anyone interested. It's as if this place
didn't exist. Or maybe a place like this can't exist in the mind of a
bureaucrat."

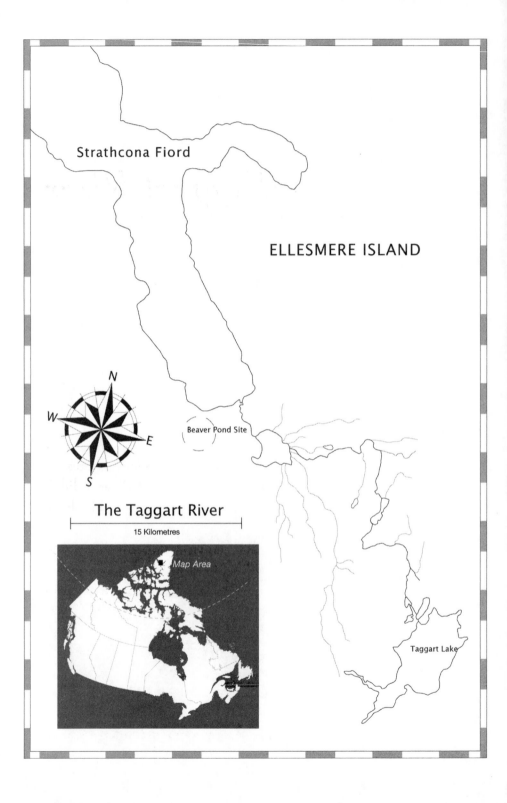

Taggart River
Ancestral Bears, Three-Toed Horses, Miniature Beavers

I had been wide awake although unaware that a white wolf had been sniffing around my tent that morning, but paleontologist Dick Harington and his good friend John Tener had seen it minutes before I joined them for breakfast. After a quick meal of runny eggs and gritty camp coffee, the only signs I could find were its tracks loping across the sandy shores of Strathcona Fiord toward the mouth of the Taggart River. I didn't know it then, but I would have one more encounter with this phantom of the High Arctic, only under different circumstances.

It was early July on Ellesmere Island, in the extreme northeast corner of Canada, and it seemed as though the coming summer had stalled somewhere south of Lancaster Sound. It was no more than 5 C. The surrounding mountainsides were dusted with a fresh coat of white powder and a brisk northeast wind had swept squalls of snow and freezing rain toward the Prince of Wales Ice Cap. The Taggart, big and silty, was racing madly out of the southern-exposed mountain lakes, but failing to make much of a dent in the thick sea ice that was jammed into the river's mouth.

Ellesmere is home to a small community of Inuit at Grise Fiord in the south and the world's most northerly military post at

Alert near the Black Cliffs on the island's northern tip. In between the highest mountains east of the Rockies, the land mostly covered with giant ice caps, big valley glaciers and a number of tiny oases like this one, which explode with life during the 24 hours of summer light. But we were not experiencing any respite on this lonely spot on the middle of the island. Harington and John had been at Strathcona Fiord 10 days before I arrived on the supply plane from Resolute Bay. On only four of those days had the weather been warm enough for them to climb 300 metres up the lifeless dirt and gravel hill behind their camp where they were searching for teeth, bones, plant fragments and other organic remains that might have been swept into an ancient beaver dam. Looking out onto the frozen fiord, searching for the yellow, tell-tale sign of a polar bear that might be heading our way, I found it difficult to imagine there had been a forest on this treeless tundra three million years ago. It was even harder to believe that the three-toed horses, miniature beavers and the primitive black bears that Harington and his associates had already unearthed, once thrived here.

"It's a unique place," Harington said as we bundled up in our parkas, preparing for a stiff climb to the beaver pond site. According to him, no other site of this age, with this diversity of fauna, had ever been found this far north. "The only comparable boreal forest habitat I know of today is in northeast Siberia where larch, rather than spruce, are dominant," said Harington. "We even have signs that forest fires may have passed through here."

The notion of a tropical or more temperate Arctic dates to 1580 when geographer William Bourne suggested that the long summer days in the northern latitudes could create enough energy to melt the ice around the North Pole and allow ships to pass through. Gerhard Kramer (Gerhardus Mercator), the leading cartographer of the time, was also convinced of the existence of an open polar sea. One of his most famous maps depicted a polar maelstrom swirling around a mountain of rock in the middle of four islands inhabited by Pygmies. Kramer's Pygmies might have been inspired by a popular Scandinavian legend, but the tales are similar to Inuit stories of little people living on the tundra and sea ice. A northern passage can be clearly identified cutting through these islands on his map.

So ingrained was the idea of a warm polar world that many 19th- and early 20th-century writers, including Mary Shelley (*Frankenstein*), Edgar Allan Poe (*A Narrative of Arthur Gordon Pym of Nantucket*) and Jules Verne (*Journey to the Centre of the Earth*) exploited the theme in their writings. In *Frankenstein,* an Arctic expedition figures prominently in the story, and narrator Robert Walton, notes in a letter to his sister that "There — for with your leave my sister, I will put my trust in preceding navigators — there snow and frost are banished; and sailing over a calm sea, we may be wafted to a land surpassing in wonders and in beauty every region hitherto discovered on the habitable globe."

More than one explorer — Constantine Phipps (1773), David Buchan (1818), William Penny (1850-51), Elisha Kent Kane (1853-55) and Isaac Hayes (1860-61) — headed off on Arctic adventures believing in an open polar sea. Both Penny and Hayes returned, convinced they had found the mythical body of water. Although, they had merely encountered polynyas — open bodies of water that are surrounded by ice and rarely freeze over because of wind, currents, upwellings and tidal flows.

Only after nearly 400 years of failure did the dream of an open polar sea, or semi-tropical Arctic, finally fade. Still, the petrified remains of trees found on Ellesmere, Banks and other islands of the North remained a puzzle. Since the fossil fragments were scant or poorly preserved, no one could explain how they had arrived there. These fossils were considered little more than curiousities until the 1970s when American scientist Mary Dawson and her colleagues unearthed the remains of flying lemurs, prehistoric crocodiles and other semi-tropical and temperate dwelling animals that had lived at Strathcona Fiord 40 million to 50 million years ago. This was the beginning of the reign of mammals that followed the extinction of dinosaurs 65 million years ago. It was also when the crustal plates that joined North America and Europe were beginning to separate and ending the migration of animals along the Thulean land bridge.

Paleontologists were astounded by the exotic findings. But they could only imagine what the landscape had looked like. That changed in the summer of 1985 when helicopter pilot Paul Tudge, on assignment with the Geological Survey of Canada, caught sight of some unusual objects sticking out of the ground on Axel Heiberg, the uninhabited island immediately west of Ellesmere. After circling and then landing for a closer look, he found the entire area littered with wood and metre-wide tree stumps. When scientists James Basinger and Jane Francis arrived the next year, they realized they had found the Holy Grail of High Arctic paleobotany. It took Basinger and his colleagues nearly 12 years of digging before the site stopped yielding its treasures. By 2000, he had assembled a picture of a redwood swamp filled with royal ferns and swamp cypress and an upland environment in which pine, spruce and walnut trees grew. The closest thing today would be found in the Carolinian forests of Georgia.

While Basinger was excavating, other smaller pieces of the High Arctic puzzle trickled in. Not far from the fossil forest site, Jaelyn Eberle and John Storer discovered the remains of *Brontotheriidae*, a rhinoceros-like animal that lived 38 million to 45 million years ago. They also found the remains of an alligator and three families of tortoises. Then Mary Dawson returned to Strathcona Fiord to unearth some rodents that had likely crossed the Thulean land bridge 50 million years ago from Eurasia.

The beaver pond was first discovered in 1961 when geologist John Fyles flew to Ellesmere Island to conduct research for the Geological Survey of Canada. He was sitting on the banks of the Taggart River scanning the hillsides with his binoculars when he stopped to focus on a patch of dark brown earth. Fyles knew that he had come upon something special the moment he saw branches. But it would be some time before he got a chance to establish the true significance of the specimens that he brought back to Ottawa.

No one has yet been able explain why it was so warm 45 million years ago and why it continued to be so hot right up to the time the miniature beavers — about two-thirds the size of modern beavers — lived at Stratchona Fiord four million years ago. But the fossil evidence suggested a cooling — climates still far warmer than today — from the age of dinosaurs that ended 65 million years ago to the time of the hot spike that started four million years ago. Harington says that several lines of evidence suggest that the beaver pond environment was similar to what is found at Dawson City in the Yukon today, where summer temperatures can rise to 28 C.

Forty years ago, it would have been difficult, if not impossible, to reconstruct this world of beavers as Harington has done. But now that we understand the depths at which various freshwater diatoms and other algae thrive, collaborators at the University of Toronto were able to use the remains of 16 ancient species that Harington had found on the beaver pond site to determine that the pond was no more than three-metres deep. And knowing now the climatic limits in which beetles and other insects can survive, paleontologists Scott Elias and John Matthews were also able tell from those which Harington found at Strathcona Fiord that it was at least 10 degrees warmer than presently during summer and 15 degrees warmer during winter.

Harington believes that the ancient boreal forest and grass meadows near this pond would have been suitable habitat for the three-toed horses and the fanged, antlerless miniature deerlets that he has identified. Not only were beavers building dams along the pristine boreal streams four million years ago, they were also probably on the lookout for ancestral black bears, Eurasian badgers and several weasel-like carnivores whose remains have been excavated from the site. So fine is the preservation of some fossils that Harington has been able to determine what the tundra bunnies (*Hypolagus*) in his collection ate.

The current look for the Arctic researcher is youth, ballcaps and beards, so Harington and Tener were a rare breed. Harington was pushing 70, Tener was approaching 80 — but neither seemed to be slowing down. They got up every morning at 5:30 a.m. to shave and wash. Breakfast was eaten and dishes put away well before their daily 7 a.m. radio report to Polar Shelf headquarters at Resolute Bay. Neither dared to venture into the field looking as if they had just gotten out of bed.

Lean and slight, Tener had the reserved but gracious nature of an academic who had been schooled at the University of British Columbia and Oxford. After a career in wildlife science, he became assistant deputy minister of the federal Environment Department. At six-feet-four-inches tall and 225 pounds, Harington was a much more imposing figure. As the son of a Royal Canadian Mounted Police officer who once led a murder investigation into the Headless Valley of the Nahanni River, he was well-versed in Arctic lore. So when the Defence Research Board offered him the opportunity to work at Lake Hazen on Ellesmere Island in 1957, he seized it. Most graduate students would have gone mad or beat each other senseless had they been forced to endure an entire year in a small hut near the northern tip of the world with three other men. But Harington was so engrossed by the challenge he never let the 24-hour days of darkness and 121 days of -40 C temperatures get him down. Nor did he mind when their radio failed shortly after their arrival, depriving them of news from the outside world. Visitors were few during this year-long residency conducting meteorological research. One of them was Tener, a muskox specialist for Canadian Wildlife Service.

Long retired, Tener relished this opportunity to return to the world where he started his career. He said as much as we headed up the hillside. "Every day, I stop here to pat this old muskox skull for good luck," he said, bending down to touch a weathered bone that was covered with orange and black lichen. "It's amazing what you see up here. I once saw an Arctic hare suckling her young no more than three feet from where I am standing now. She didn't budge an inch. We haven't had a polar bear come into camp, at least not yet, but we have had muskoxen and caribou, and of course, that wolf which passes through on a fairly regular basis."

Age, I discovered with some humility, was clearly no impediment to Tener's ability to climb. Neither did it seem to slow down Harington who had opted to take the shorter, but much steeper route, up the slope. In hindsight, I shouldn't have been surprised when we found Harington already sorting through a pail of peat by the time we arrived. This, after all, was the same man who took a three-day walk to the coast without a stove or tent in -40 C temperature while he was on the island more than 40 years ago.

———

Harington was still working in the Arctic in 1961 when Fyles first discovered the beaver pond site. But by this time, he had started to follow a different path than the one he had started on at Lake Hazen. As a scientist with the Canadian Wildlife Service during the early 1960s, he had studied the ecology and behaviour of polar bears while living and travelling with the Inuit for a number of months. But as fascinating as the work was — a tranquilized bear once woke up in the middle of a rectal examination — he found he had little stomach for shooting the great white animals, then considered an accepted part of research protocol. And the truth of the matter was that his interest in modern-day mammals had been overtaken by a fascination with the origins of Arctic fauna. In 1965, when legendary scientist Frank Banfield asked Harington if he would like to study ice age animals at the National Museum of Canada in Ottawa, he jumped at the opportunity.

At the museum, Harington found the collection overflowing with dinosaur fossils while the cabinets containing ice age mammal bones were not quite full. Determined to correct this, he pored through every back issue of *Canadian Geographic* — including its forerunner *Canadian Geographical Journal* — and many other sources to find somewhere in Canada where he might start building the collection. An article by geologist Hugh Bostock helped him decide on the northern Yukon.

Harington's travels with the Inuit served him well enough in getting to know the Aboriginal Peoples of the North so intimately that they felt comfortable telling him stories about the country. During the 1960s, the Gwich'in First Nation of Old Crow was still living a traditional life on the land, hunting and fishing for food and communicating with the outside world largely through the fur trade. Harington was intrigued by the story of an enormous creature that had risen from the depths of a big lake in the northern Yukon and then walked up the Whitestone River where it died along the banks. Harington figured this was as good a place as any to see whether the myth had a core of truth to it.

Harington's upstream slog up Whitestone River proved to be a bust. He and Peter Lord, a resident of Old Crow, had travelled by boat to an abandoned Gwich'in camp. They had hauled the heavily loaded craft over sandbars and shallow passageways until they were exhausted. There weren't any signs of ancient mammals, nor were there any farther upstream toward the Richardson Mountains. In the end, they turned back before winter had a chance to close in.

On the return, Harington saw something on the riverbank that they had missed on their way upstream. He was securing the boat when Lord called for him. On his way along the riverbank, Harington nearly tripped over a giant jawbone imbedded in the sand. Lord was pointing to a similar fossil submerged in the clear water. Harington could barely contain his emotions when they went on to find an enormous tusk and other bones of a woolly mammoth. That, he realized, was probably how the Gwich'in legend got its start. Some hunters must have come across these fossils or some similar specimens along the river.

The Whitestone mammoth was only a small part of the mother-lode of ice age treasures that Harington, Lord and other assistants unearthed in the years that followed. Their collection eventually contained everything from tiny shrews and lemmings to ferocious scimitar cats and sloths the size of an ox. One of Harington's favourite finds — a giant beaver the size of a black bear with incisors as long as knife blades — got him thinking about what Fyles had found at Strathcona Fiord. By this time, the marks on the branches that he had brought back to Ottawa were clearly identified as the tooth marks of a beaver. "When I first heard of John Fyles' discovery through Bob Christie of the Geological Survey, I had assumed that it might have been *Castoroides*, the giant beaver," said Harington. "But I didn't think much more of it at the time because I had assumed that there were no bones there to be found. So I left it at that."

Not much more was made of the beaver pond site until 1988 when Fyles returned as a semi-retired chief geologist of the Geological Survey of Canada. With him was paleobotanist Jane Francis who discovered the partial skeleton of a beaver. The animal turned out not to be *Castoroides*, the giant beaver, but *Dipoides*, a beaver two-thirds the size of its modern-day relative. A second fossil turned out to be the heel bone of an *Ursus abtrusus*, an ancestor of the modern black bear. "John Fyles really has to be given credit," Harington emphasized. "He not only found the site, he discovered the first bones as well. And it was through his co-operation that we went up to Strathcona Fiord to take a closer look."

In 1992, Harington and Tener finally got the chance to fly up to Ellesmere Island with Fyles and his granddaughter Jennifer Adams. The plan was for Fyles and Adams to conduct geological observations while Harington and Tener concentrated on excavating the beaver pond. Not long into the dig, Harington found a perfect neck vertebra of the primitive bear along with the remains of a "deerlet" that had fangs but no antlers.

Satisfied, they were about to leave when Tener noticed a chunk of peat near the edge of the site. "It was like a concretion," he recalled. "I opened it up carefully, which was probably the smartest thing I'd done in years. To my surprise, it came apart like a peach, and when I looked inside, I realized that I had come across something really important, so I immediately passed it over to Dick."

"I didn't see what it was at first," said Harington. "Only when I got it into the light could I see the vertebrae, ribs and skull parts of what turned out to be a fish, probably a new genus and species of perch. It was really quite exquisite."

Since that summer, Harington and Tener returned to the site six times with various assistants: Clayton Kennedy, a senior technician with the museum, Natalia Rybczynski, a graduate student, Kim Aaris-Sorensenm, a vertebrate paleontologist from Copenhagen and David Gill, an experienced Arctic field worker. Harington recorded more than 150 significant finds in 1995, including the teeth and partial skull of a horse. Harington and Richard Hulbert Jr. of Georgia Southern University later identified the horse, a three-toed colt with characteristics similar to the Asiatic hipparionine *Plesiohipparion*. The species would have migrated to North America by way of the Bering land bridge five million years ago.

"You should have been there," Tener said. "Clayton Kennedy was working this area alone while Dick and I were back at the main site scraping away. Then Clayton's trowel hit something, and there was this dead silence. Dick went over to look and I heard him say 'wow.'"

"Clayton had uncovered the outer surface of a very large tooth," explained Harington. "I could see that it was that of a large animal, such as a horse. It's almost most certainly the most northerly find of a hipparionine thus far." The resemblance of this horse to the Asiatic hipparionine may well be the result of convergence, meaning two separate species may have adapted in the same way under similar environmental conditions. If not, then it is the first record of these animals moving from Eurasia into the High Arctic of North America. In either case, the find represents a fascinating study in evolution.

This glimpse into ancient life during this particular period is unprecedented in Arctic America. But what made it especially intriguing to scientists is the fact that the Arctic world was as warm as some climatologists believe the High Arctic will be some time within the next 50 years. That's why Harington believes this find is of value to both paleontologists and natural historians, but also to climatologists trying to determine what the Arctic world will look like as the Earth continues to heat up.

"You need only to look at this stark landscape all around us to realize what a different place this must have been four million years ago, when the beavers and other animals were here," said Harington.

Why the Arctic was warmer then than today is not entirely clear. Elevated carbon dioxide levels, resulting from undersea methane eruptions, volcanic activity or increased circulation of the oceans could be responsible. What is known is that by the beginning of the last ice age two million years ago, the environment near the beaver pond was gradually cooling even though the circulation of warm ocean currents in the North was apparently strong. "It is easy to imagine the massive snout of the glacier that left these high mounds of rubble moraine just before it melted back some 8,000 years ago," said Harington as he led me to view the fiord from the top of the plateau. Clearly marked, raised beaches on its margins, he explained, tell of the rapid rise of land during the last few thousand years. "It is remarkable, when you consider it," he said, "how catastrophic the changes were when the glaciers enveloped this part of the world."

Harington's project had not been without its setbacks and slow periods. The weather had also produced its share of drama. One of the most memorable incidents was on the night of July 12, 1994. Camped well above the highest storm beach berm, all four people in the research party had gone to sleep in their tents, assuming that the 60-knot winds that had held them captive in camp all day would eventually abate.

"Around midnight though, we could hear the ice in the fiord cracking and scraping," recalled Tener. "I thought nothing of it at first. Then there was this crashing of pails and smashing of boxes and I knew that all was not well outside. It was quite the sight when we got out to look. The cook tent was being crushed by the weight of all the ice being driven up the shore. We managed to salvage some food and the stove, and were lucky to have dug out some blocks of chocolate for breakfast. That was an awful summer. It rained or snowed almost every day, and we got little done."

On my trip with the two scientists, Harington made the 45-minute hike up the hillside twice and returned with a barrel of peat so that we could work out of the wind, snow and rain at the base-camp tent. But while inside, wearing down-filled winter coats, we

still struggled to keep warm. In the end, all we had to show was a
handful of exquisitely preserved snails, some galls from fairly large
larch trees and more branches that had been chewed by beavers.
Harington was expecting that this might be his last year at
Strathcona. But as time went by that summer, he was coming to the
conclusion that he might have to return to the site one more time.

On the morning I was to depart, I was once again wide awake when
the white wolf came into camp. I had no hint that it was there until
I stepped out of my tent and found one of my hiking boots missing.
I thought neither Harington nor John was the type to play practical
jokes — a point they confirmed when I asked them about the boot
at breakfast. But I still hadn't got it. It wasn't until I took one last
walk toward the Taggart River that I finally realized that it was the
wolf that had visited my tent that first morning. There, in the sand,
were the fresh tracks of the animal leading away from camp. I could
see where it had stopped to sniff the remains of a long-dead, long-
tailed jaeger — and where it had stopped to mark its territory.
There, I found my boot lying at the mouth of the great river. But I
did not see the white phantom. So, instead, I looked, as John Fyles
might have done 40 years ago, at that brown spot on the plateau. I
still found it difficult to imagine there had been a forest there four
million years ago. I did find myself able, however, to consider the
possibility of the mysterious animals that once inhabited this place
— the three-toed horses, miniature beavers and primitive black
bears that had also disappeared from sight.

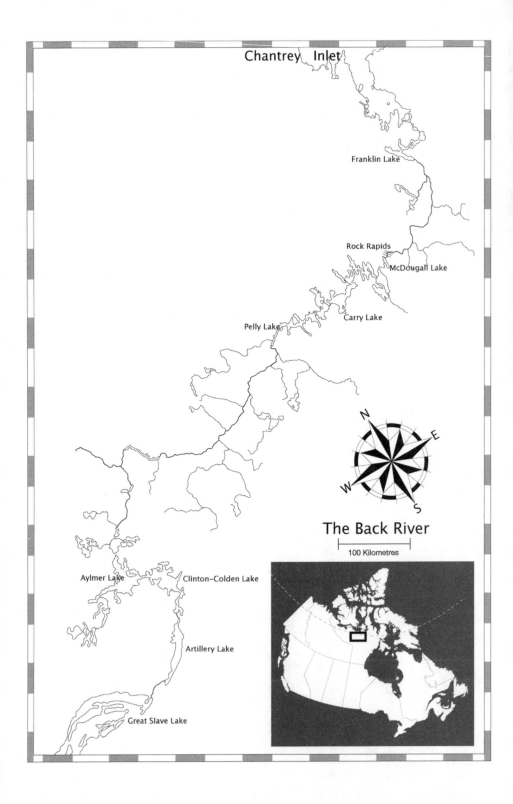

Back River

Thlew-ee-cho-desseth — The Great Fish River

Far above the treeline northeast of Great Slave Lake, there's an insignificant height of land that represents a critical divide between the waters that flow southwest into the Mackenzie River drainage and those that flow directly north into the Arctic Ocean. On August 29, 1833, British explorer George Back climbed this hill that overlooks Sussex and Aylmer lakes hoping to spot some caribou that seemed to him to be so "exceedingly numerous," they left several miles of tracks on the treeless tundra. Up on top, Back failed to detect a single animal. He was, however, delighted to see a line of whitewater trailing off to the northeast. When his Dene guides returned the next day to report that the river was big enough to carry a fully loaded canoe, Back pulled out a bottle of grog to celebrate. After months of hard-slogging and paddling from New York and Montreal, and various northwest points, the 37-year-old naval officer had finally found the fabled Thlew-ee-choh-desseth, the Great Fish River, he had been looking for.

Back wintered in the sheltered forest along Great Slave Lake before returning to this spot the next summer. He and a crew of 10 men then floated 853 kilometres down the river unaware that they would face 83 rapids and waterfalls along the way. Not only did they successfully steer through most of the whitewater, they also made it back

upstream to their camp at Great Slave before their second winter in the
Canadian North had a chance to set in. It was, and will likely forever be,
the greatest overland boating expedition in North American history.

I had long had the idea of following in the path of Back after
reading his account of the trip. I was struck by the scenes and
sketches that he had described and drawn and I was equally
impressed with the manner in which he had confronted the many
challenges on the long journey. Back was not only an exceptional
explorer, he was a talented artist who was able to use his skills to
describe the wilderness experience in a way that was far more imag-
inative than the institutional nature of most Arctic travel literature
of his time. He was also one of the first Arctic explorers to equate
wilderness travel with pleasure.

The Back, however, is among the most inaccessible rivers in
mainland Canada. Getting there requires an expensive bush plane
flight from Yellowknife, or a long, arduous upstream paddle from
the shores of Great Slave Lake. The return trip requires an even
more costly flight from Chantrey Inlet where the Back River ends,
or alternatively, a perilous trip across the Arctic Ocean to the Inuit
community of Gjoa Haven or Ursuqtuq. The fact that the Back is
also one of the longest and most isolated rivers in North America
didn't help my cause either. Not only does it demand advanced paddling skills, it also requires from those who dare to run it, the
strength and resolve to line and portage long distances in conditions that may, at times, be miserably cold or deathly hot and buggy.

Finding prospective partners with the money, skills and time to
join me in such an undertaking proved to be impossible until the editors at *Equinox* magazine, sensing perhaps the imminent sale and
demise of the publication, agreed to underwrite part of the expedition. It was, I think, a way of rewarding two of their veteran field cor-
respondents for long service. Brian Milne, a friend and celebrated
wilderness photographer, was my partner on this journey. Although
both he and I had worked well together on a number of stories, we
recognized that the psychological and physical strains associated with
a summer-long trip like this one might prove to be the undoing of

one or both of us. So we decided to bring some company. Tom Carpenter and Andrew Nikiforuk, both accomplished writers and editors as well as friends of ours, were to join us on the first leg of the trip from the shores of Great Slave to Muskox Lake, which was a-day-or-two's paddle downstream from the Back River's headwaters. They would go home on the supply plane that was to bring in my friend Miriam Wideman and her friend Jane Bishop, a Yellowknife doctor. The women would then complete the trip with Brian and me.

Ultimately, we were unsuccessful at trying to keep pace with the 1833 leg of Back's expedition. We also failed to make it anywhere near the Arctic coast, which is what we had hoped to do on the second half of the trip. Weather, rapids, waterfalls, illness, injury and long portages played a part in the failure. So did my plan of attack. I had had a run of good luck paddling northern rivers. It ended on this trip.

George Back was on leave from the British navy and living in Italy during the autumn of 1831 when he got word that fellow explorer John Ross and a crew of men had been missing in the Arctic for nearly three years. Judging from his letters and journals, Back seemed to be content with the sensual life in Europe. He was spending most of his time painting, going to the theatre, attending balls and dinners and romancing a married woman whom he referred to only as "Lady XXXX". He even managed to find time for adventure in his busy social schedule. Shortly after Mount Vesuvius erupted, Back climbed to the top of the simmering peak and descended into the crater with "thoughts of being blown into little atoms by an eruption." Inside the hot volcano, Back was struck by the contrast between him sitting there on a smouldering cloak and the "frost-biting blasts" he had so often endured on two overland Arctic expeditions with John Franklin in 1819-22 and 1825-27.[1]

[1.] See Peter Steele's *The Man Who Mapped the Arctic,* Raincoast Books, 2003 for more on Back's life in Europe.

Evidently, the prospect of returning to the polar world was too compelling for him to stay put in Europe. Recognizing a unique opportunity for adventure and future advancement in the navy, Back went home to England with a plan to find Ross and his crew. However, he had no intention of sailing another ship into harm's way. Instead, he borrowed an idea from fellow explorer John Richardson by volunteering to lead an overland canoe trip across the unmapped Barren Lands of the New World to the region where Ross and his crew were thought to be.

William McTavish, a veteran Hudson's Bay Company factor, gave Back little chance shortly after the naval officer arrived in Montreal to prepare for his trip west. "You'll hear what a fine story they'll make out of this bungle," he wrote to his family back home in Scotland. "They will, you may be sure, take none of the blame themselves. They will return next summer and like all other Expeditions, will do little and speak a great deal."

McTavish may have been resentful about being ordered to help Back in whatever way he could. Company men like him were not as enamoured about the British navy's search for a northwest passage through the Arctic as the public was back in England. The navy's track record was also not an enviable one. In addition to Ross's disappearance, Back's first overland expedition with Franklin in 1819-22 had been a disaster. Eleven of the 20 men had died on the return trip up the Hood, Burnside and Coppermine rivers to Franklin's base camp at Fort Enterprise. Many of those who perished starved to death. One was murdered, another executed and two were likely cannibalized. Many more would have died as well if Back hadn't snowshoed and skied 1,930 kilometres for help. Notwithstanding that heroic effort, Back was never able to win over his many critics. Noted Thomas Simpson, cousin of the governor of the Hudson's Bay Company, Back appeared to be "deficient in that commanding manner with people, so necessary on this savage country."

Back may have been arrogant, prickly and guilty of a number of other personality deficiencies, but unlike most of his contemporaries, he connected with the aboriginals in ways that the stiff-upper-lip officers of a higher, more rigid social class either could or would not contemplate. As a prisoner of war for five years in France, Back learned to speak perfect French. On both of his Arctic trips, he used that skill to join the voyageurs in song around the campfire. (Back, in fact, published a compendium of voyageur songs in 1823.) He appeared to enjoy their company, and they, in turn, must have appreciated his genuine interest in spending time "tippling" with them after a day of hard paddling.

Personality issues aside, McTavish and Simpson may have had another reason to doubt Back's ability to successfully complete the journey. For all they or anyone else at the time knew, the Thlew-ee-choh-desseth may not have existed. And even if it had, as some Yellowknives had told Back and Richardson on that first overland trip with Franklin, there was no guarantee that it flowed into the Arctic Ocean.

Out of Montreal, Back made his way west towards Norway and Cumberland House and the confluence of the Clearwater and Athabasca Rivers. Back's crew included two Canadians, a couple of Métis, three Iroquois, naval surgeon/naturalist Richard King and Alexander McLeod, a Hudson's Bay Company employee whom he met at Pine Portage. Although ill and heading east with a boatload of furs, McLeod readily agreed to come on the journey when Back presented him a letter from the governor of the company instructing him to assist Back in whatever way he could. All McLeod asked was that he be allowed to bring his wife, three children and a servant with him.

With 13 people in a boat built for eight or nine, it made for an interesting dynamic. "Babel," wrote Back, "could not have produced a worse confusion of unharmonious sounds than was the conversation they kept up." So overloaded were they by this time that one of the steersmen warned Back the boat would surely sink along the way.

Downstream at Salt River past what is now the Alberta/Northwest Territories border, Back was reassured by a group of that the Thlew-ee-choh-desseth did, in fact, exist. But they also cautioned that it was "narrow, shoal, and dangerous – destitute of wood, even for fuel – full of dangerous cascades and falls – and after a course more torturous than that known to the oldest and most experienced of their tribe, tumbling over its northern barrier in a foaming cataract to the sea."

Undeterred, Back pushed on to Fort Resolution on the southwest shore of Great Slave where it became all too apparent why his guide was so concerned about the weight of the boat. Covering an area of more than 28,000 square kilometres. Great Slave is the second largest lake in Canada and one of the deepest in the world. Exposed as the southern shore is to the prevailing northwest winds and the huge waves they often whip up, boating of any kind can be extremely dangerous.

Looking north towards a shore he could not see, Back evidently recognized the perils and divided the crew into two parties. He had five go with McLeod and King in the big boat they had paddled north in while four others accompanied him in a smaller, lighter canoe. Back then used the faster boat to speed ahead so that he could find a wintering site and a route that might lead them northeast through the forest into the tundra.

It took more than a week to get from one end of the big lake to the other. After hugging the reedy, swampy southern shoreline, Back and his crew "paddled with spirit" toward a high point of land – an island as it turned out – that they spotted in the north, praying along the way that a gale would not suddenly come up and drown them. Back was awestruck by the 360-metre cliffs that he found on the other side of the lake. "Never, either in Alp or Apennine, had I seen a picture of such rugged wildness," he wrote; "...the rocks were rent, as if by some violent convulsion, into deep chasms and rugged fissures, inaccessible to the nimblest animal."

At Taltheilei Narrows, a sliver of a channel that led the party into the east arm of Great Slave, the water was no longer "turbid and yellow," but a "pellucid green." Here, Back and his crew ran into the last of the winter ice that damaged the bark of their small canoe and forced them to stop several times for repairs.

Continuing on this northeastward course, Back passed Mountain, Waldron, Harnston, Hoarforst and finally Ah-hel-dessy, or Lockhart, where he found a wintering spot that suited him. Then, he sent one of the men back to King and McLeod with instructions to build the appropriate winter quarters there. In the meantime, he and his small party headed west to the Hoarfrost, which Maufelly, the Dene guide, assured them would eventually get him to the Thlew-ee-choh-desseth.

———

Maybe it was Back's sketch of Beverley's Falls at the mouth of the Hoarfrost River that convinced me to try and get us into the tundra from there. Or perhaps it was Back's poetic description of the scene that enticed me. "Nothing can be more romantically beautiful than the wild scenery of its course," he wrote. "High rocks beetling over rapids like towers, or rent into the most diversified forms, gay with various coloured mosses, or shaded by overhanging trees – now a tranquil pool. Lying like a sheet of silver – now the dash and foam of cataract."

I should have known better than to trust Back's description. Franklin era explorers like him had a tendency to metaphorically tame Arctic landscapes to fit into the more familiar schemata of the English countryside back home. So invariably "hill and dale" would be used to describe what was, in reality, a frozen pingo surrounded by boot sucking tundra ponds and swamps. As I. S. MacLaren, a friend and wonderful historian, once noted in an essay touching on the subject, picturesque depictions of the Arctic landscape may have been good for the morale of an expedition and for book sales back in England, but it did not prepare others who followed for the environmental realities they would inevitably face.[2]

---

2. See I. S. MacLaren, "The Aesthetic Map of the North 1845-1857" in *Arctic*, Volume 38 No. 2, pp 89-103, as well as "The Aesthetics of Back's Writing and Painting" in *Arctic Artist, The Journal and Paintings of George Back, Midshipman with Franklin 1819-22*, edited by C. Stuart Houston, commentary by I. S. Maclaren, McGill-Queen's, 1994.

It wasn't until the four of us started making our way up the Hoarfrost River that I realized just how big a mistake I had made. The waterfalls we found there were just as picturesque as Back had drawn them in 1833. But upstream, the route was far worse than anything the explorer had hinted at in his journal or drawings. We spent a day without our packs, bushwhacking through thick forest and swamp trying to find the so-called "path" that Back mentions in his narrative. But no matter how hard we tried, there was no way we could figure out how he and his men managed to haul their canoe and gear up through this tangled mess of spongy muskeg, fallen-down trees and continuous stretch of whitewater. In the end, we were left with no other choice but to retreat.

Following our return to Great Slave Lake, we were faced with two alternatives, three if you consider Brian's blunt suggestion that we just pack it in right then and there. We could spend a couple of days paddling over to the Lockhart River, then line and portage our gear upstream as Back had done on his second trip into the tundra in 1834. Or we could follow the longer Chipewyan route (Pike's Portage) that arcs around this dangerous waterway. Having canoed down one side of the Lockhart and hiked up to Parry Falls on the other, I had no intention of subjecting my partners to the misery of bushwhacking through that impossible country. We would go the other way even if it the detour was going to put us a few days behind schedule.

Pike's Portage, however, was hardly a cakewalk by comparison. The 38-kilometre route follows a chain of 10 lakes that string out from the boreal forest around Great Slave Lake through the taiga and eventually into the tundra that begins at Artillery Lake. Explorer Samuel Hearne may have used this route when he and his Dene guide Matonabbee visited the shores of Great Slave Lake on route to the mouth of the Coppermine River in 1770-72. But it was Warburton Pike who got the honour of having his name put on the map of this part of the world. Passing through this landscape in 1890, Pike, who was one of the first people to explore the Arctic purely for sport and adventure, described it as the "prettiest part of the country that I saw in the North."

This was the first time that Brian, Andrew and Tom had canoed so far north and none of them had ever done a portage that was longer than a few hundred metres. So the initial leg to Harry Lake, which is five and a half kilometres long and mostly uphill, was not appreciated. Nor were they happy about holding a canoe over their heads in a way that left them unable to defend themselves from the endless assault of blackflies. The bug dope they liberally sprayed on themselves proved to be useless. Every time they doused themselves with the poison, it came streaming down into their eyes along with the sweat that liberally poured from their heads.

Sensing a mutiny, I used a lunch break to point out that Back and his men too had endured the "torture inflicted by these puny bloodsuckers" and that one of his voyageurs was so "subdued by the pain and fatigue," that came with trying to fight them off, he threw himself "in despair with his face covered to the earth." My partners, however, would not be consoled.

It took us three trips and more than 30 kilometres of walking to complete the first leg of the portage to Harry Lake. By the time we tucked into our sleeping bags in the early hours of the following morning, Andrew was so badly bitten by the blackflies that had crept into the folds and holes of his shirt, I feared he might go into shock. Having worn no underwear beneath his button-up blue jeans, Brian was, if one can imagine, in even worse shape. Bright and early the next morning, it was left to Tom to wryly note that "we made camp precisely where all those bugs we'd seen the day before had been heading."

Humour is much appreciated in wilderness travel, and for Tom, it came easily, even when the best of his lines were delivered at his own expense. We all had a good laugh when he joked that the nice fit between the top of his head and the moulded curve in the seat of the canoe suggested that his skull was the shape of the average buttock. And we chuckled again when he complained that no one had instructed him on the morning etiquette of washing your private parts and brushing your teeth in the icy lake. "Should you, say, first wash your derriere and your willy in one spot and then perhaps move up-sink before you wade in and dip your toothbrush?"

What made us appreciate Tom even more was his willingness to do twice as much as any one of us to complete the long portage to Artillery Lake. Where one heavy pack was more than sufficient, he carried two (one on his back, the other in his arms). An 80-pound canoe wasn't enough for him. He had to shoulder a backpack as well. Thanks to his strength and unflagging energy, we managed to gain some of the ground we lost when we failed to find the route up the Hoarfrost. Unfortunately, for Tom and for us, he paid a price for his heroics.

As if often the case on wilderness adventures, Tom's moment of crisis arose exactly at the halfway point of our trip from Great Slave to Muskox Lake. Four of us were lining our two canoes along the whitewater of the Upper Lockhart River, which connects Artillery to Ptarmigan Lake. We were slipping and sliding on the wet rocks, occasionally falling chest deep into the icy river, and generally feeling pretty sorry for ourselves when Tom stopped and asked me the last question I expected to hear: "I'm peeing blood," he said. "What do you think I should do?"

I could have offered him the antibiotics I had packed for the trip, but my medical kit, along with our coveted bottle of hot sauce, had disappeared a few days earlier when we nearly tipped over in our canoe while eating lunch on some rough water. He obviously needed help. But heading back to experience more of the same physical stress that was likely the cause of his infection was not the answer. Nor was plowing ahead at the speed we were going. So all I could suggest was that we stop at the first suitable site and take a day or two to rest up.

No sooner had we decided to do just that than several flashes of lightning lit up the dark skies ahead of us. It had been deathly hot up until this point and the cold front that appeared to be moving in was obviously going to put an end to the enervating heat in a violent way. Recognizing that we might wind up as crispy casualties in this fast approaching meteorological light show, we hastily paddled to shore to put up a tent. The best site we could find, however, was a soggy one that sloped into the river. Sitting there, crowded uncomfortably against each other, listening to the hail pinging against the walls of the tent, ducking with each ear-splitting crack of thunder and wincing every time we felt lightning strike the ground around us, I was beginning to wonder if we would ever make it to Muskox Lake and the start of the descent of Back River.

———

It was early June in 1834 when George Back's crew shuttered up his log cabins at the mouth of the Lockhart River and started hiking upstream towards the headwaters of the Thlew-ee-choh-desseth that they had found the year before. Back wasn't sorry to leave Fort Reliance as he called the place. All winter long, he and his crew had been surrounded by starving Dene begging for food. Back had little to give them, and it didn't help matters that the scientific instruments they used in their observatory were seen by the Dene as the reason why the caribou didn't come to the lake that winter. It was also bloody cold. Temperatures dipped to as low as –60 C. It got so frigid on the fourth day of February, they couldn't get the inside temperature to rise above –25 C no matter how many logs they put on the fire. Back noted that after washing his head within three feet of this fire, his hair iced up before he had a chance to dry it.

News of John Ross's rescue by whalers the year before meant a slight change of plans for the summer of 1834. Instead of searching for the missing crew, safe as they were in England, Back was now instructed to proceed down the Great Fish River with the purpose of completing the exploration of the northeast coastline of the Arctic. That seemed to suit him fine. It had been a long hard winter and like the true adventurer that he was, he was desperate to get going. "In turning my back on the fort," he wrote, "I felt my breast lightened, and my spirit, as it were, set free again."

The return to the tundra was even more difficult than the grueling journey up the Hoarfrost the year before. Artillery Lake was still frozen that June. So Back's men were forced to haul the big nine-metre boat that McLeod had constructed from wood near the treeline across the ice on sledges. It was exhausting work and many of the men faltered. Back took no pity on any of them. When the carpenter was overcome with snowblindness, Back refused to give him a break. "Indeed, squeamishness is little heeded in travelling such as this," he wrote, "and shirking is quite out of the question. I could not dispense with a single individual. . ,"

The first week out, Back nearly lost boatman Hugh Carron after he slipped on the icy shores of the Upper Lockhart. Then Orkneyman James Spence almost disappeared when he plunged through a patch of thin ice. Had Spence not had his rifle to break his fall that day, he would have almost certainly been swept under the ice by the powerful current.

Snow and freezing rain also chilled the expedition to the bone that June. "Never was seen a more gloomy sky than which ushered in Midsummer's day," Back wrote as only an artist might. "It was of a leaden colour with horizontal streaks of dirty, brick-red clouds — except to the north, where in strong contrast with the cold whiteness on which it rested, were accumulated, in one black mass, the horrors of an hyperborean winter."

Back refused to let up in spite of the weather, knowing as he learned on the 1819-22 expedition that a day or two forfeited could mean death for any one of them on the return trip. There were days when he himself was still up at 2 a.m., dreaming about a hot supper that had not yet, or could not be made, because they had no wood on the tundra to build a suitable fire. Through it all, Back somehow managed to maintain a sense of humour. "As I had not yet dined," he wrote on yet another day that ended in the early hours of the following morning, "gnawings began to intimate the propriety of supplying the organs of digestion with some occupation that might keep them quarelling with themselves. ... 'We can not build a fire' said my servant to me ... 'but I have brought you some pemmican and a little cold water, Sir.'"

It was the end of July when Back and his men finally made it to Muskox Lake, the turnaround point of the previous year's foray.

There, he was reunited with Akaitcho, the great Yellowknife chief, who had helped him rescue the surviving members of Franklin's first overland journey. Among the party travelling with Akaitcho that day, Back spotted Greenstockings, his "old acquaintance and belle," — the woman he and midshipman Robert Hood nearly fought a duel over in 1820. Although 14 years had passed since he last saw her, Back noted that "she was still the beauty of her tribe." He politely asked if he could sketch her portrait. She coyly accepted the offer. Back made no mention of the child that Greenstockings and Hood had produced.

In the hours before Back set off on his great adventure, Akaticho warned him of the evil reputation that the Thlew-ee-choh-desseth had among his people and of the warring Inuit he would meet along the way. There would be no Dene to help him when he returned this time, "They will attack you," Akaticho said. "I am afraid I shall never see you again."

———

Although the Back is not a well-travelled river, it has claimed its share of victims over the years. Joseph Buliard, a Catholic missionary, likely drowned while canoeing the river in 1950 trying to reach the nomadic Inuit at Garry Lake where a mission had been set up by the legendary Oblate order of missionary adventurers. Yellowknifers Peter Bromley and Ian Calder also vanished when they paddled the Back in the summer of 1967. The pair were with Peter's 16-year-old son Bob when they got sucked into one of those big, boat-swallowing holes that typically occur behind a protruding boulder in the middle of a big, fast flowing river. It was cold and snowing at the time and once the canoe swamped, Peter urged his son to swim to shore. When Bob woke up some hours later, paralyzed from the waste down and with his jacket and sweater on in reverse order, there was not a soul to be seen on the tundra. It was all Bob could do to crawl around and set up the tent that he found washed up on shore a couple of days later. Fortunately, the paralysis didn't last. But it was 10 days before legendary Yellowknife pilot Brock "Rocky" Parsons flew in with Bob's mother in nasty, foggy weather that was, at best, marginal for aviation.

Many others, however, have successfully paddled all or parts of the Back since the historic 1834 expedition. James Anderson, chief factor of the Hudson's Bay Company, and a party of 10 did it in two canoes in 1855.[3] Warburton Pike made it to Beechey Lake in 1890 and artist/naturalist Ernest Thompson Seton got as far as Aylmer Lake in 1907. John Tener, the retired scientist working with Dick Harington at Strathcona Fiord canoed from Beechey to Pelly Lake in 1955 while paddling part way up the Baillie River as well. But it wasn't until 1962 that people started paddling the river purely for pleasure. Two groups, one led by John Lentz; the other involving a British naval group, did it that year.[4] Two fine books have been written about the Back: Robert Perkins's *Into the Great Solitude, An Arctic Journey* (Little Brown, 1983) and David Pelly's *Exploration, An Arctic Journey Through History on George Back's River* (Beteguese, 1981).

The journey from the end of Pike's Portage to Muskox Lake had the potential to be a heartbreaker. Once across Artillery Lake, we had to line, paddle and portage several miles up the Lockhart to Ptarmigan and Clinton-Colden lakes. Huge as Clinton-Colden is, we could have been wind-bound for several days trying to get to Thanakoie Narrows, the river channel that connects Clinton-Colden to Aylmer Lake — which is a few hundred metres from where the Back River begins.

But our fear that the thunderstorm that hit us that evening on the Upper Lockhart would bring in strong winds and nasty weather proved to be unfounded. All we got when the hail and heavy rain stopped after a couple of hours were brilliant blue skies, slightly

---

3. William Barr, *Searching for Franklin: the Land Arctic Searching Expedition 1855: James Anderson and James Stewart's Expedition via the Back River*, Hackluyt Society, 1999.
4. *Sport's Illustrated*, August 26, 1963.

cooler temperatures and a dry, stiff tailwind. The weather change proved to be a good omen, at least for awhile. At Clinton-Colden Lake, Tom happily confided that he was no longer afraid to pee or to wash in water that contained fish bigger than his dog. The hordes of blackflies had also thinned considerably and everyone stopped complaining about the lack of wildlife when we spotted dozens of caribou and muskox and listened one night to a loon interrupting, and thoroughly confusing, a pack of wolves that were howling towards each other.

My ability to use a compass also did not fail us when we made the decision to cross the wide expanse of Clinton-Colden instead of spending an extra day or two following its winding shoreline. But even with everything we had going for us, we were unable to cover half the distance that Back and his men typically travelled in the same time. Looking at the maps when we got to Thanakoie Narrows, I was humbled. I estimated that Back and his men had to be going 18 hours a day to achieve the mileage they were making. And try as I often did on that first leg of the trip, I could not imagine what must have been going on in Back's mind when he climbed to a high point of land, as he routinely did at the end of a long day, fatigued and bloodied by bugs, searching for a northern waterway in the unmapped wilderness that he wasn't absolutely sure existed.

We were closing in on the northeast corner of Aylmer Lake two days later when I recognized beyond the distant shore the chain of sand hills that Back had drawn in 1834. A steady rain was falling at the time, but the air was so warm, soft and still that no one bothered to suggest that we pull out and take shelter. Upon our landing, I spotted a long line of caribou tracks, and was reminded of what Back had also seen here. After more than 160 years, the Bathurst herd — 186,000-strong and one of the biggest herds in the world — was still using the same migration route.

More than two weeks earlier, I had had serious doubts about whether we'd make it this far. Now that we were almost where we needed to be at Muskox Lake, I set out to do what Back had done

in August 1833. I climbed the height of land to see if I could spot
that line of whitewater — the sign that we'd arrived at the Thlew-
ee-choh-desseth — trailing off to the northeast. I even carried with
me a flask of 18-year-old Scotch that I had saved for the occasion.

Up on top, however, my heart sank. The line of the river was
there, but from where I was standing, it didn't look like there was
much water in it. In a panic, I ran back down the hill and then
downstream to see if it I might have been mistaken. I wasn't. Then,
after conferring with my partners, I hiked alone for more than six
kilometres to see if I could find the volume we needed to transport
us to Muskox Lake. Again, I had no luck.

Arriving back at camp late that night, Brian, who had still not
forgiven me for losing the hot sauce, seemed to take perverse pleasure
in giving me some more bad news. "That putrid smell?" he said.
"There's a dead animal somewhere around here, but we haven't been
able to find it. I think a grizzly bear must have buried a caribou. It's
going to make for an interesting night when it comes back for supper."

Over our own supper that night, we tried consoling ourselves
with the knowledge that the pilot bringing Miriam and Jane in
would come looking when he didn't find us at Muskox Lake. We
could then get him to fly our gear to a spot upstream that was deep
enough for our canoes. It would cost us, but it was better than the
alternative of portaging our gear for three or four days.

It was not meant to be. By the time the pilot tracked us down
late the next day, he had burned up so much fuel there wasn't enough
left for him to help us out. His only option was to fly directly
back to Yellowknife. So that night, while Tom and Andrew were on
their way home, Brian and I had to explain to Miriam and Jane what
had happened and the kind of portaging they faced in the days
ahead.

We were a sad looking foursome sitting there in the midnight
sun, fending off thick clouds of blackflies and mosquitoes that were
taking full advantage of the stillness of that unusually warm night.
Before we could descend into total despair, however, the silhouettes
of two sets of antlers popped up from behind the hills above us. The

animals looked down at us, then back again as if something was driving them forward. By the time we got up the hill for a closer look, there were tens of thousands of caribou filling up the lakes and valleys for as far as our eyes could see. For nearly three hours, the animals kept coming in, kicking up clouds of dust, clacking and grunting as they do while they are on the move. At one point they were so thickly packed together around us that we had to go running, waving and yelling to stop them from knocking down our tents. "Whatever lies ahead," said Miriam after the last of the caribou had passed from sight early the next morning, "this alone was worth it."

We were consolidating our gear later that day, readying ourselves for the long portage when our attention was diverted by the sound of a plane coming towards us. The drone of a Twin Otter is unique in its ability to excite the heightened senses of tired, weather-beaten paddlers like Brian and me. Initially, I assumed that this one was shuttling passengers between Yellowknife and Gjoa Haven. But then when I saw that it was descending towards us, I realized it was going to land on Aylmer Lake near our camp.

Without needing to say much, Miriam and I grabbed one of the canoes and paddled as hard as we could. Fifteen minutes later, the pilot didn't disappoint us when we asked if he could hopscotch our canoes and us over to Muskox Lake. He was more than happy to lend a hand once he finished unloading all of the gear that he had brought in with a diamond exploration crew. It looked as if our nightmare was over.

———

In the three weeks it took Back and his crew to get to Muskox Lake, they did not enjoy two consecutive days of fair weather. That didn't change after they bade farewell to Akaitcho. By midnight that day, the sky "assumed an aspect so decidedly stormy," wrote Back, "it really looked as if the watery saint, old Swithin, had taken it into his head to leave his favourite abode in England." It stormed for five days straight after that, and by the time they had repaired the boats and packed up, an icy fog had moved in, making it difficult to see the hazards that lay ahead on the river. Sure enough, seconds after they launched the boat, James McKay, the Scottish steersman, nearly capsized the boat after he inadvertently slammed onto a rock shelf in the middle of the river.

Despite all of the bumping, the boat held through the many rapids that lined a good part of the 117 kilometres to Beechey Lake. Back, however, got a scare halfway along when artilleryman William Malley disappeared while portaging a particularly dangerous section of whitewater. When the search party finally found him, several hours later, "tired and rambling" through swamps, Back adhered to voyageur tradition and named the rapids in his honour.

As he closed in on Beechey Lake, the stark, rugged hills of the surrounding tundra reminded Back of the lava at Mount Vesuvius. Here, he counted 1,200 to 1,500 caribou in a space of 12 hours. There were likely thousands more. But most eyes were focused on the river, lined as it was with "long and appalling rapids" and "hemmed in by a wall of ice." At Beechey Lake, McKay and the other steersman finally got an opportunity to relax on the calm water, but not for long. The "loud roar" they heard at the end of the 53-kilometre-long lake signaled that more rapids awaited them. These were particularly daunting. Scouting what lay ahead, both steersmen reported "that it was possible the boat might be got down, but they did not see how she could ever be got up again."

The idea of having to take more time to portage once again clearly worried Back. So did the horseshoe bend in the river that sent the water flowing southeast in the direction of Hudson Bay. Sensing that the season was rapidly closing on him, Back made the decision to run most everything they faced from here on in, even after the river reverted to its northeast course.

Throwing caution to the wind almost proved to be fatal at Hawk Rapids where the river violently squeezes through a narrow canyon lined by steep cliffs. There, Back dismissed the steersman's suggestion that it was too dangerous, reasoning that he was not "equally anxious to proceed as myself." At the outset, the boat was "twirled about in whirlpools." Once the steersman miraculously managed to straighten it out, Back noted there was a "deep and settled gloom in the abyss, the effect of which was heightened by the roar of the rapid, still in deep shade, and by the screaming of three hawks, which frightened from their aerie were hovering high above the middle of the pass, and gazing fixedly upon the intruders of their solitude."

It was July 19th when the expedition reached Pelly Lake, the first of four large bodies of water on this section of the river just below the Arctic Circle. The ice had not yet melted so the crew was forced to use axes to chop channels through many sections. Back also had a difficult time finding a current. When he finally did, he was distressed to discover that it flowed in an easterly direction. The expedition by this point had come "double the distance" the Dene suggested would be required to get them to the Arctic sea. Once again Back wondered whether they were on the right track. Finally, after four long days on Pelly, Upper and Lower Garry and McDougall lakes, Back found the outlet that sent the river flowing once again on a northeast course.

The river, however, did not flow gently into the sea from this point on as Back had hoped. Spilling out of McDougall Lake, Rock Rapids represented the first of a long line of whitewater challenges the paddlers faced in the days ahead. Escape, Sandhill, Wolf 8 and many other stretches of impossible whitewater followed in succession. "The current, always swift," Back wrote in describing this part of the river, "now rushed on still faster and soon became a line of heavy rapids, which more than once made me tremble for our poor boat, for in many parts, not being able to land, we were compelled to pull hard to keep her under command, and thus flew past rocks and other dangers with a velocity that seemed to forebode desperate termination."

On Lake Franklin, the last of the big lakes on the river, the crew finally encountered the Inuit that Akaitcho had warned them about. Back initially interpreted their waving from a distant hilltop as a sign of welcome. But when the boat got close enough to allow him to appreciate what was actually going on, he could see them running toward him "brandishing their spears, uttering loud yells, and with wild gesticulations, motioning us not to land." For this, Back boasts that he was "well-prepared." Once on shore, 35 hostile Inuit surrounded the crew. Remaining calm, Back called out *Tima*, the Inuit word for peace. Then he approached each one, confidently shook their hands in "John Bull fashion," and gave them shining buttons, fish hooks and other objects, "being strongly opposed," as he explained in his report, "to the customary donation of knives, hatchets and other sharp instruments which may be so easily turned against us." (Back had no cause to distinguish one group of Inuit from another, so his confrontations with bellicose Inuit on the Yukon and Alaskan coast during the second Franklin expedition nearly a decade earlier would have sprung to mind at this encounter.)

The gifts and gestures of goodwill had their intended effect. So did the likenesses that Back sketched of several of them. Studying the map that he had drawn, the Inuit added to the picture and assured him that he was within striking distance of the Arctic Ocean. Then they helped his crew transport the boat and the gear around the last waterfall.

Two days later, Back and his men finally tasted salt water. The weather was "fine and calm" that day and with the "tide ebbing" the crew was much amused by the seals that popped up all around them. Looking out into Chantrey Inlet, Back was optimistic about the coastal survey that lay ahead. But after clambering up a 245-metre hill to gain a better vantage point, he was mortified by what he saw awaiting them.

———

I might have taken some inspiration in the fact that it took Back and his crew just three weeks to get to Chantry Inlet from Muskox Lake. But I wasn't going to kid myself. There was no way we were going to maintain the pace of the 1834 expedition. The first half of our journey proved that. And once we encountered Malley, Hawk and many of the unmarked rapids downstream, it was evident that we could not risk running all the whitewater that Back and his crew routinely shot.

It was hot and dry the first week out. At times, it felt like we were paddling through a desert. The blackflies were as thick as I've ever experienced them. More than once, we took our dinners into the tent to avoid them blackening our plates. It didn't matter that the lingering smell of our food might entice hungry grizzly bears to come visiting while we were asleep. Miriam and Jane suffered the most. Each time they went to the bathroom on the tundra, they would have to return to their tents to remove hundreds of the "puny bloodsuckers" that got into their pants and underwear. Compelled as we were to kill thousands of them each night before we zipped up our sleeping bags, I unhappily discovered that piled in sufficient quantities, dead blackflies smell like fish.

The hundreds of caribou we spotted along the way were similarly tormented. Heading downstream from Muskox Lake, we spotted several bulls running back and forth along the river, oblivious to our presence, trying to escape the misery that the flies inflicted on them. It looked as though they would go mad before dropping dead from exhaustion as they sometimes do. We also saw many muskoxen standing in the middle of shallow parts of river water trying to find relief from their attackers.

The country was so thick with caribou on the second half of the journey that they eventually ceased to draw excitement from any one of us. The one notable exception occurred when we were camped on an island in the middle of the river, fast asleep in our tents. During the dusky hours of the early morning, at least one caribou swam over to where we camped. Startled perhaps by what it found on shore, it made a hasty escape in the dark, but not before slamming into and knocking over the canoe that we had been using for a cooktop. The adrenaline pumped for some time when we woke up, desperately trying to find our flashlights and bear deterrents, thinking that a grizzly was tearing into our food containers.

Remarkably, we hadn't seen a grizzly bear up until this point but for the next three consecutive days we were more than a little concerned to find fresh tracks at each of the spots we chose for a camp. It seemed that the phantom bear was keeping pace with us as we headed downstream. We were at the confluence of the Back and Baillie rivers when I thought I caught a glimpse of it. A thick fog had blanketed the river that morning, and with it the spectre drifting in and out of the mist, I couldn't tell for sure.

When we headed downstream a half-hour later, it wasn't a bear that ultimately presented itself on shore, but a bearded man, in his 50s I guessed, standing waist-deep in the water by his kayak, beckoning us to come visit. "Do you have cigarettes?" he asked in a thick German accent before we could get to him. Without introducing himself, the man hastily explained that he had been a heavy smoker for more than 30 years and that the decision to stop on this trip was a horrible mistake. He had finished his last pack a week earlier and now realized that he could not function properly without the noxious weed. "I will die in one of these rapids if I don't get a smoke," he said. "I've tried everything, even rolling up lichen in toilet paper. But that nearly burned off my beard."

On and on he went until we gave him the news that none of us smoked. Our friend wasn't much in the mood for chit-chat after that. Instead, he went into a deep sulk. All we could discern from what little more he told us was that once he reached Chantrey Inlet in mid-September, he was planning to cross the sea to Gjoa Haven. We were all stunned. The trip is dangerous enough in the best of conditions, but attempting it alone during the storm season seemed to us to be suicidal. A short time after, we said our good-byes unable to convince him to alter his plans. I will never forget the last thing he said, however. Just as we were about to continue on, he pulled out a map and asked, "Can you tell me where we are? I've lost track."

In the days that followed, our progress was slowed by a number of developments. Jane came down with an intestinal illness that sapped her of strength and energy for a time. The need to stop and scout many rapids, including those we might have shot in a less isolated environment, also was a factor. But the real show stopper was the north wind that blew in that second week and fought us for 10 days straight.

Headwinds are a fact of life on tundra rivers like the Back. Many paddlers avoid them by travelling at night when the weather is generally calmer. But the cold wind never seemed to let up on the latter part of the trip no matter what time of day it was. I can't count the number of times I picked out a rock on shore downstream for the purpose of measuring our progress only to discover that after 15 or 20 minutes, we had barely made any headway, even when we doublestroked. So instead of covering 20 or 30 kilometres in a day as we had planned, we were often lucky to do eight or 12. By the time we got to the McKinley River upstream of Pelly Lake, it was clear that we would be lucky to make it to Rock Rapids that summer.

In the end, a three-day gale stopped us short of getting even that far. I clocked the winds gusting to speeds of more than 50 knots during that storm. It blew so hard that we spent nearly a half-day chasing down Jane's tent after it was ripped from its anchors. We would never have caught up with it had it not collapsed into a tundra pond. Also, Miriam's hand and arm were burned one day when a pot of boiling water was literally lifted off the gas stove.

Just as the storm was abating toward the end of that third day, we were all mortified to see the yellow Turbo Beaver that was coming in to get us flying high and well past us on a northeastward course. We realized that the pilot had been instructed to start looking for us at Pelly Lake. What we didn't know was whether he would or could come back upstream once he realized that we hadn't made it that far.

———

The sight that mortified Back on that 240-metre hill overlooking Chantrey Inlet, was "one solid body of drift ice, connecting both shores." It was clear to him then and there that whatever progress might be made mapping the coastline in the coming days would only come by "slow and laborious efforts." The crew had an impossible

time trying to get their battered boat up the coastline after that.
Fresh meat and drinkable water were hard to come by and the
stormy weather chilled them to the bone. Even when they managed
to shoot some caribou, they couldn't find enough fuel with which to
cook them.

Back had strict instructions to begin his return to Great Slave
on August 12 and no later than August 19. So on the 15th with
little accomplished, he climbed to another hill on the coast – a bluff
he named after his friend Captain Maconochie R.N. – to have
another look at what lay ahead in the distance. Seeing a stream of
ice wedged tightly to shore, Back finally decided to call it quits.
"There was no expedient by which we could overcome the obstacles
before us," he wrote, "every resource was exhausted, and it was vain
to expect that any efforts, however strenuous, could avail against the
close-wedged ice and the constant fogs which enveloped everything
in this impenetrable country."

Richard King, the surgeon/naturalist on the expedition, later
wrote that it had been a bad decision to retreat, but it was not. Had
Back split up the party and headed east on foot as he had contem-
plated doing, the journey could have ended up as badly as Franklin's
first overland expedition. They were smart to return when they did.

In truth, I can't imagine what was going on in Back's mind
when the party started heading upstream to Fort Reliance that cold
August. It was hard enough getting down the Back River through or
around all of the rapids and waterfalls along its course. Paddling,
lining and portaging upstream would have been something altogether different. What Back was thinking along the way will never
be known, however. His journal devotes just a few pages to the
return journey. In that brief summary, he notes that they were
chased off by 60 or 70 angry Inuit they encountered at the narrows
in between Pelly and Garry lakes. They also nearly lost the boat in
Hawk Rapids when the tow line snapped. The site of Alexander
McLeod waiting for them at Sandhill Bay at Aylmer Lake in the
middle of September seemed to be one of the few uplifting
moments on the return to Reliance. The other was the sight of Parry

Falls on the last day of their four-month trip. True to the artist that he was, Back couldn't help waxing poetic in describing the scene that day.

"The whole face of the rocks forming the chasm was entirely coated with blue, green, and white ice, in thousands of pendant icicles:," Back wrote. "And there were, moreover, cairns, fissures, and overhanging ledges in all imaginable varieties of form, so curious and beautiful as to surpass any thing of which I had ever hear or read. ... Niagara, Wilberforce's Falls in Hood's River, the falls of Kakabikka near Lake Superior, the Swiss or Italian Falls — although they may each 'charm the eye with dread', are not to be compared with this for splendour of effect."

When they finally got to Fort Reliance, Back and his men found the cabins leaning and in bad shape. It had been a miserable, rainy summer and the Indians who were camped there were predicting that it would be another terrible winter. Even with that prospect and all that he had gone through, Back couldn't help consider the possibility of returning and completing what he had not accomplished on this journey.

Shortly after reaching England in October 1835, Back discovered why the Inuit at Garry Lake had reacted so aggressively towards them on the return trip. Based on the testimony of one member of the expedition, an inquiry was told that while on a hunting trip on the Arctic coast, three artillerymen were confronted by some Inuit. When the Inuit shot a volley of arrows in their direction, the artillerymen fired back, killing some of them. King apparently discovered what had happened when the men returned to camp acting in "an evasive manner." For some reason, he neglected to inform Back.

George Back's reputation did not suffer as a result. In addition to being awarded the Royal Geographical Society's coveted Founder's Gold Medal and the Patron's Silver Medal as well, he was eventually promoted to the rank of post captain even though he had not served a full year at sea as required. He could have retired or assumed a prestigious role in the navy, but he chose instead to return to the Arctic one more time in 1837 on a trip through Hudson Bay that nearly cost the lives of him and his crew when the ship became hopelessly trapped in a sea of crushing ice. More honours followed in his career and Back continued to be a celebrity. In 1856, Charles Dickens wrote an adaptation of a Wilkie Collins play in which two Arctic explorers – no doubt Back and Robert Hood – fall for the same girl (Greenstockings). Back, however, never did forget the Arctic. Before explorer John Rae headed out on his own expedition to the Arctic in 1850, Back had given him a handsome knife which he hoped Rae would deliver to Ouligbuck, the Inuit guide on the 1825-27 expedition with Franklin.

Back in Yellowknife, we weren't altogether surprised to learn that of the four parties that were on the Back River that summer, none had made it to Chantrey Inlet. Halfway between Great Slave and Muskox lakes, a Japanese kayaker was injured on one of the many portages and had to set off his emergency locator transmitter to get rescued. An American paddler also decided to cut short his solo trip down the Baillie and Back rivers when it became apparent that his dog couldn't cope with the blackflies. It was another six weeks before I learned the fate of our German Canadian friend. The news came in a short two paragraph newspaper article that caught my eye by chance. Two pilots flying over Garry Lake that September spotted him on a hilltop, far off course, out of food and fuel and nearly out of his mind. He had been overdue for nine days. It was only by chance that the pilots, out on other business, had spotted him.

Talking to one of the pilots a short time later, I learned that they nearly didn't get to him. The weather was so stormy that it was all they could do to land the Twin Otter on the rough, icy lake. Concerned that they might be flipped or sunk in the storm, they insisted that he leave his kayak and gear behind. He apparently didn't protest.

Back's legacy lives on in Canada. The journal of his first overland expedition is archived at the McCord Museum in Montreal and thanks to I. S. MacLaren and Stuart Houston, his sketchbook, which was found in the possession of a distant relative in England, has been returned to Canada. It is stored at the National Library and Archives of Canada.

In an essay, MacLaren eloquently summarizes the significant contribution that Back made to Canadian history, representative as it is of the way the aesthetic mind influenced early perceptions of the Arctic landscape. Back's art and his narrative were a refreshing departure from the institutional nature of so much Arctic travel literature of the time. Like his contemporaries, Back's main aim was to get from one point to another as expeditiously as possible and without a loss of life or injury. But like most modern Arctic travellers, he also hungered for adventure and saw in wilderness much more than the promise of material gain. He took from this sublime and picturesque landscape a spiritual inspiration that transcends anything that is man-made.

Epilogue

There is an unnamed stream on one of the High Arctic islands that haunts me in my dreams. It is clear and cold, like the favourite stream of my youth, and it is filled with char at certain times of the summer. Although it flows out a high boulder-strewn plateau that looks like the surface of the moon, its lowland banks are lined with lush stands of sedges, grasses and willow bushes suitable for flightless snowy owl chicks to hide in. Arctic foxes are constantly walking up and down this shoreline looking for a quick lunch. One night while camped here, my partners and I were wakened by the sound of wolves barking. I popped my head out of the tent to have a look and was surprised to see just how close they were. The big white alpha male was making the most noise, bounding forward each time it barked, and then stopping as if it had reached the end of a rope. It went on like this for a good half-hour before the big wolf walked in, peed on our gear and loped off with the others.

The next day, it rained hard for quite some time, which is unusual for this part of the polar world. When it let up, I went for a long walk to see what the snowy owls were up to. They were nowhere to be found. Neither was their mother, which was always perched on a hilltop nearby keeping an eye out for predators. Searching the sand to see if I could figure out where they might have gone, I came across the tracks of a polar bear in the fresh mud. I was stunned, not only by the recent presence of a bear this far inland but by my own foolhardiness. Hiking alone without a gun or a serious bear deterrent in the High Arctic was not the wisest decision.

I headed back to camp that afternoon and then walked upstream to the top of a big rock spire that signaled the dividing line between the boulder-strewn plateau and the sandy desert. I sat up all night staring at the line of water flowing northward into the Arctic sea and at a herd of muskoxen that had bedded down on a hillside. Around midnight, a thick, white fog that had hovered all day on the coast slowly moved inland covering everything but the hilltops. The sun was low on the horizon and the sky was a dark purple-blue. It was a sublime, dreamy landscape, one that only the hand of God or some other supernatural force could create, I thought.

It has been suggested that the Arctic is not so much a geographical location as it is an idea, a cultural artifact or a metaphor for human perseverance and ingenuity[1] – "a pattern of "places, prospects, and possibilities" as anthropologist Bernard Saladin d'Anglure once put it, drawn from "an archaeology of dreams, myths, beliefs and facts."[2]

For centuries, the long days of summer, the dark nights of winter, mirages, aurora borealis, Perihelia (mock suns), whiteouts and ghostly fog banks have confused, fascinated and overpowered those who visited this landscape under the constellation Arktos or the Great Bear. The sublimity of it all, the struggle the explorers went through trying to describe the New World to people back home, the inability of scientists to keep up with the many environmental changes that take place over a relatively short period of time, partially explains why the idea of the Arctic continues to enchant and bewilder.

---

1. Sherrill E. Grace, *Canada and the Idea of North*, McGill-Queens, 2001.
2. Bernard Saladin d'Anglure, "The Route to China, Northern Europe's Arctic Delusions, in *Arctic*, Vol. 37. No. 4, pp 446-452.

Although the Arctic has enticed and repelled, gratified imperiled generations of explorers, adventurers, scientists and artists, it has also been the backdrop to a reckless struggle with nature. It began with the desire to find a commercially viable sea route from Europe to the Orient through a northwest passage. It continues with mining and the search for new energy sources. The desire for wealth and security is an understandable one – a necessity in many ways. But the pace at which it is occurring is quickly overtaking our ability to protect and preserve what makes the sum of the Arctic's many disparate parts so special. David Schindler, one of the great scientists of our time, recently noted that while environmental pressures – climate change, ozone depletion, long distance transportation of pollutants, oil and gas and mining developments – are increasing dramatically in the Arctic, the corresponding funding for research necessary for predicting and mitigating ecosystem impacts has not nearly kept pace.

When I first started paddling and hiking in the North in the 1970s, most of the major rivers were wild. Today, there is a mine along the headwaters of the legendary Coppermine River, another proposed for the Back River area and one that sits ready to go on the banks of Prairie Creek which flows directly into the South Nahanni. There's another being looked at south of the Thelon Wildlife Sanctuary, as well as at several spots in the Yukon. There's serious talk about a deep water port at Bathurst Inlet into which the Hood, the Burnside and the Western rivers flow.

Development has taken precedence over all other considerations in some instances. In 2003, 5,000 square kilometres of land along the Brown River was removed from the proposed boundaries of Ukkusiksalik, the new national park at Wager Bay, so that a future mine might be established. The Kendall Island Migratory Bird Sanctuary in the Mackenzie Delta has already been so carved up by seismic lines and drilling pads that some species of nesting birds like the Lapland longspur appear to be avoiding them. If this could happen in a national bird sanctuary, one might naturally ask, then what's in store for the rest of the unprotected Arctic?

There has been talk about putting two dams on the Mackenzie, one on the Great Bear River, another on the Talston and one on the Slave. There was even a suggestion a few years ago that the waters of the Lockhart, a river that is sacred to the Dene of Lutselk'e, be blocked to provide power for future diamond mines. Oilsands developments in northern Alberta are also threatening to cause huge environmental change in the North. If developments go ahead as planned, a significant diversion of water from the Athabasca, which flows into the Slave and Mackenzie River system, will occur in order to provide steam for oilsands extraction.

One would have thought that after the mining disasters at Mount Nansen, Faro, Colomac and dozens of other spots in the Canadian North, lessons would have been learned. High up in the alpine country of the south-central Yukon, the people who ran the Mount Nansen gold mine left behind a toxic mess that required a multi-million dollar emergency intervention to prevent what one expert described as a "rolling wave of death" downstream. The company declared bankruptcy in 1999 and then left the territory before it was tried in absentia. In denouncing the operation as "inept, bumbling, amateurish," and "consistent with raping and pillaging" the judge hearing the case exhorted federal officials to find ways of putting people like this behind bars. It never happened. And so, more than $4 billion of taxpayers' money is now being spent to clean up the environmental legacies left behind at Mount Nansen, Colomac, Faro and other abandoned mines.

It's not all terrible news. The Thomsen River Valley on Banks Island continues to be a remarkable haven for muskoxen — in July 2005, scientist John Nagy estimated there were 47,274 muskox on the island, down from 69,000 in 2001 — and for other animals just as the Firth River in Ivvavik is for the Porcupine caribou herd. We have the Inuvialuit to thank in large part for Ivvavik, for Aulavik — the national park that protects the Thomsen — and for another park at Tuktut Nogait through which the Hornaday and Brock rivers flow. We also owe a debt to the Inuit of the eastern Arctic and Labrador for Ukkusiksalik, the Torngat Mountains and for several other national parks. And we should be obliged to the Dene of the southern Mackenzie Valley for setting aside a huge area of land they will own in the near future to protect the headwaters of the Nahanni.

Not all industry players have been bad either. A few years ago, the Mining Association of Canada worked with Nature Canada and the Inuit of the High Arctic to set aside an area on Bathurst Island in the High Arctic for a national park. So, the template is there for similar agreements in the future.

Sitting on that pillar of rock that night, I learned that there is something about this landscape that causes even the agnostic, the atheist or the hard-core scientist to believe, or at least be tempted to believe, in the Inuit, Inuvialuit and Dene legends that reflect the mystery, power and beauty of this part of the world — and to question the liberty that humankind has to do as it pleases here. What else can be said about a place that was once home to giant beavers, woolly mammoth, scimitar cats and three-toed horses[3] and is now a refuge for polar bears, muskoxen, belugas and narwhals, white wolves and nearly two million caribou?

---

3. See the Yukon's Beringia Interpretive Centre's excellent website: **www.beringia.com/what** for more on the natural history of the early North American Arctic.

Acknowledgments

There were many people who helped me with this book. In particular, I would like to thank those who kindly read various chapters and offered suggestions, clarifications or corrected mistakes: Parks Canada biologist Doug Tate, Chuck Blyth, superintendent of Nahanni National Park, Fisheries and Oceans scientist Jack Orr, grizzly bear biologist Grant MacHutchon, Jack Anawak, Ambassador for Circumpolar Affairs with Foreign Affairs Canada, University of Alberta historian Ian MacLaren, University of Alberta scientist Andrew Derocher, Richard Harington, Curator and Researcher Emeritus with the Canadian Museum of Nature, Arctic scientist Tom Smith, Northwest Territories biologist Bob Bromley, Steve Catto, Manager of Resource Conservation, Nahanni National Park and Margaret Bertulli, an archaeolgist with Parks Canada. Thanks to my editor Lynn McAuley for hanging in there even after she took on a new job. I was humbled by Lynn's razor sharp eye for detail and her attention to felicity of style and grammar. And to Meredith Birchall-Spencer and Carole-Ann Hayes for their enthusiasm in getting this to print.

I would also like to thank Tom Smith, Dick Harington and Andrew Derocher for graciously allowing me to accompany them in the field and Canadian Wildlife Service scientist Ian Stirling for sharing his extraordinary insights into the world of Arctic science over so many years.

Thanks as well to Parks Canada's Jane Chisolm, Ron Larsen, Steve Travis, Paul Dixon, Steve Catto, Sophie Borcoman, Barry Troke and others for helping me with maps, identification of plants, times and dates, and other pertinent matters; to Harvey Locke who arranged to have the Canadian Parks and Wilderness Society include this book in the venerable organization's Henderson Book Series. And to Rick Pape, a masterful illustrator who came in at the last minute to produce the maps.

I would like to note that I am not the first to write about river adventure in the North. Many fine books have on the theme have been produced. Apart from those mentioned in the various chapters, I'd like to recommend David Finch's wonderful biography of Raymond Patterson, *R. M. Patterson, A Life of Great Adventure* (Rocky Mountain Books), Karsten Heuer's *Being Caribou* (McClelland and Stewart), Neil Hartling's *Nahanni River of Gold* (Key Porter), James Raffan's *Summer North of Sixty, By Paddle and Portage Across the Barren Lands* (Key Porter), and Alex Hall's *Discovering Eden* (Key Porter). Paddling enthusiasts would also be well-served and entertained by subscribing to *Che-Mun, The Journal of Canadian Wilderness Canoeing*, which is edited and published by Michael Peake, who, along with his brothers, has a remarkable paddling record in the Canadian North.

And to all my paddling partners and companions: Peter Clarkson (who saved us both from drowning on the Burnside River), Tom Carpenter, Andrew Nikiforuk, Miriam Wideman, Ian MacLaren, Allan Mayer, Chuck Blyth, Steve Travis, Merv Joe, René Fumoleau, Brian Milne, Dawn Goss, my sister Sam, my brother Rick, my brother-in-law Randy, my son Jacob, my daughter Sigrid, my wife Julia and many, many more wonderful people for the great times.

Special thanks to Eric Sommer for providing me with additional details of his brother's tragic death on the Little Nahanni and for encouraging me to include his brother's story in the book.

Last but not least, I'd like to acknowledge that the writing of this book was assisted by Linda Hughes and Allan Mayer, publisher and editor of the *Edmonton Journal*. They gave me the time and encouragement I needed to get this done.